THE ROMA AND THE HOLOCAUST

Perspectives on the Holocaust

A series of books designed to help students further their understanding of key topics within the field of Holocaust studies.

Published:

HOLOCAUST REPRESENTATIONS IN HISTORY (2ND EDITION), *Daniel H. Magilow and Lisa Silverman*

POSTWAR GERMANY AND THE HOLOCAUST, *Caroline Sharples*

ANTI-SEMITISM AND THE HOLOCAUST, *Beth A. Griech-Polelle*

THE HOLOCAUST IN EASTERN EUROPE, *Waitman Wade Beorn*

THE UNITED STATES AND THE NAZI HOLOCAUST, *Barry Trachtenberg*

WITNESSING THE HOLOCAUST, *Judith M. Hughes*

HITLER'S 'MEIN KAMPF' AND THE HOLOCAUST: A PRELUDE TO GENOCIDE, *John J. Michalczyk, Michael S. Bryant and Susan A. Michalczyk (eds.)*

THE HOLOCAUST AND AUSTRALIA: REFUGEES, REJECTION, AND MEMORY, *Paul R. Bartrop*

ISRAEL AND THE HOLOCAUST, *Avinoam J. Patt*

Forthcoming:

SITES OF HOLOCAUST MEMORY, *Janet Ward*

THE PERPETRATORS OF THE HOLOCAUST: THE FOLLY OF THE THIRD REICH, *Nathan Stoltzfus*

THE HOLOCAUST IN EASTERN EUROPE (2ND EDITION), *Waitman Wade Beorn*

THE ROMA AND THE HOLOCAUST

THE ROMANI GENOCIDE UNDER NAZISM

María Sierra
Translated by Margaret Clark

BLOOMSBURY ACADEMIC
LONDON • NEW YORK • OXFORD • NEW DELHI • SYDNEY

BLOOMSBURY ACADEMIC
Bloomsbury Publishing Plc
50 Bedford Square, London, WC1B 3DP, UK
1385 Broadway, New York, NY 10018, USA
29 Earlsfort Terrace, Dublin 2, Ireland

BLOOMSBURY, BLOOMSBURY ACADEMIC and the Diana logo are
trademarks of Bloomsbury Publishing Plc

First published in Great Britain 2024

Copyright © María Sierra, 2024

Translation copyright © Margaret Clark, 2024

María Sierra has asserted her right under the Copyright,
Designs and Patents Act, 1988, to be identified as Author of this work.

Series design: Jesse Holborn
Cover image: A group of Romani prisoners, Belzec, 1940.
© United States Holocaust Memorial Museum, courtesy of
Archiwum Dokumentacji Mechanicznej

All rights reserved. No part of this publication may be reproduced or transmitted in any form or by any means, electronic or mechanical, including photocopying, recording, or any information storage or retrieval system, without prior permission in writing from the publishers.

Bloomsbury Publishing Plc does not have any control over, or responsibility for, any third-party websites referred to or in this book. All internet addresses given in this book were correct at the time of going to press. The author and publisher regret any inconvenience caused if addresses have changed or sites have ceased to exist, but can accept no responsibility for any such changes.

Every effort has been made to trace the copyright holders and obtain permission to reproduce the copyright material. Please do get in touch with any enquiries or any information relating to such material or the rights holder. We would be pleased to rectify any omissions in subsequent editions of this publication should they be drawn to our attention.

A catalogue record for this book is available from the British Library.

A catalog record for this book is available from the Library of Congress.

ISBN:	HB:	978-1-3503-3309-3
	PB:	978-1-3503-3308-6
	ePDF:	978-1-3503-3310-9
	eBook:	978-1-3503-3311-6

Series: Perspectives on the Holocaust

Typeset by Integra Software Services Pvt. Ltd.
Printed and bound in Great Britain

To find out more about our authors and books visit www.bloomsbury.com
and sign up for our newsletters.

CONTENTS

List of illustrations — vi
Foreword *Philomena Franz* — viii

Introduction: One history, many stories — 1

Part I A scantly known and under-acknowledged genocide

1 The Roma and anti-Gypsyism: Parallel histories — 13

2 The Romani genocide under Nazism — 43

3 The long road from denial to acknowledgement — 99

Part II Memoirs: Remembering events long ignored

4 Neither heard nor believed: Survivors' accounts — 123

5 What language are memories written in? — 139

Annotated bibliography — 179

Notes — 194
Index — 210

ILLUSTRATIONS

1	Romani woman telling German troops' fortunes in Poland, October 1939	8
2	Map used as an illustration in *Accounts of the Gypsies of India*, 1886	15
3	*The Fortune-Teller*, Georges de la Tour, *c.* 1630	20
4	*Gypsy Woman Dancing the Zorongo*, 1874, by Gustave Doré	22
5	Poster for an adaptation of Mérimée's *Carmen*, 1896	25
6	Paola Negri, silent movie star, in *Screenland*, October 1923	26
7	*Rose Merton and the Gypsies*, 1850 scrapbook	32
8	Members of a successful Romani French and Hungarian interwar period band posing with their instruments	34
9	Bamberger family posing for a studio photo in the 1930s	35
10	Romani family at Neudorf bei Landsee, Austria, German General Intelligence Service photo, 1934	39
11	Karl Heilig, soldier in Rommel's Afrika-Korps	45
12	Marzahn internment camp for Roma outside Berlin established on the occasion of the 1936 Olympic Games	48
13	Family caravan at Halle Camp	51
14	Sparta Boxing Club, 1929	52
15	Dr Robert Ritter in 1938 at Stein in der Pfalz, Germany	54
16	Craniometric studies and racial science. Eva Justin [?] and Dr Adolf Würth measuring the head of a young Sinto, 1938	55
17	*Unku*, Ena Laubinger in 1936 at Dessau-Rosslau, Germany	56
18	Magdeburg criminal police photos of Ena Laubinger, 1939	56
19	Walter Winter in German Navy uniform, 1942	59
20	Rosa Lehmann (maiden name, Höllenreiner) in the 1920s at her house at Munich with her father and nephew	61
21	Anthropometric ID used to control 'nomad' peoples in France	63
22	Polish Romani women	66
23	Romani prisoners taken to Jasenovac Camp in Croatia, 1942–3	68
24	Roma on their way to execution, photo taken between 1941 and 1943	69
25	'Gypsy' camp at Haarlem, the Netherlands, 1940	75
26	Two Romani children at Haarlem, the Netherlands, 1940	77
27	Else Schmidt (centre) with her two older sisters	88
28	Sinti and Roma child genocide victims	90
29	Josef Mengele, head physician at the Auschwitz *Zigeunerlager*, 1944	91
30	Theresia Seibel acting in a stage play before the war at Würzburg, Germany	93

Illustrations

31	Marion Kaufmann (centre), Jewish girl given refuge by a Romani family in 1944, the Netherlands	96
32	Jan Yoors and Pulika family members	96
33	Ionel Rotaru, activist and Communauté Mondiale Gitane President, c. 1965	107
34	Pond at the memorial monument on Sinti and Roma genocide, Berlin	110
35	Ceija Stojka, one of the Romani Holocaust's most powerful narrators	114
36	Laubinger family, Romanies	115
37	Settela Steinbach, photogram from the documentary filmed at Westerbock Camp, the Netherlands, 1944	118
38	Group of Romani men and boys at Belzec Camp, Poland, 1940	119
39	'Romani prisoners lined up for execution'	124
40	Hildegard Stein ('Lulu') holding a baby in a Hans Weltzel photo taken at Dessau-Rosslau, Germany	146
41	Sonderkommando works at the Auschwitz crematory, 1944	146
42	Georg Laubinger in the 1930s	154
43	Three Pulika family teenagers smiling for their non-Roma friend Jan Yoors	158
44	Gustav and Rudolf Thormann at Dessau-Rosslau, Germany, 1936	160
45	Romani family alongside their caravan photographed by Jan Yoors between 1934 and 1939	161
46	Uniformed police in charge of watching over the Marzahn-Berlin Camp	163
47	Laubinger family men posing for a group photo, Dessau-Rosslau, Germany, 1935	170
48	Eva Justin interviewing Romani women and children in Racial Hygiene Unit, photograph taken between 1936 and 1940	171
49	Hedwig Laubinger-Steinbach posing for Hans Weltzel at Dessau-Rosslau in 1939	172
50	Musicians Lolo Adell (violin), Frans Basili (laud) and Josef Basili (rear) at Haarlem, the Netherlands, 1940	178
51	Pauline Thormann (Lotte)	178

FOREWORD
Philomena Franz

Dearest Maria,

I've finally got around to writing you a few lines; as you know, I'm still busy with work and my literary pursuits. I can hardly thank you enough for writing this book, a unique combination of Sinti and Roma history with Auschwitz memorial literature. I hope from the bottom of my heart it will find a wide readership. I'm delighted you've written it and send you my very best wishes for its success. We need to stick together, right up until our dying breath. We must not allow the stories of the Holocaust, no matter whose, to be forgotten. We must ensure they get written down, and tirelessly persist in that endeavour. They should never be forgotten. The world must know what happened in Auschwitz, what happened in the relentless, grinding horror of that place and must never be allowed to happen again!

When you're in Auschwitz, you're powerless: there's no way you can defend yourself. You're utterly impotent. That was how I felt as a young inmate in the camp.

They'd shout: 'Out of the barracks!' 'Stand still!' In winter and summer, rain or snow, they'd leave us standing out there. They harassed and abused for sheer enjoyment. One woman in my row died. She just collapsed. It was too much for her.

You no longer felt anything, only fear. Along with humiliation, fear, like a watchdog, just stood in waiting, it never went away. You felt nothing else, didn't feel like a human being, didn't know if you were a man or a woman; you were too exhausted to think or even feel.

I loved God, I loved Jesus Christ. Christ was very important to me: that divine human being shed his holy blood, died on the cross as his Father had sent him to do. At home, we always prayed in the evenings. Grandpa was a devout man. He lived with us and raised me. We children were in good hands.

Escape was always on my mind, in my plans. One day, I thought, I would find my way out of there. That belief gave me strength, gave me the courage to escape. Eventually, the day would come! Patience! Never give up! Never!

Later, people said that my belief in God was all my hope could cling to. He charted my course. In His name I swear I never got scabies in the camp. That was nothing short of a miracle. My cousin, with whom I had to share a bed because the camp was overcrowded, was infected, but I never caught the disease. Everyone else did, for they had lost faith. I trust entirely in my Lord God, he leads me and guides me and delivers me from fear.

Auschwitz was Hell for us. There was nothing worse.

If there is a Hell, then we have already atoned for our sins. The children and old people, in particular, couldn't help or defend themselves.

I experienced Hell, once. I was 19 then, and I had wanted to go so far in life! If it hadn't been for the camp … but after the camp, there was nothing left.

Foreword

If we hate, we lose.

Perhaps, of all of us, I'm the only one who has forgiven. Perhaps. Sinti are often mistaken for Roma and vice-versa. I can only speak for the Sinti. Princess Irina von Sayn Wittgenstein Perleburg was my friend at the Frauen Europas (women of Europe). She loved my energy, the way I would push to make something happen, win or lose. When you've lived a life like mine, it's not hard to come out on the losing end.

I hope with all my might there will never be another Auschwitz.

Not like it was then, with the smoke from burning people billowing skyward.

People. Smoke from the people who were incinerated there.

I pray there will never be such furnaces again.

Do you think that goes away? What dreams do you think I have?

I wouldn't wish anyone in the world the moments of genuine terror I feel when Auschwitz invades my dreams.

I close my eyes, and I can still see the smoke rise from the furnaces.

In the spring I used to sit behind the barracks, when the sun came out for a bit. The fear I felt for having managed to get a piece of bread, the hunger, the cold.

The early summer bathed the desolate camp of Birkenau in sunlight.

I'd go out of the barracks, out into the warmth of the sun. I'd sit behind the barracks and let the sun beam down on me. As I'd close my eyes that wonderful warmth, with a little effort on my part, would carry me home. Then the memories of life outside would take over. I'd sit in the sun, eyes closed, and let my spirit drift free of my body. Suddenly I'd be outside, strong and full of energy! At home eating bread, eating good food. I'd sit back there for hours on end, wandering elsewhere, far away from my physical self. But then I'd come to, wake up to grim reality. Waking up from those out-of-camp escapades to the horrendous present was what was the hardest. For it was then I felt the misery. I'd cry my eyes out, quite beyond my sense of propriety. On Sundays.

I set no store by prosecuting the perpetrators. I always used to look for someone who was to blame. But who would that be? The Gestapo? Adolf Hitler? The people at the top? Who could have the burning of human flesh on their conscience? It stank like the plague. Such a revolting smell. Human beings can endure a great deal. You need wits to come through this. Being dull could get you killed.

'If I die, take me with you. Don't leave me to perish here in this human Hell!'

For me, dear Maria, this book is about keeping such memories alive and ensuring that they are still shared with other people. Today, things are once again building up to a crisis we simply cannot afford. We must not allow that horror ever again. I'm worried.

Yours,

Philomena

'Author, speaker, Auschwitz survivor'[1]

Foreword translated from the German by Andrew Godfrey Collins and Michael Walker

INTRODUCTION: ONE HISTORY, MANY STORIES

It's 1942 and spring in Vienna.

Seventeen-year-old Rosa Mettbach boards a train to Munich. Once in her car she is frightened to see the only other passenger, an elderly Hungarian soldier with several medals pinned to his uniform. She is well dressed. She has to do everything in her power to hide her recent escape from Lackenbach Camp. It's not easy, she has no papers. But this wouldn't be the first time she managed to slip through Nazi police fingers.

At each stop, Rosa rushes to the toilet to hide from the inspector checking all passengers' documents. But when the train stops at the German border near Salzburg, the official arrives before she can get up from her seat. 'I'm done for' she thinks but, giving it one last try, closes her eyes pretending to be asleep. And then she hears the elderly soldier say, as he stops the inspector from 'wakening' her: 'Leave that girl alone. She's been checked ten times since we left Vienna. Let her sleep. I know she's legal'. The inspector obeys.

When they're alone again, he tells Rosa: 'You can open your eyes now'.

***

That may be one of the few episodes from the war years Rosa Mettbach remembers fondly. Born in Austria to a Sinti family of musicians, she was fourteen when her country was pressured into unification with Germany in 1938. Soon after, she was expelled from school and her family forced to live in an area under police control. They were later imprisoned at Lackenbach, an internment camp for Austrian 'Zigeuner' from which many were deported even farther afield, outside the areas reserved for allegedly pure Aryans. On the journey with her family to the Polish ghetto at Łódź she managed to escape and hide for a while, but was again arrested and sent back to Lackenbach. After her second escape, she made it to Munich, where she married Hamlet Mettbach, who had been a soldier in the German army until he was expelled on racial grounds in 1942. Shortly after bearing her first child, Rosa was arrested for a third time and sent to Auschwitz. In the interim she'd been informed that her mother, sister and nephews all died at Łódź. She survived imprisonment at both Auschwitz-Birkenau and Ravensbrück. Her testimony as a Holocaust survivor was recorded by Toby Sonneman in a book essential to understanding the Romani genocide perpetrated by the Nazis, from which the narrative of her escape to Munich was drawn.[1]

Rosa Mettbach's is just one of the thousands of personal stories that contribute to the history of the genocide of the Roma people under Hitler. Although the exact number of victims of that persecution has yet to be determined, on the order of half a million so-called 'Gypsies' are currently estimated to have perished in Nazi concentration camps, ghettos, mass executions by mobile killing units and other scenarios. The stories of those half million direct victims, most lost, form part of a much broader narrative. Whilst not a mortal victim of Nazi persecution, Rosa Mettbach, like many thousands of Romanies, had her possessions confiscated, was jailed, obliged to engage in forced labour and tortured by a regime that murdered most of her immediate family. Hers is a story that should be told and heard. The handful of accounts selected for this book constitute a record of names and faces, emotions and reasons. Its author, however, is deeply frustrated by the keen awareness that there are countless others she will never be able to tell.

Those personal tragedies have gone essentially unknown in Europe and America, not only to the general public but also to researchers at universities and other institutions engaging in the study of the recent past. European Romanies were persecuted and murdered by the Nazis and targeted by the same racial policy as millions of Jews and other communities. Nonetheless, for a long time after Hitler's defeat Romanies were denied acknowledgement of their status as Nazi victims, a denial that lies at the root of both the social and academic tendency to overlook and generally ignore such mass murder. This book aspires to help raise public awareness of the matter in the conviction that it should prompt an analysis of racism in today's societies, as well as the self-criticism imperative to future social harmony. Prejudice against groups collectively characterized by disparaging stereotypes is fertile soil for the banal, second-nature racism ingrained in self-presumed non-racists that rises to the surface as jokes or common expressions tainted with prejudice. That variety may be as dangerous today as it was in interwar Europe when Nazi policies geared to exterminating 'inferior races' were met with widespread social support. While still injurious to Romanies, what used to be exclusively anti-Gypsyism is being redirected today against other vulnerable communities such as recent refugees.

This book is structured around two parts. Part I systematizes research on the Romani genocide perpetrated during the Third Reich, furnishing an updated review of publications in a host of languages that although useful have made only a minor impact on historiographic dissemination. Research on the Romani genocide has progressed fractionally and very few overviews have come to light to date. This book adopts a rather different approach, with broader coverage of geography, timing and subject matter. The aim is to furnish an updated summary of the most relevant facts and figures. The resulting synopsis of the basic known data is supplemented by a critical look at significant research problems and an analysis of controversial issues (such as the delay with which such mass murders have been researched, leading some voices to designate the respective events as the 'forgotten Holocaust' or draw comparisons between the Jewish and Romani genocides).

Part II peers into the history of the Romani genocide from the perspective provided by memoirs published by its survivors. Those testimonies, varying in format, intention and chronology, failed to encounter a social or cultural environment willing to listen to their authors' voices until the 1980s. Most were published in German, although some have now been translated into English and a few into French and Spanish. No study has yet used them jointly as material to trace the history of the Romani Holocaust. They have, however, been analysed by some authors with a cultural or literary focus and by others as background for the development of this minority's individual and collective identity based on autobiographies (most prominently a PhD thesis authored by Marianne Zwicker).[2] Part II combines the narratives of Romani women and men of varying origin and age to describe the emotional dimension of the Holocaust experience. These accounts can be read from many vantage points. The present review highlights the use made by their authors of the language of emotion (fear, sorrow, hope, dejection etc.) to chronicle their life stories. Such words and notions constitute a way for survivors to draw from the remembrance of those events to compose a discourse intelligible to readers, viewers or listeners who were not there, breaking out of the narrow confines of the 'predictable empathy' among Holocaust victims. Understanding the internal logic of such accounts, which converge in a series of essential elements, calls for a reappraisal of their value as testimony and communicational bridge-building between author and reader. Although here emotion is by no means meant to serve as a universal language, for the way sentiment is expressed depends heavily on social and historic context, it is nonetheless a cultural resource of enormous communicational power when set in a biographical dimension. It is up to today's generations to discover the names, faces, families and pre- and post-camp life stories of people resorting to such expression to formulate and convey the memory of their experience.

Before going into these accounts certain terminological decisions adopted in this book merit explicit discussion, for they mirror more than merely linguistic issues. The first has to do with the use of the words 'Gypsy' and 'Rom' (plural 'Roma')-'Romani' (plural 'Romanies'). The latter is the term most widely accepted in the international arena to refer to this community ('Rom' and 'Romani' as nouns, 'Romani' also as the name of this people's language and as adjective), for it is an endonym, i.e. the name the people historically called 'Gypsies' by others have more or less recently begun to use to refer to themselves. The term was chosen at the First World Roma Conference held in London in 1971 as part of the campaign to demand those peoples' rights as well as their acknowledgement as Nazi regime victims. The choice of that name, drawn from the Romani language, should come as no surprise given the contempt with which the words used in other languages were (and still are) charged. 'Gypsy' in English, 'Gitane' in French, 'Zigeuner' in German and so on are all labels applied from outside the community and synonymous with other traits disdained in mainstream society, as discussed in Chapter 1. Such words have also served to criminalize and persecute those so branded, words with ever more offensive connotations detrimental to their targets. The supreme example may be the letter 'Z' (for 'Zigeuner') tattooed onto the arms of Auschwitz-Birkenau extermination camp prisoners. The Romani struggle for the recognition of group dignity consequently necessitated rejecting such terms and adopting a name of their own, a decision with political intentions that may be questioned but that has proven to be effective and operational.

Nonetheless, the Romani protest movement itself, which is plural, has on occasion resorted to the word 'Gypsy' as a sort of self-assertion of identity that is particularly common in Spain as regards the term 'Gitano'. Inasmuch as the term has been generally preferred among Spanish Romanies, the original Spanish version of this book[3] accords it the same legitimacy as Roma and Romani. The term 'Gypsy' would appear to be less acceptable to Romanies living in English-speaking areas, however, and should not be used by non-Roma authors, such as in this case. Therefore the terms 'Rom' and 'Romani' have been chosen systematically in this translated version, except in citations or where the focus is on past discourse. Where they are used, words such as 'Zigeuner', 'Gypsy' or other expressions with demeaning connotations in the language of the historic actors involved are consistently set in quotes and contextualized.[4] Sinti, Kalderash, Lovara, Manouche and others, in turn, the names of Romani communities historically settled in different areas of the world, denote generally accepted geographic and cultural identities. For instance, Philomena Franz, the author of the letter that opens this book, introduces herself as a Sinti, the majority Romani community traditionally settled in Germany.

A second group of terminological choices that need to be justified here revolves around the difficult task of naming a historic development of such extraordinary nature and dimensions as the 'Holocaust'. Recognition of the difficulty involved does not imply the absence of precedents or the unsuitability of analogy, however. The original religious meaning of the word refers to ritual burning at the stake. Although previously used to describe other events, starting in the late 1950s and throughout the 1960s Jewish scholars introduced it to refer to the murder of millions of European Jews as a result of Nazi racial policy. The term, both for its original meaning and for its subsequent consolidation, is rife with (religious, nationalist, scientific) connotations that may cast the suitability of its use today in doubt. Nonetheless, as Dominick LaCapra[5] contends, no name is free of intention or fully objective. In this case the choosing from among the options implies interpreting the event(s) in question as unique and incomparable or otherwise and hence in need of a name that to be understood must be reframed. The same author also notes that the popularization of the term 'holocaust' (particularly in the wake of the 1978 television series titled *Holocaust*) is indicative of public appropriation and social usage that have abetted the dissemination of scientific knowledge. Claude Lanzmann's 1985 film *Shoah* had a similar effect on the widespread adoption of the Hebrew word with the same meaning (literally translated as 'catastrophe'). At this time general academic consensus defines the term 'Holocaust' as 'the systematic state-sponsored killing of six million Jewish men, women, and children and millions of others by Nazi Germany and its collaborators during World War II'.[6]

The reader will note that the expression 'other victims' in the foregoing definition masks or attributes secondary relevance to the identity of groups such as European Romanies subjected to the same mass destruction as Jews. That would explain why the Romani case has often been referred to as the 'forgotten Holocaust'. Although as discussed below much research has now been conducted on the matter, the scant transfer of scientific knowledge to public awareness has limited its social and political impact, which is not even vaguely comparable to that prompted by the Jewish Holocaust. The emergence of names in Romanes for the Nazi genocide recently proposed by Romani intellectuals must be viewed in that light, for the intention is to demand the acknowledgement of

Introduction

and a tribute to these victims of Nazi racial policy. Ian Hancock (2005), a researcher residing in the United States, has proposed the word *Porrajmos*, a neologism meaning 'to destroy' or 'to devour'. Given certain sexual overtones inherent in the term, however, other authors such as linguist Marcel Courthiade have questioned its use. His proposed alternative, *Samudaripen*, meaning 'destruction of all' or 'mass destruction', is the expression preferred by the International Romani Union and most local associations.

These names seek to raise the curtain of silence and invisibility long lowered on Romani victims of Nazi racial policy while also stressing the singularity of their experience. The persecution of Romanies across Europe by the Nazi and other fascist governments has certain specific traits, as discussed in Chapter 2. That notwithstanding, the reasoning invoked here is that viewing the Romani genocide in the context of the whole suite of Third Reich genocide policies explains more than it conceals. A fragmentary study of that complex historic development would 'ghettify' knowledge, thereby unwittingly corroborating the social 'ghettification' pursued by the Nazis. In contrast, detecting relationships and establishing comparisons (with the concomitant identification not only of similarities but also of differences) between the various scenarios of racial persecution and collective murder perpetrated by the Nazi regime afford greater understanding. And that understanding is useful to better defusing the racist platitudes used to describe European Romanies then and now.

This book uses the word 'Holocaust' in its very title. The first reason is that it implies comparison among experiences and favours general comprehension. A second argument for its application, namely its widespread use in academia and mainstream society, also supports the primary intention pursued: to contribute to the transfer of scientific knowledge to public awareness. Given the connotations of the word and its origin mentioned earlier, its consolidated use emphasizes the specificity of a historic event with a particular moral impact not only on historians, but on mindful citizens everywhere. The reference is to a programme for systematic elimination of millions of people pertaining to racial groups deemed inferior, instituted with all the State's administrative resources, implemented by a generously endowed bureaucracy that included scientists and engineers as well as police and military forces, conducted via an industrialized system of mass destruction and applied to a civilian population quite beyond any combat-related military logic.

Moreover, any approach that stresses the incommensurability of the historic development so branded should also include comparative references that render it intelligible. The Holocaust must be understood in its historic context (one of extreme violence) so as not to afford it such exceptional status that its social impact is construed by today's generations as an extraordinary, monstrous or unparalleled event. As Enzo Traverso[7] notes, from 1914 to 1945 Europe, battered by events comparable to civil war, was characterized by a culture and scenarios of extreme violence. The outcome was societal tolerance of a premised 'total war' that would blithely ignore the traditional distinction between front and rear guard or between armed forces and civilian population. Although the First World War may be thought to have set the stage for that drama, Traverso and other authors agree in identifying the Nazi invasion of the Soviet Union in 1941 as a point of no return in the dehumanization of the enemy and concomitant violence. Unless those general coordinates are understood, sight will be lost of all that was served to the Nazi regime 'on a silver platter' in the form of pre-existing, resolutely racist legal measures, scientific studies and cultural products. Failing to acknowledge such circumstances would be tantamount to ignoring a sizeable proportion of society's complicity in the harassment, abuse, deportation and murder of those branded as the nation's racial 'enemies'. It would mean forgetting that the murder of millions of people for those reasons had intellectual and material perpetrators, some but not all of whose names are known. In short it would involve refusing to be warned against the 'banality of evil' identified by Hannah Arendt in her chronicle of the Eichmann trial in Jerusalem and interiorizing the ingenuous conviction that the Holocaust is an issue anchored in the past, over and done with.

In the terminological tension in which this book is set, then, the word 'genocide' is very likely the most suitable. As explained at the beginning of Chapter 2, it is in all certainty applicable to the destruction inflicted on the Romani population by the Nazi regime. The term was first used immediately after the Second World War as the one applied to a legal category with which to rise to the challenge of instituting legal and judicial grounds for defining Nazi crimes. Raphael Lemkin, a Jewish jurist exiled in the United States, one of the pioneer advocates of the use of the term, explicitly included 'Gypsies' as victims in his earliest defence of the category. Beyond its legal definition, however, 'genocide' is the academic term most widely used today in studies of the persecution and destruction of Romani communities in Hitlerian Europe. The most relevant reference for the debate on the suitability of its application is (primarily the introduction to) Anton Weiss-Wendt's book,[8] particularly in light of evidence found in recently accessed eastern European country and former Soviet Union archives. Those documents attest to the magnitude and ideological determination underlying the persecution afflicted on Romanies merely because they were deemed 'Gypsies'.

In his book Weiss-Wendt addresses a related issue likewise broached by other scholars: the comparison between the Jewish and Romani Holocausts. The present discussion revolves not around the differences between the movements that have driven the study and acknowledgement of the two experiences, but to the positions from which research has been conducted. Some objections to or otherwise avoidance of that comparison have been voiced both by Jewish historians (Yehuda Bauer in particular) reluctant to view the suffering inflicted on all groups of victims in the same light and by Romani activists (such as Romani Rose), who have preferred to emphasize the singularity of the persecution of Roma people. Whilst lying in neither one camp nor the other, the research conducted by historian Guenter Lewy[9] can be positioned within that spectrum. His studies have significantly advanced knowledge of the Romani Holocaust, although deeming the scope of that genocide to be minimal compared to dimension of the Jewish experience. That premise is rebutted in Part I of this book, for the differences in the determination and degree of centralized management of Nazi anti-Jewish and anti-Gypsy racial policies entailed a no less destructive effect on Roma than on Jewish people.

Introduction

As discussed later, most researchers presently stress the similarities in the racial policy of aggression against the two communities and its effects. Building on Sybil Milton's and Henry Friedlander's key studies,[10] historians have drawn from the records to show that couching the problem posed by the Roma minority for the Nazi regime (the 'Gypsy plague') in racial terms is wholly appropriate. The same perspective has been applied to the deprivation of both groups' legal rights, their deportation to the same ghettos and concentration/extermination camps (singling out the highly symbolic Auschwitz), the execution of Jews and Romanies at the hands of the *Einsatzgruppen* (special mobile killing units accompanying the German army as it advanced eastward). Unsurprisingly, many of the first historians to analyse the Romani genocide were originally engaged in studying the Jewish Holocaust, for the archives they reviewed also contained evidence of the similar fate that befell European Roma. That inclination to compare and relate the two does not mean that differences are obviated or singularities denied. As Weiss notes, the idea is not to engage in a blunt comparison of numbers of victims, but to place the focus of research on the constant contextualization of new data and to study Nazi racial policy as a whole.

The review of the state of the art in Part I of this book aspires to follow that line of reasoning, comparing both the similarities and differences between the two (Chapter 2), tracking long-term precedents for the processes studied (Chapter 1) and reflecting on the intensification of the sequelae of Nazi persecution as a result of the subsequent disregard for its Romani victims (Chapter 3). All references have been consistently included in endnotes, specifying authors' names and dates of publication. Their contributions are then discussed in the annotated bibliography included at the end, intended as a guide for interested readers wishing to delve more deeply into the subject. Part II draws from the survivors' memoirs listed at the beginning of that section and in the bibliography, and explicitly cited in the text.

The book's illustrations were drawn from a number of archives. The effort deployed to locate and reproduce these materials was a venture in itself worthy of detailed description. Although that will have to wait for another occasion, be it said that such a discussion would aptly complement Chapter 3, in particular as regards the issue of how research and dissemination impact public knowledge and social awareness of a matter of such civic relevance as the issue at hand. Direct contact with the centres where this material is in custody revealed that whereas some institutions are fully compliant with their stated aim to participate in the dissemination of Holocaust history and memory, others fail to meet the expectations of survivors and their families donating personal documents.

The end list of illustrations, in turn, cites all possible references, including the present location of the respective photos. Switching to a more personal voice, as author of these pages I also urge readers to take a critical view of that part of my discourse. As Susan Sontag says, photographs never depict, but rather interpret or even re-create supposedly objective reality [Illustration 1]. The present selection of illustrations, partially mediated by the aforementioned documentary accessibility, constitutes just that, a selection, one of the various options adopted in this study. Although such

Illustration 1 Romani woman telling German troops' fortunes in Poland, October 1939.
Panzer driver souvenir or propaganda? In this photo, titled 'Behind the lines humour', the woman was forced into a pose that necessarily attracts the viewer's gaze [NIOD, Institute for War, Holocaust and Genocide Studies, Amsterdam].

choices are my sole responsibility, I am indebted to all those who contributed to the task. Any long-term academic study is conceived in an environment where exchange with colleagues is consistently rewarding. In this case I benefitted from the activities and discussions arising around two collective research projects: *Beyond Stereotypes: Cultural Exchanges and Romani Contribution to European Public Spaces* (*BESTROM*) (with funding from HERA – Humanities in European Research Area, Joint Research Programme, 2019–2022) and *Discursos y representaciones de la etnicidad: política, identidad y conflicto en el siglo XX* (ethnic discourse and depiction: twentieth-century politics, identity and conflict); PID2019-105741GB-I00, Spanish Government RUDI Project, 2020-3.

I also wish to express special thanks to a number of colleagues who generously found the time to critically review the book as it was being written, while providing material of interest and sharing their experience: Eve Rosenhaft, colleague and friend at the University of Liverpool; Miguel Martorell, author of an indispensable book on Nazi cultural looting; and Juan Pro, my most critical and trusted travelling companion. In the long journey involved in this research I also had the enormous fortune of making the personal acquaintance of Philomena Franz, Romani genocide survivor and author of one of the memoirs used hereunder. I benefitted greatly from dialoguing with her. The merit is not mine, but Philomena's: her intelligence, courage and generosity would inspire anyone. I encourage readers to view the online multi-language documentary *My Holocaust. Philomena Franz*[11] produced from videos of my interviews conducted with her in 2021 with the invaluable assistance of Sidonia Bauer and Virginia Maza. Lastly, I am deeply grateful to all the Roma who read the original Spanish version of this book and sent me feedback in the form of their comments and encouragement.

PART I
A SCANTLY KNOWN AND UNDER-ACKNOWLEDGED GENOCIDE

CHAPTER 1
THE ROMA AND ANTI-GYPSYISM: PARALLEL HISTORIES

The systematic liquidation of Europe's Romani (like its Jewish) population, designed and perpetrated by the Nazi regime, is only understandable if set into the historic background of anti-Gypsyism, a complex bias as long-running as the very history of the Roma people in the Western world. This chapter consequently broaches the precedents for the Romani genocide under the Nazi regime. Irrespective of the specificity of events that took place in preceding periods, the outcome of different mentalities and approaches to societal organization, nations all across Europe have consistently rejected and harassed their Romani minorities, denying their culture and even attempting their annihilation. In other words, Nazi policies against the Roma peoples fell on fertile soil, given the long legal and cultural tradition that had stigmatized this community, deemed foreign and a social peril. Without that background, the programme for exterminating the people branded by the Nazi regime as 'Gypsies' would have barely been feasible.

Abuse and persecution have been (and still are) so persistent that the reaction prompted in the group so labelled was understandably to build defensive barriers, rendering the task of defining these people even more vexed. The naming issue referred to in the introduction is a clear example of the complexity plaguing an often-debated and controversial identity. The derogatory term 'Gypsies' was used from outside that community. In the wake of the abuse inflicted on so-called 'Gypsies' during the Holocaust, after the Second World War they attempted to redefine their collective identity with other names. The memory of that abuse, one of the keys to Romani post-war identity, has a number of readings among those who, deeming themselves heirs to the Roma of those times, continue the struggle to eliminate the adverse stereotypes that served the purposes of such treatment.

Coming to Europe in troubled times

Philological reconstructions trace the origin of Europe's Romanies to north-eastern India, which they left at some indeterminate time in the Middle Ages. They settled in a number of areas in the former Byzantine Empire: first in Asia Minor and then on the Balkan peninsula, where there are historic records of their presence and economic activity. Later, in the context of other migrations related to the Turkish invasion of those areas, they spread throughout Europe. In the fourteenth and fifteenth centuries groups of misnamed 'Egyptians' or 'Bohemians' began to settle in most of the Old

Continent: Moldova, Wallachia, Hungary, Poland, Germany, Switzerland, Italy, France, the Netherlands, England, Spain and so on. Not long after, they travelled to the New World with Christopher Columbus in his earliest transatlantic voyages.

That at least is how the origins of Europe's Roma are normally described, an account that glosses over huge documentary voids in the earliest times. More strikingly, its assimilation in Nazi racist policy entails an inherent contradiction, for it would imply an Indo-European or Aryan ancestry for these peoples, as defended by eighteenth-century German scholar Grellmann [Illustration 2]. Irrespective of such considerations, that account of Romani entry into European history is plagued by a scientific and political issue that tends to be overlooked. Viewing them as immigrants of a distant and even mysterious origin attributes (though perhaps inadvertently) 'foreigner' status to peoples who have been living on European soil continuously since the lower Middle Ages. Europe has historically been a demographic flood basin. But the same criteria are not applied to all the human groups occupying, crossing and populating the area, for some are saddled with an indelibly exotic and distant origin. The historic narrative is not neutral, integrating some communities naturally while stressing others' foreign ancestry. The English word 'Gypsy', the French '*Gitane*' and the Spanish '*Gitano*' are all rooted in the term 'Egyptian'. Whether they refer to an area of Peloponnese known as Little Egypt or African Egypt itself, they are misnomers that identify these people as a group foreign to the social corpus historically rooted on the respective national soil. (Their denomination in France as '*Bohemien*' as an allusion to their arrival from Bohemia can be similarly construed.)

The reasons for depicting Romanies as foreigners have much to do with the cultural shock generated by the new arrivals among Germans, Italians, Spaniards and Dutch, to name a few. According to the diary[1] authored in the first third of the fifteenth century by a self-styled 'Parisian bourgeois', the year 1427 is recalled for the expectation prompted by a group of over 100 people from 'Lower Egypt', whose strange language, dress and customs induced both curiosity and apprehension.

> Nearly all had both ears pierced and wore one or two silver earrings in each, which they said was a sign of nobility in their land. The men were very dark, with curly hair. The women, darker and uglier than any ever seen […] Despite their poverty, the group included sorcerers who could tell people the future that awaited them by reading the palm of their hand.

For all those reasons, during their stay in Paris 'more people gathered to see them than had ever assembled for the Bishop's blessing'. From the very outset, then, societies that deemed themselves civilized rejected nomadism, a lifestyle suspect to them for any number of reasons that heightened racial prejudice.

But the specific timing of the arrival of these peoples in Europe was an even more decisive factor in the institution of conclusively anti-Gypsy legislation than any such societal fear of the unknown or different. The circumstances definitively driving the construction of the modern nation-state happened to fall in place at just that time.

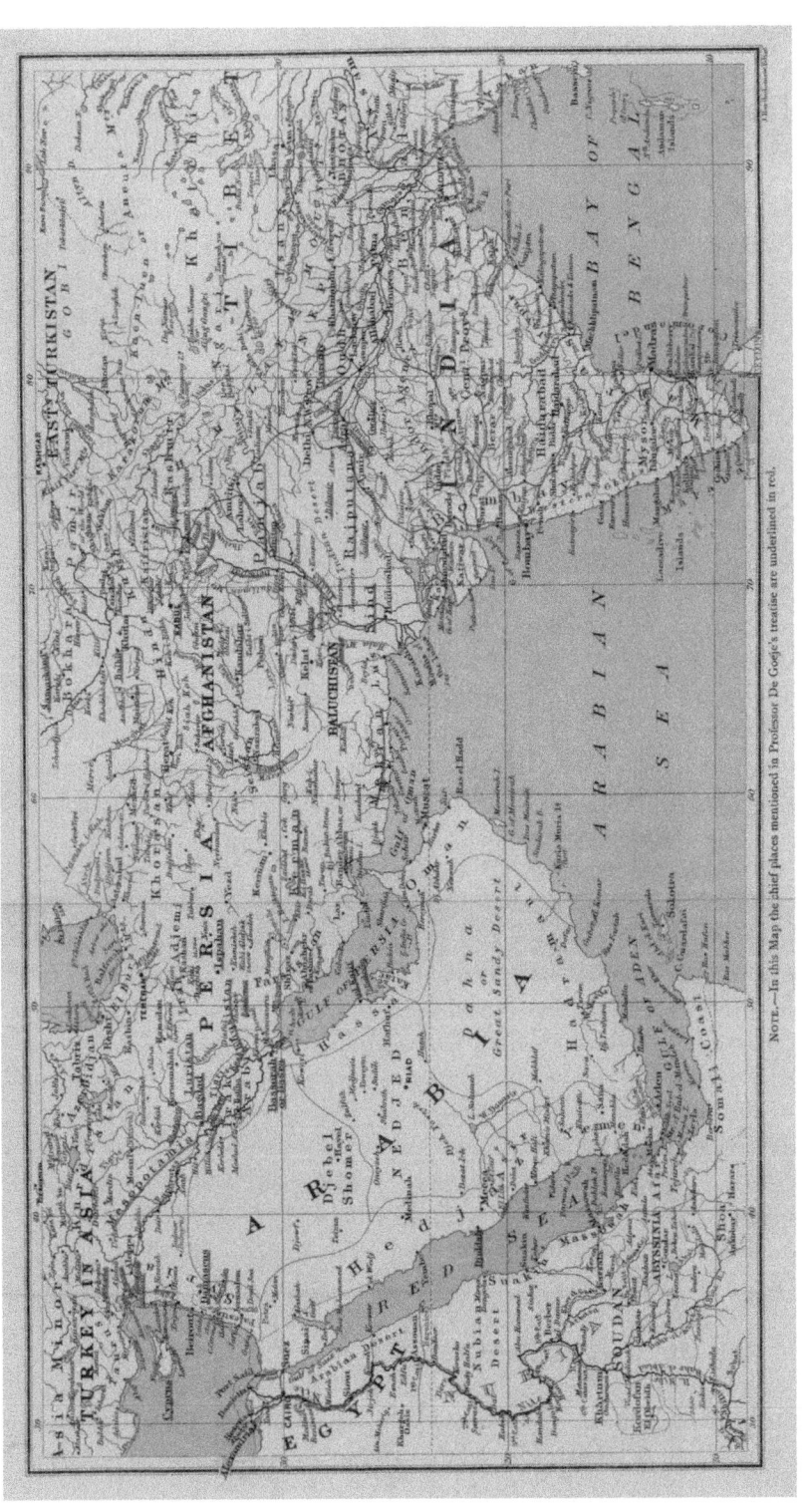

Illustration 2 Map used as an illustration in *Accounts of the Gypsies of India*, 1886. Collected and edited by Gypsy Lore Society member D. MacRitchie, this book was subtitled *An Historical and Cultural Study of the Gypsies of India* (from whence it was believed the 'Gypsies' of Europe originated)' [British Library, London].

The Roma and the Holocaust

Many fifteenth-century European sovereigns undertook the difficult task of vesting royal power with a higher civil status than other powers and institutions, fuelling processes that defined the nation-state, with the concomitant inter-territorial conflict. From the advent of this complex historic development and through its consolidation in the sixteenth century, sovereigns attached utmost importance to controlling populations and their movements and to securing cultural uniformity among different groups of subjects. Romanies arrived when diversity, never an object of political esteem, was viewed as particularly undesirable. Legislation on their settlement was consequently enacted just as European monarchs were embarking on political and cultural isolation. At the same time, the pressure exerted by the Turkish-Ottoman Empire from the Balkans and Mediterranean highlighted the religious dimension of operations contributing to the political definition of European nations. From the outset, Romani groups residing on Christian soil began to be branded as suspect on the grounds of presumed espionage in favour of Muslim power. They continued to be deemed spies protected by a nomadic lifestyle up to and including the First and Second World Wars. During both wars, a considerable number of Romanies were arrested for espionage and executed in the name of national security, with utter disregard for the fact that many members of the community had served in the front lines of their respective countries' armies.

To return to their origins, for all the foregoing these groups were tainted with the stigma of permanent foreigners on national soil. Sixteenth-, seventeenth- and eighteenth-century legislation sought their disappearance across Europe through mandatory assimilation via the elimination of their specific cultural characteristics, expulsion or annihilation. The accumulation of specific anti-Gypsy measures in the various European kingdoms throughout the Modern Age acquired incommensurable dimensions. The laws, edicts and decrees ceaselessly instituted everywhere were all cut to the same basic pattern, seeking to control a group legally defined as an internal enemy encrusted in the social body. That entailed acknowledging their distinctive culture, albeit with persecutory intentions, while at the same time denying any such specificity, contending that the term 'Gypsy' was a mere cover-up for vagabond and delinquent.

Despite the safe-conducts initially granting Romanies the right to enter German lands as religious pilgrims, for instance, their presence set off an increasingly restrictive series of local and regional provisions against them. The city of Frankfort was the first to legally expel them in 1449, whilst in others they were only allowed to camp on the outskirts. An edict enacted by the imperial Diet in the latter years of the fifteenth century revoked all the safe-conducts issued earlier by Emperor Sigismund that allowed Romanies to enter the Holy Roman Empire, rendering their presence on its soil illegal. From the mid-sixteenth to the mid-eighteenth centuries approximately 120 laws of differing scope imposed physical punishment and forced labour on Romanies if found on lands forbidden to them. In some cases transgression meant the death penalty, such as in a 1661 decree issued by the Prince-Elector of Saxony. Other laws provided for the mandatory separation of children from their parents to be raised in families or institutions deemed Christian.

Although the eighteenth century brought an enlightened approach to governmental tasks, perhaps surprisingly the governing classes adhering most enthusiastically to modernizing reform were the ones that prioritized control of the population and subjects' economic utility. Without revoking the earlier measures, the policies newly introduced imposed permanent settlement and assimilation on Roma people. During the reigns of Empress Maria Theresa and her son Joseph II of Austria and Fredrick II (also called the Great) of Prussia, Romanies were confined to a scant few legally condoned and fiercely enforced encampment sites and allowed to engage in only a short list of occupations.

The events taking place in that area of Europe in the Modern Age were hardly exceptional. It would be a mistake to extend earlier legal abuse to Nazi Third Reich measures on the assumption of an exclusively or primarily German pattern of pre-existing anti-Gypsyism. A quick look at English legislation on 'Gypsy travellers' also attests to a flurry of laws of differing rank specifically targeting Roma peoples or associating the term 'Gypsy' with 'peddler' or 'poor'. The former included the 1530 Egyptians Act that banned their entry and ordered the exile of those present in England. In 1554 an eponymous act also prohibited entry to 'Egyptians', while providing for mandatory permanent settlement of Romani families already living on English soil. It also harshened the penalties for non-compliance, adding capital punishment to the confiscation of possessions and deportation already on the books. Laws and judicial practice were no more benevolent in Elizabethan England, although by then Roma peoples were viewed not as an exotic peril of foreign extraction but an autochthonous social problem.[2] Fingering them as an especially criminal component of the cast of nomadic and delinquent rogues, beggars and vagabonds, in practice the new measures vested local judicial authorities with substantial discretionary power. As Morgan notes, in some cases exemplary punishment was imposed on those who looked, dressed or lived like 'Gypsies'. In other cases 'the possibility of the discretionary commutation of an indictment from a charge of being a "counterfeit Egyptian" down to being a "rogue" or "vagabond"' entailed greater judicial benevolence. That of course also called for concealing and eliminating Romani identity, for what the courts offered was the 'opportunity to renounce an identity or face the death penalty.'[3]

The severity of these provisions was in line with measures in other countries, even in places such as Spain, where the local Romani population, the 'Gitanos', was paradoxically assimilated as a symbol of the national identity. There also, Roma peoples who were initially granted royal authorization (and even welcomed by the nobility) to live on national soil witnessed the revocation of their status as pilgrims on which it was based. In the Spain of Ferdinand and Isabel, sovereigns keen on building a nation united around a common culture and religion, 'Gitanos', like other minorities such as Jews and Moors, were threatened with expulsion. Under a 1499 law, 'Gitanos' preferring to remain on national soil were required to renounce their language and dress and submit to the authority of a lordship. The penalties for non-compliance announced at the time, slavery and forced labour, were maintained by subsequent monarchs. In 1619 Philip III decreed that transgression would entail capital punishment, while subsequent laws opted for mandating assimilation rather than expulsion. The respective provisions required 'Gitanos' to appear in court to be censused, limited the places they were allowed to live and crafts they were allowed to practise, and prohibited the use of their language, construed as 'gibberish'. In one of the cruellest moments of eighteenth-century Enlightenment Spain, in 1749 Ferdinand VI, acting on the advice of the Marquis de la Ensenada, decreed the arrest of all the country's Romanies. Known as the 'Gran Redada' (the mass raid), the operation dragged whole families out of their permanent homes, confiscated their goods, subjected men and women to forced labour and kept them separated to secure the community's biological extinction.

The arguments underlying this dense legal apparatus in the countries involved, as well as the accompanying political discourse formulated by royal counsellors, members of Parliaments and Diets, local authorities, scholars studying the nation's problems, police orders and so on are revealing in a number of ways. First, they imply that Romani groups had come to stay, for the reiterative measures and punishments constitute implicit acknowledgement of the failure of any attempt to expel them. Second, they stand as proof that Roma peoples were integrated into the life and economy of mainstream society to a greater extent than suggested by the stereotype that reduced them to itinerant bands of vagabonds and delinquents. Whilst the legislation supposedly targeted nomad Roma, it actually impacted the sedentary community as well, limiting the crafts they could practise, confining them to certain areas, capitalizing on the strength of their labour and mandating censuses to keep track of their existence. Consequently, the legislation supposedly targeting unoccupied nomadic outlaws, an obsession at a time when banditry intensified due to the severe social facture generated by the Thirty Years War, actually impacted sedentary, censused Roma as well.

Read against a broader background, those measures are indicative of the presence of a number of Romani groups settled across Europe, on whom they imposed constraints regarding where they could live and what they could do to earn a living. Some, such as farming tasks, were shared with the working class in the host societies. Others were associated more specifically with occupational profiles, such as iron and other metal forging, the repair of a variety of objects, horse husbandry and trading or musical and theatrical performances for the entertainment of the public at large. In countries such as Hungary and Russia their presence in musical circles was deemed characteristic of the respective national cultures as early as the eighteenth century. Their frequent engagement in minor-scale trading and object repair necessarily involved mobility, which had to do as well with the ban on membership in established guilds.

Paradoxically, that sort of policies presumably geared to assimilating Roma peoples generated alienation and induced criminality. Some of the measures prevented them from practising certain crafts or required them to move to certain locations. Others banned practices that were not exclusive to Romanies, such as begging or nomadism, but for which as 'Gypsies' they were doubly criminalized. For all the foregoing, the roots of the governmental logic that remained in effect until the onset of Nazism and even later can be traced back to that period, That reality is attested to by the fact that the legal and regulatory discourse formulated by Modern Age monarchies created criminal categories meant to be applied to a whole community as such. They activated a three-pronged operation that translated into a long-lasting political synthesis: categorization, whereby a community is assigned a name; branding, in which its members are identified; and stigmatization that results from the application of adverse value judgements.[4]

One of the primary problems encountered by the Romani community was the extra-legal effect of such laws. As a regulatory instrument they not only punished those deemed delinquent or a social peril, but quite beyond any specific judicial or penal activity, conveyed to the rest of society a globally disparaging image of so-called 'Gypsies', much to the detriment of many generations of Roma. In addition, the prevailing adverse legislative and political discourse fed into parallel narratives that contributed to spreading such a detrimental multidirectional image and above all including it in what might be termed societal 'second nature'. Literature and the plastic arts are known to be particularly influential in defining the suite of presumptions unconditionally accepted by a community and assumed to be entirely natural. Those and other cultural vehicles erase the tracks of how the respective images are generated. The outcome is that the target public rarely poses objections to their artificial and temporary nature or questions the political intention of their authors.

During the Renaissance and Baroque eras, novels and stage plays resorted to 'Gypsies' to portray delinquents and social outcasts. At times they were not even named directly, but used as ambience or excuse. They constituted a very effective literary resource, for they served as symbols of the unlawfulness that drives any plot, not to mention their value in defining the moral of the story or other edificatory formulas. Hence the vast number of tales where 'Gypsies' were assigned the role, no explanation needed, of bandits who defy social laws, fearsome witches, dangerously attractive women or child abductors. From Cervantes' *La Gitanilla* to Molière's *Les Fourberies de Scapin*, Sallebray's *La Belle Egyptienne* and Dafoe's *Moll Flanders*, pre-Romantic writers in all countries used 'Gypsies' to introduce intrigue and social tension in their plots. The benign traits exceptionally vested in certain characters or specific situations were utterly compatible with the stigma that smeared the group as a whole.

Paintings and engravings also tapped into the vein of thematic ore personified by 'Gypsies' as an exotic element, a colourful mobile component in a landscape or an occasion to introduce the contrast between 'normal' and 'other' characters in a plastic narrative. The portrayal of Romani women as fortune tellers was adopted as a subject by Georges de La Tour, Nicolas Régnier and Watteau, among many others [Illustration 3]. For many a landscapist such as David Teniers, Jan Steen and Thomas Gainsborough, Romani campgrounds and caravans served to illustrate the contrast between nature and humanity, suggesting something that might be construed as a missing link in the development of civilization. In such depictions, the typification of a generically 'Gypsy' appearance for readier identification drew from the dress codes and adornments attributed to them. Racial differentiation was also deployed (albeit not without hesitation) in the form of physical traits such as dark skin and eyes and black hair. That outer appearance was intended as well to match the personalities portrayed: vagrancy, indolence and an inclination to deceive and steal in their dealings with 'honest citizens'.

Illustration 3 *The Fortune-Teller*, **Georges de la Tour,** *c.* **1630.** Stereotyped images of Roma people, fortune telling and burglary, with a social impact above and beyond the scope of art [Metropolitan Museum of Art, New York].

That literary and plastic but in any event fictional portrayal of 'Gypsies', more than depicting the social reality of the various Romani lifestyles, interpreted and fed into the legal and political discourse formulated by governing elites. It also contributed substantially to creating simplified stereotypes that sullied the collective history of these minorities. Nonetheless, the era that followed brought a decisive qualitative leap in the depiction of Romanies that, in addition to governing their everyday lives, deprived many generations of their right to define their own image.

The long nineteenth century and Romantic stereotypes

As the period when Western modernity's cultural paradigm crystallized, the nineteenth century is a key era for understanding the depictions of and discourses around 'Gypsies' that even today inform Roma people's societal image. The cultural processes and their political implications addressed below sprouted in the latter decades of the eighteenth century and extended, generally speaking, through the first few of the twentieth, very closely matching what Eric Hobsbawm termed the 'long nineteenth century'. Throughout those years, at least in countries where liberalism began to prevail as a political project, the institutional harassment referred to above was mitigated to some extent. Laws were still on the books specifically referring to 'Gypsies' as a collective target for penal and police measures, but at least the legal stigmatization disappeared from higher-ranking provisions such as constitutions adhering to the premise that the entire citizenry was equal under law. That was not the case, however, in the areas of Europe where the new liberal regime had not yet been instituted. In regions such as Wallachia and Moldova most of the Romani population was enslaved until well into the nineteenth century.

Where it did prevail, such relative political-legislative progress did not translate into the deactivation of the stereotypes with which Romanies had been branded since they arrived in Europe. On the contrary. Whilst the legislative dimension underwent a temporary relaxation of the attention to what had by then been categorized as the 'Gypsy question', 'Gypsies' continued to be an object of growing cultural interest among high- or mid-ranking artists, scientists and essayists. The voice of those outside observers was decisive in solidifying images which, drawing from past centuries' materials, were projected forward to the world wars. Both art and science portrayed Romanies as a uniform community so frequently and insistently that they may be said to have had the effect of rendering real people indistinguishable, invisible to the gaze of contemporary society in general and concealed to later eras under a thick layer of exogenous depictions.

In the hands of Romanticism, 'the Gypsy' as subject matter became genuinely popular in the nineteenth century. The spread of a particular cultural sensitivity across all of Europe for one reason or another favoured the observation and use of these communities as a subject for artistic representation or scholarly reflection. Romantic travel, a development that grew into an early tourist industry in the Western world, contributed greatly to enhancing that popularity. Ever larger swathes of the European and American bourgeoisie, particularly self-deemed artists, took to travel as an experience in pursuit of lifestyles that differed from their own or even as an attempt to discover supposedly lost or endangered cultures. 'Gypsies' became one of the trophies of that endeavour and travellers' narratives recorded their existence wherever they found them. The alleged realism with which such accounts were narrated made them particularly misleading. In that context guidebooks, paintings, engravings, poems and photographs became a source of inspiration for those who had not directly experienced travel, generating ever denser fantasies around Romani exoticism and otherness.

In that setting, Spain became a romantic destination par excellence. For the earliest English, French, American and other tourists (and through them, their readership), Spain meant not only proximity to Africa but monuments attesting to a Muslim past and Medieval Age that could be readily mythicized. In addition to all those alluring features, it had a particularly large 'Gypsy' population, especially in Andalusia [Illustration 4]. Many European and universal romantic stereotypes attributed to 'Gypsies' were generated in that specific space, at once real and figurative: understood as the epitome

Illustration 4 *Gypsy Woman Dancing the Zorongo*, **1874, by Gustave Doré.** Andalusia, Spain and 'Gypsies': convergence of romantic myths [Antonio Machado Library, University of Seville.]

of the Spanish psyche, the construction of a 'Gypsified' Andalusia afforded romantic travellers fertile soil in which to sow exotic fantasies.[5]

From the ethnocentric perspective of those observers, the southern and eastern peripheries of Europe were logically related. And stimulated by such awesome monuments as the Alhambra at Granada and other remnants of Andalusia's Muslim past, 'Gypsies' could be interpreted as a fragment of that Far East encrusted in the West, as an explanation for their presence and appearance. One English traveller kept a travelogue where she described her impression, shared by others, when seeing a group of Romani women dance in Granada. 'Colonel H., who had just returned from India overland, was struck with the similarity existing between these dances and those of the Nautch girls of India and Persia; and I, for my part, found very little difference between them and the performances of the dancing girls I had seen in the harems of Turkey'.[6] More than a few local cultural entrepreneurs capitalized on that presumption, setting 'Gypsy' or 'Gypsified' characters in Moorish scenarios when producing post cards, photographs and other very popular souvenirs. As discussed later, Gypsyism is a close parallel to 'Orientalism' as defined by Edward Said: appropriation of the image of 'others' in the name of expert knowledge and from a position of cultural superiority that forms part of a device for cultural domination more pervasive than mere territorial and economic control.[7]

The power of the images of 'Gypsies' portrayed by romantic artists draws from the tension inherent in depicting positive and negative traits as inseparable parts of one and the same identity. The community hosting those features is consequently characterized by a wealth of nuance and potential, rendering it more credible and intuitively acceptable to the rest of society. The discourse is ostensibly benevolent and even admiring. 'Gypsies' in that narrative are special inasmuch as they are a reservoir of primitive humanity whose nature has been unaltered by industrial progress, endowing them with a collective personality highly appealing to the romantic mentality. They would presumably be freer, more spontaneous, authentic, sensitive and closer to the natural world. That would make them collectively more artistically inclined and better suited to enjoy life. Braver and bolder, they would entertain social relations less constrained by bourgeois hypocrisy. Along those lines, nearly from its inception, Romanticism used 'Gypsy' camps in fiction as a hideout for persecuted heroes, sheltered by tribe seniors and possibly enamoured of a pretty young girl. Prototypical heroes were even cast as 'Gypsies' in some romantic fiction, good and brave bandits protesting a manifestly unjust order and extraordinarily beautiful women able to dissolve social boundaries. That role-casting mirrors bourgeois gender standards which, like any stereotype, provide a more telling depiction of the social group generating the image than of the group portrayed.

The freedom admired in 'Gypsies' as a community could also entail undesirable traits, however, on which nineteenth-century cultural discourse also tended to insist. As rebels against common constraints, they could at the same time be irremediably asocial and extra-legal or even criminals, fruit of primitive morals that had not advanced in the understanding of good and evil in the same way as civilized society. In that discourse 'Gypsies' were dangerous because they honoured no rules and were used to living in caravans, homes on wheels that favoured disregard for borders and national loyalties. Although they lived in close communion with Mother Nature and were able to capture her magic, they were materially and rationally backward. Their rejection of progress could readily translate into barbarian behaviours.

Further to that reasoning, their peculiar sensitivity was conducive to both natural artistic talent and uncontrolled passion prompted by primary instincts, likening them to archaic humans or even animals. Literary descriptions often based their metaphors on animal (bird, wolf etc.) or infantile conduct, at least as frequently as they eroticized 'Gypsy' presence in all manner of fictional scenarios. That insistence on sensuality, voluptuosity and sexually free behaviour was particularly intense when inspired by women, often portrayed as attractive but lewd and as such dangerous. Positioning the Spanish 'Gypsy' on the higher rungs of seductive artistry, Gypsylorist George Borrow contended that 'no females in the world can be more licentious in word and gesture, in dance and in song, than the *Gitanas*'.[8]

Any number of paintings, photographs and novels, read as discourses about a presumed 'other', clearly reveal the lust in the (masculine) authors' gaze on the objects of their portrayals. The best known example is indisputably Carmen, the 'Gypsy' woman created by French author Prosper Mérimée in a short novel published between 1845 and 1846 and raised to the altar of worldwide fame by Georges Bizet in an eponymous opera that premiered in Paris in 1875. 'There was something strange and wild about her beauty (…) Her eyes, especially, had an expression of mingled sensuality and fierceness which I had never seen in any other human glance. "Gipsy's eye, wolf's eye"'.[9] That is how the author introduces this fascinating woman whose 'Gypsy' exterior mirrors an even more perilous interior, for Carmen is a free spirit subject to no social or moral rules, governed only by impassioned sexuality. Her lover loses his head and his honour in her pursuit, 'Gypsyifying' his behaviour to delinquency. Only her death puts an end to the rabid passion inspired by such an irresistible woman. Her story has given rise to many subsequent interpretations, in view especially of the versatility of the readings given it in thousands of cultural products. That issue is not addressed here, although the following two reflections on the history of the figure help set the plot in the context of the present discussion, namely its role and concomitant effects as a dense stereotype of Roma people.

First, bourgeois gender models that attributed to women domesticity and motherhood were consolidated in that period, depicting the 'angel in the house' as man's perfect (silent and obedient) partner. Men in turn (rational, productive, self-controlled) were believed to assume their natural role in the liberal public sphere. The institution of counter-models has been a consistent and effective way to reinforce and uphold the value of a society's ideal standards. Hence Carmen and in general Romani women were depicted as the antithesis of genuine (and proper) femininity [Illustration 5]. Her presence was consequently perilous for men, as a seductive, ravenous *femme fatale*. In some fictional narratives 'Gypsy' women were compared to panthers for the way they moved and especially the way they danced. In music, Franz Liszt described them as sorceresses of beauty and hypnotic song, much to the terror of young Russian aristocrats' mothers and tutors.[10] Nonetheless, the moral teachings contained in all manner of stories and images not only failed to hinder but in fact enhanced male sexual and emotional fantasies. They induced a view of Romani women in much the same racial light as other female figures, one of many in a suite of exotic beauties that served as an escape valve.

The second reference alludes to the length in time and breadth in space of the success of that depiction of Romani women, in which gender plays into and reinforces the general racial stereotype applied to 'Gypsies'. Since the opera was first composed in the mid-nineteenth century, *Carmen* has been performed continuously in any number of media. It leapt from the live stage to cinema, where it engaged even larger audiences. The first motion picture version of *Carmen* was a short film in Britain in 1907. It was

Illustration 5 Poster for an adaptation of Mérimée's *Carmen*, 1896. Dangerous 'Gypsy' women, a long-lived nineteenth-century myth [US Library of Congress].

soon followed by a host of silent films, some by directors as renowned as Charles Chaplin (1915) and Ernst Lubitsch (1918). The latter cast emergent star-system actresses such as Paoli Negri in the role [Illustration 6].

All these developments denote the compatibility between sublimation and stigmatization inherent in any complex stereotype. Whilst the 'Gypsy' women who drove these fictions were 'drop-dead gorgeous', their personalities fated them to a frenzied and unhappy life. The cultural inferiority of their race served to explain their nature and behaviour, as well as to draw moral and social borders between the various characters. That was reinforced by the appearance of secondary 'Gypsy' characters, rarely endowed with the exceptionality that made the Carmen character so powerfully attractive. Her appeal was so strong that in the nineteen forties Leni Riefenstahl, Hitler's favourite director, scripted a film[11] about an irresistible vagabond dancer, object of a perverse nobleman's lust, and decided to play the lead role herself.

Illustration 6 Paola Negri, silent movie star, in *Screenland,* **October 1923.** Daughter of a Romani Slovakian violinist born in 1897, she played the lead role in Ernest Lubitsch's *Gypsy Blood* [US Library of Congress].

In one particularly striking scene in *Tiefland* (lowland), Riefenstahl fails woefully in her efforts to dance seductively as a 'Gypsy' might, despite her use of all the necessary props: flounced skirt, shawl, large earrings and even castanets. The background for this film is exemplary in helping understand how stereotypes contribute to the banalization of evil. The scene at issue was shot at the same time as the Nazi regime was consistently engaging in persecuting nomads, identified with 'Gypsies' as discussed in a later chapter. That circumstance is particularly enlightening in terms of how sublimation and stigmatization can go hand in hand, affecting the lives of real people. The extras in Riefenstahl's film, Romanies imprisoned in camps such as Marzahn and Maxglan, later perished at Auschwitz with many other members of their community.

The role of science

The cultural schizophrenia that exalts fictitious 'Gypsies' while persecuting real Romanies rests on nineteenth-century romantic stereotypes. At the same time, however, presumably scientific expertise, in fields ranging from anthropology to medicine, furnished comprehensive grounds for twentieth-century anti-Gypsy political measures. Racially slanted, although ostensibly rational, science consolidated the depiction of Roma people as a community defined by a given genetic nature that according to reputed scientists accorded them a subordinate place in the world. In an assessment of the historic contributions made by a number of the world's peoples, Scottish anatomist Robert Knox broke the ground in that regard with the rhetorical question: 'but were Central Africa, from the Edge of the Sahara to the Cape of Storms, sunk under the ocean wave, and with it the gypsy race, what should we lose?'[12] Nothing, was his reply, or at least 'nothing to distinguish man from brute', for no authors of discoveries, inventions or artistic creations or sublime thoughts would disappear with them. That influential mid-nineteenth-century treatise foreshadowed what was to become the standard approach in European scientific circles when addressing Romani communities and their place in the cultural ranking of known peoples.

The modernist racial cosmovision of humanity emerged as early as the eighteenth century, revealing the darker side of the Enlightenment according to historian George Mosse, which affected not only 'Gypsies', of course. Kant, in a little known aside on racial classification, compared the tendency of America's freed black slaves to shrug work and live as vagabonds to the behaviour of European 'Zigeuner'. Piasere traced the application of physical anthropology to the Romani population back to the Enlightenment. He noted that in the eighteenth century Johann Friedrich Blumenbach, MD, used a 'Zingaric' skull in his famous morphological comparison of known races, combining anatomic observations with popular prejudice, in particular the belief that 'Gypsies' were child abductors.[13]

In the nineteenth century, before craniometry and ancillary disciplines evolved into deeply racist anthropological organicism, the scientific approach to the 'Gypsy' problem moved in other directions. Such disciplines should not, however, be viewed separately from the general racial cosmovision applied more widely to other racialized ('black', 'yellow') groups by authors such as the Count of Gobineau, whose writings had a powerful impact on contemporary society. The application of such precepts to Romanies formed part of the general racial metaphysics that was assimilated into the basic logic and culture of modern Western societies.

Other intellectuals, more influential than nineteenth-century racist philosophers, also formulated ostensibly scientific canons on the collective personality attributed to Roma people. Decisive in that regard was the presumed enigma that drew the scholarly attention of varied groups of philologists, ethnologists and historians, i.e. social scientists, in an age when those pursuits were coming into their own as academic disciplines. Following in Grellmann's tracks, English, French, German, Austrian and other academics set out in pursuit of the 'true Gypsy'. They deployed scientific parameters to determine the traits objectively characterizing Roma people, a community living in Europe whose differentiation from the rest of society constituted an epistemological challenge.

There was, then, no need to travel outside the Old Continent to remote jungles or virgin islands to find exotic peoples. For those observers 'Gypsies' were a readily accessible 'other'. Romani lifestyles, deemed ancient and endangered, piqued their scholarly curiosity. Many authors studied them empathetically, genuinely attracted by what they viewed as Romani singularity, and more than likely unaware of their self-attributed, culturally patronizing position of superiority. 'Gypsy' research consequently contributed to the construction of Romanies as 'others', beings whose anthropology necessarily differed from that of their observers.

One of the most prominent groups of early social scientists, who combined a part amateur, part professional knowledge of linguistics, history, archaeology and ethnography, included the members of the Gypsy Lore Society, dean of associations engaging in Romani studies (that still publishes a prestigious academic journal). Although the society was not founded until 1888, the original group of scholars had been meeting informally and working prior to that date. And George Borrow, maestro of several subsequent generations of Gypsylorists, had initiated his studies even earlier. Traveller, writer, Protestant Bible evangelist, Borrow built his opinions of Romanies out of interest and some empathy, but with the attitude of the racial and cultural hierarchy characteristic of a mid-nineteenth-century Briton. In studies that proved to be extraordinarily influential in defining the 'true Gypsy', Borrow combined a typically romantic travel spirit riddled with an indisputable leaning toward anthropological observation and a no less remarkable linguistic talent whereby among other languages, he learnt Romanes. With that as his introductory letter, he broached Romani communities in a number of countries, recording his observations quite extensively in some, such as in a book[14] on Spanish 'Gitanos' that was to become famous in these circles.

The book contains sections on the 'Gitano' languages and comparative tables to demonstrate its Indian origins, with a core common to the Romanes spoken in other European countries, thereby countering theories that ventured a northern African origin. True to the author's folklorist spirit, another section addresses supposedly 'Gypsy' songs and poems not conserved in writing and consequently at risk of being lost. Quite beyond the disputable rigour of those two tasks, they consistently endorsed Borrow's expertise in 'Gypsy' lore acknowledged by his contemporaries and long after. He, in turn, contended to be an insightful observer of Romani nature, knowledgeable of the community's traditions and even their secrets, thanks in part to his command of Romanes. His writings combined historical information, anthropological observation and interviews to furnish a detailed and truthful depiction of Roma people. Nonetheless, his genuine liking of certain specific Romanies and overall interest in 'Gypsy' lifestyle did not soften his very harsh assessment of the group's collective inclinations. 'Much will have been accomplished, if, after the lapse of a hundred years, one hundred human beings shall have been evolved from the Gypsy stock, who shall prove sober, honest, and useful members of society'.[15] Theirs is a 'stock [...] degraded', he warned. According to Borrow, 'Gypsies' earned their living by duping 'non-Gypsies', whom they hated intensely and for whom they were a peril. He found the men to be violent and the women lewd, contending they had no history, interest for the past, or religion. Interestingly, the nuances stemming from sharp observation he noted on occasion had no impact on his general conclusions. Although he described the specific trades in which he observed some Romanies to engage, he insisted that 'Gypsies' the world over made a living by cheating the rest of society. Although the information Borrow himself recorded contradicted or at least questioned his universal assertions, the resulting inconsistency failed to prompt any doubts in his mind about the validity of his conclusions.

The key to understanding that gap in his logic can be found in his physical description of 'Gypsy' people, for which he resorts to metaphor. What he contended as characteristic features, dark mulatto-like skin, thick lips, black, horse main-like hair, fit an invariable, universal pattern 'as if they were not of the human but rather of the animal species'. Not only their outer appearance, but also the activities in which they engaged exhibited a 'striking similarity [...] in every region of the globe to which they have penetrated'. One key to such racism was, then, to link outer appearance to inner inclinations. Hence the contraction of their lips when speaking or the observation that their 'very smile has an expression hard and disagreeable' would be obvious proof of 'all the customs of barbarous people'. In that same vein sorrow, the most prominent feature of their physiognomy, was 'like unto the savage man'.[16] The classification of peoples into culturally hierarchized races that was developing in Borrow's times constituted the foundations on which that collective definition of Romanies rested. While addressing other Romani case studies and varying the approach adopted, subsequent generations of Gypsy Lore Society members continued to apply scientific evidence to defend that racial organization of humanity, which they did not view as inconsistent with their folklorist enthusiasm for a lifestyle they deemed endangered. David Mayall's and Wim Willem's studies[17] are essential to understanding how that process evolved.

The profiles of some late-nineteenth-century scholars engaging in 'Gypsy' research are indicative of the initial premises informing the scientific field they created. Charles G. Leland, first society president, was an American philologist and ethnographer; Francis H. Groome, a British folklorist married to a Romani woman; John Sampson, an Irish dialectologist and scholar of Gaelic music. Similarly expressive is the term 'Romani *rai*' used by the foremost among them as a self-definition to highlight their expert understanding of Roma people, qualifying them as mediators between 'Gypsies' and mainstream society. Their toolbox contained both an empathetic approach and impulsive pursuit of romantic adventure. After all, as Dora Yates, editor-in-chief of the *Journal of the Gypsy Lore Society* wrote in the early twentieth century, 'Gypsies' embodied the world's last remaining romantic spirit.

That approach was compatible with the academicism deployed by those scholars as endorsement of the scientific validity of their work. They contended that anthropological, ethnographic and philological research was conducted in a very specific laboratory, 'Gypsy' campgrounds, and was informed by scientific spirit and methods. The result was to pour into the category 'Gypsy' content drawn from popular stereotypes, nourishing an ideal that had more to do with what they chose to project onto the group studied than with actual Romani lifestyles. They consequently contended that genuine 'Gypsies' were characterized by a love of freedom and nature, rejection of progress, a Bohemian and romantic personality and marginality relative to mainstream society. The focus of their discourse was the identification of 'true Gypsies' under the conviction that they would be extinct by the end of the nineteenth century. From the perspective of their various disciplines, they described Romanies in terms that associated the conservation of their staunchest traditions with racial purity, fearful that Romani culture would disappear with the miscegenation of its bearers. Most particularly, defining a command of Romanes as the indisputable sign of racial purity, they engaged in intricate philological interplay, among other documentary tasks.

That concern for racial purity and in particular Groome's genealogical investigations have been deemed a turning point in the political readings based on the definition of 'Gypsies' as an object of study. As discussed later, purity within the 'Zigeuner' was a major factor in Nazi racial policy, both for racial scientists such as Robert Ritter, whose definitions of 'pure' and 'mixed' race Roma were applied by Nazi police, and for the Nazi camp organizer himself, Heinrich Himmler. The earlier activity of other European experts emulating the British Gypsy Lore Society also attested to the formulation by late-nineteenth- and early-twentieth-century ethnology and similar disciplines of the components of the racial trap subsequently set by the Nazi regime. In the Austro-Hungarian Empire, for instance, Anton Hermann, Romani studies spokesman and founder of a journal modelled on *Gypsy Lore*, furnished the Government with analyses in support of official policy geared to assimilating the Romani population.

Other academic disciplines were accorded scholarly status in the nineteenth century. The ideas applied to 'Gypsies' were later used by the Nazi regime in defence of its creation of a racial device against Roma people in which that ostensibly scientific bias was carried through to its ultimate consequences. Foremost among those disciplines was physical anthropology, consisting largely in craniometric studies geared to categorizing and hierarchizing different known populations. In conjunction with other anthropometric measurements and data such as skin, hair and eye colour, a series of medical doctors, anatomists and other specialists established Eurocentric racial canons that assumed the white Caucasian race to stand innately at the pinnacle of human evolution.

The measurement of skulls entailed variables such as facial angle and cranial volume or shape to establish classifications as widely (and questionably) used as dolichocephaly-brachycephaly. Such studies are known to have been geared and applied to so-called 'blacks' since the late eighteenth century. Piasere[18] has recently showed how the data were collected and rearranged to include 'Gypsies' in such racial scales. The construction of the so-called 'Zingaric' skull was advanced by medical doctors including Augustin Weisbach, who typified the Romani populations' skulls as the smallest (and therefore presumably with the scantest intellectual capacity) in the entire Austro-Hungarian Empire. Leopold Glück, in turn, concluded from his measurements that Romanies' initially Indian dolichocephaly was diluted in proportion to their miscegenation with other peoples. Swiss scholar Eugène Pittard combined engagement in anthropometric studies and active participation in the Gypsy Lore Society. In his writings he defined 'Gypsies' to be a race whose anthropological primitivism hailed back to humanity's earliest evolution, a characteristic deemed consistent with features such as their tendency to nomadism.

A further series of scientific disciplines also participated in creating an extremely detrimental stereotyped image of Roma people (based on presumed cultural underdevelopment) with implications for political and police endeavour and the formulation and application of penal measures. Two that emerged in the late nineteenth century are of particular interest here due to their involvement in developing Nazi racial science in the context of the academic institutionalization discussed above in connection with other fields of study. Criminology and eugenics mirrored governing elites' urge to control populations in times of growing social mobilization and acquired ever greater influence in the design of official police protocols and other policies. Such discourses nourished social fears, affording affluent classes with scientifically endorsed grounds from which to broach issues such as delinquency and what influential Italian criminology referred to as the *mala vita* (the underworld), both viewed as symptoms of social degradation. The direct relationship between these disciplines and the adoption and enforcement of the legal measures applied to the Romani population shortly before the emergence of the Nazi regime are addressed in greater detail in the following section.

Here the aim is to draw conclusions around the dual process of the artistic and scientific generation of 'Gypsy' stereotypes emerging in modern Western culture throughout the nineteenth century. Much of the material used to build such stereotypes, which can be traced to earlier times, had been assimilated by mainstream society. Nonetheless, the arguments put forward in that century differed both in intention and in persuasive power. 'Gypsies' became a passive object of depictions in which they were viewed as the ideal vehicle for 'otherness', the physically nearest and hence perfect contrast to the bourgeois society under development. Whilst travel and colonial conquest set the example of many exotic and primitive populations within the sight of such observers, being much closer, 'Gypsy' presence could be conveniently perceived to be threatening.

In an attempted characterization of Roma people, intellectuals of different backgrounds were actually building a collective image of the community that served to ensure social order. That task was performed through a number of cultural vehicles that used a stereotyped image of Romanies to depict attitudes and lifestyles diametrically opposed to what was officially deemed acceptable behaviour. As noted by Jean Kommers, authors writing stories for children and youths introduced 'Gypsy' characters as the embodiment of child abduction to impress on their readers the importance of obeying family rules. Disobeying parents' orders not to leave home or the immediate surrounds could result in being stolen by a 'Gypsy' tribe, disappearance from civilized society and submission to nomadism and delinquency [Illustration 7].[19]

Successive generations of Europeans were indoctrinated into obeying family rules and national law with such stories, which prevented real Roma from being seen as anything other than child thieves. The impact of fiction on reality can be highly troubling, such as in the memoirs authored by Rudolf Höss, commander at Auschwitz, where thousands of Romanies perished during the Holocaust. In his autobiographical writings drafted in prison after the war, looking back on the family environment of his childhood, Höss recalls an attempted abduction, presumably at the hand of 'Gypsies', and his parents' subsequent orders not to stray far from home. He adds that fortunately a neighbour rescued him from his potential abductors.

Illustration 7 *Rose Merton and the Gypsies*, **1850 scrapbook.** Children were often coerced into parental obedience through bedtime stories portraying 'Gypsies' as presumed child 'thieves' [Private collection of Jean Kommers (Nimega)].

Romantic and scientific stereotypes mutually reinforced their power of persuasion. Just as age-old traditional artistic depictions and popular images furnished content for the 'true Gypsy' category invented in academia, Romantic artists used scientifically sourced ideas and arguments in their oeuvre to create more realistic fictional 'Gypsies'. The influence exerted by Borrow's anthropological-philological study of Spanish 'Gitanos' on an example of romantic fiction so apparently distant from the scientific spirit as Mérimée's *Carmen* is obvious when the two texts are compared. The former inspired the 'realistic account' technique deployed in the latter. Mérimée's apparent familiarity with the Romani community, based on the integration of scholarly knowledge (use of words in Romanes, description of ancestral tradition, inclusion of dialogue in the first person), affords his plot credibility. One of any number of examples can be found in the scene describing an encounter between Carmen and her lover when she is in the midst of duping an Englishman into gifting her with all his possessions. Responding to her lover's jealous reaction that prevents her from 'doing gipsy business', Carmen explodes: 'Are you my *rom* (man-husband) pray that you give me orders? If El Tuerto [Carmen's husband] is pleased, what have you to do with it? Oughtn't you to be very happy that you are the only man who can call himself my *minchorro* (lover, fancy)?'[20] (the word 'minchorro' is defined in a footnote to mean *Mon amant ou plutôt mon caprice* – my lover or my fancy). Romani women's engagement in delinquency as a lifestyle, their art for thievery, skill in taking advantage of their husbands, sexual promiscuity and so on form part of their portrayal in this novella written with such anthropological verisimilitude.

The opera based on the story stylizes the plot and underscores the leading lady's appeal, but does not eschew the blend of sublimation and stigmatization so characteristic of the nineteenth-century view of 'Gypsies' as a whole, defined as an object both of study and artistic depiction. In that vein, cultural products intended for mainstream society with clearly commercial aims from their inception were to be particularly effective in introducing such stereotyped portrayals. The mass culture audience typical of the twentieth century was already in place in the nineteenth. Certain instances attest to the huge success of the 'Gypsy' persona in musical and stage shows. *The Bohemian Girl* (1843), based on Cervantes's *La Gitanilla* (the little 'Gypsy' girl) and staged hundreds of times in London, was enormously popular all over England and in other countries, as was the opera *Mignon* (dating from 1866), the story of a young Bohemian girl drawn from a text by Goethe.[21]

The images from such stage productions were soon (and not unexpectedly) mirrored in cinema, the twentieth century's foremost cultural vehicle. The serial and inexpensive reproduction of pictures afforded by photography and post cards also extended the reach of such depictions, whose appeal was based on their exotic or romantic roots. Indisputably, however, the combination of mass culture and business in the form of international exhibitions and human zoos was what most aptly embodied that stereotyped depiction of 'others'. Such scenarios, shameless displays of the racial hierarchy interiorized by Western societies, exhibited groups whose 'different' physical appearance and lifestyles piqued public curiosity (and fattened business earnings). Romani communities occasionally shared such stages with Bushmen, Araucanians, Laplanders and so on. Paris's Jardin d'Acclimatation (acclimatization garden), for instance, initially designed for plant and animal species, in 1877 became the city's Jardin d'Acclimatation Anthropologique (anthropological acclimatization garden), where exotic human groups were also on display. Before the First World War a collection of traditional *Kalderash* tales was published in 1959 under the title *La Bible des Roms*[22] (the Roma bible). The collection was compiled by Alexandre Zanko, one of the members of a family who were exhibited in that type of compound. The use of their image in post card photos, flaunting the originality of their dress and ceremonies, did not save them from imprisonment with other Romani families at the Lannemezan (Hautes-Pyrénées) internment camp, operational from 1941 to 1946.

The Roma and the Holocaust

Not only in Germany: The reins tighten in the twentieth century

Romanies engaging in any of the occupations assigned to the community from times immemorial were doubly affected by the consequences of reductionist stereotypes. Their characteristic mobile lifestyle made musicians, circus artists, amusement park ride owners and similar suspect in an interwar Europe in the grips of old and new tensions. As Romani Holocaust survivor Philomena Franz recalls, her family staged works with 'Gypsy' themes in which they dressed in ways audiences expected, clearly exemplifying the paradox inherent in reductionist cliché.

The early-twentieth-century social reality suppressed by such stereotypes was much more diverse and complex, however. Quite a number of Romani families, from entertainers as successful as Django Reindhardt to street musicians whose names were never recorded, earned a living from music and other theatrical genres [Illustration 8]. Nonetheless, Romani communities' economic pursuits across Europe were more varied than perceived by the rest of society. Many entailed sedentary lifestyles not acknowledged in official discourse, where 'Gypsy' continued to be synonymous with 'nomad'. And yet alongside Romani groups who lived in their travelling caravans, other families were sedentary year round and a third group combined the two alternatives seasonally, depending on the labour market. Many interwar European Romanies were

Illustration 8 Members of a successful Romani French and Hungarian interwar period band posing with their instruments. Under Nazi rule the band's activities were prohibited and all its members were sterilized at Würzburg in 1942 [US Holocaust Memorial Museum, Washington, courtesy of Rita Prigmore].

Illustration 9 Bamberger family posing for a studio photo in the 1930s. Margarete Bamberger (seated, left) was deported to Auschwitz in 1942. Max Bamberger (seated, right) was executed by an SS killing unit in 1945 [Dokumentation und Kulturzentrum, Deutscher Sinti und Roma, Heidelberg].

farmers, whilst others were craftsmen (smithies, boilermakers), horse traders, retailers, street merchants or even civil servants [Illustration 9].

Some countries even witnessed a burgeoning Romani business and intellectual middle class that at times founded movements in defence of this minority's rights. Rather different circumstances were in place in the Soviet Union. At first at least, the communist regime officially supported Romani intellectuals and activists, enabling them to engage in both cultural and political initiatives such as the 'Teatr Romen' founded by Romani Bolshevik Ivan Rom-Lebedev or the periodical *Nevo Drom*.[23] Even after Stalin withdrew recognition of Roma as a national minority in 1936, cases such as Aleksandr Baurov's were still possible in that country. A member of a musical family, he trained as a communications engineer and served as an officer in the army that deterred the Nazi invasion. Distinguished as a war hero, he later formed part of a commission entrusted with reviewing post-surrender German space technology and of the group of Soviet engineers who launched the first rockets into orbit.

Although not to the same extreme, during the interwar period countries such as Bulgaria, Romania, Yugoslavia and Czechoslovakia were home to an extensive network of Romani intellectuals and activists later destroyed by the Nazis. Ilona Klímová-Alexander studied a number of cultural and political initiatives attesting to nascent Romani associationism in those countries.[24] The formulation of a discourse claiming their civil rights stemmed essentially from a feeling of national belongingness, of their self-perception as citizens of their respective countries. As a general rule, Romani soldiers were recruited by the armies of the nations battling in the First World War. In Germany the males in many (sedentary) Sinti families were called to arms. In France, paradoxically, some Roma were employed in the army while others were imprisoned in border penitentiaries on the presumption they posed a threat to national security. There are records of even more deplorable situations in the context of the military mobilization of Romani citizens during the war. By way of example, forty-five Serbian prisoners of war in Austria were used by racial anthropologist Victor Lebzelter in his anthropometric studies of 'Gypsies'.

Despite the sociological diversity of Europe's Romani population, in the early twentieth century governmental attention focused ever more keenly on those deemed nomadic and seen as threats to society. The official perspective saw the lack of resources, stable modus vivendi and protective citizenship that plagued such itinerant groups as characteristic of all Roma, Those outlooks masked other situations that would have called such stereotypical simplification into question. Intensified police control and harassment was only the most visible feature of that attitude which, as discussed later, also made its way into political, legal and scientific discourse on the subject. Such discourse not only broke the ground for the extreme measures instituted by the Nazi regime. As noted by Michael Zimmermann, it also and more significantly meant that in practice police harassment turned the political theory of assimilation into a policy of expulsion.[25] Legislation such as the Prussian 1906 *Bekämpfung der Zigeunerplage* (combating the Gypsy plague), an epitaph later adopted by the Nazis, was also designed both to hinder street selling and prevent Roma from staying in the cities they visited. The alienation prompted by family separation as mandated by Swiss legislation was even greater. In 1913 foreign Romani men were separated from their families and incarcerated in a forced labour camp at Witzwil. In 1926 the Pro Juventute foundation, presuming Swiss Roma adults to be inept parents on the grounds of their nomadic lifestyle, institutionalized their children in orphanages and similar when no families willing to adopt them could be found.

The premise of assimilation characteristic of nineteenth-century liberal discourse constituted an enlightened intention to turn 'Gypsies' into good citizens by mandating their adoption of mainstream lifestyles. It lost ground in the first few decades of the twentieth century, however, to the 'social peril' discourse that ultimately prevailed. In that context nomadism, generically and even genetically attributed to all Romanies, became the key to a collective depiction of the entire community as 'asocial', an image that was to have an ever greater impact on legislation and police practice. 'Gypsies' were classified as a group whose itinerant lifestyle presumably revealed, while at the same time concealing, a collective tendency to indolence and non-compliance with the law: in a word, delinquency; a community unwilling and unable to live in or like the rest of society. Consequently, their social integration, rather than desirable, would be simply impossible. From that perspective, the supposedly anthropologically determined personality attributed to 'Gypsies' encapsulated them in communities whose lifestyles were viewed as incompatible with civilized social conduct.

The term 'asocial' was a reformulation of a centuries-old fear traditionally associated with non-sedentary or uncensured people, reinforced at the turn of the century with new arguments characteristic of mass society. Concern was not limited, then, only to the generic fear of nomads or the typically liberal dread over the potential loss of a labour force, both of which had given rise to the laws against indolence and vagrancy in place until then. In addition, beginning in the latter nineteenth century the issue of collective health, whereby society was understood as a living being, became ever more pressing for sociologists, physicians, psychiatrists and of course public authorities.

Much intellectual reflection and many political decisions at the time in both Europe and America were informed by considerations around a country's collective demographic vigour and concern over the possible degradation of the national personality, in a context of social Darwinism. Concern pivoted around the presence of groups engaging in the *mala vita* (underworld) in large cities, deemed ground propitious not only for prostitution but also homosexuality and other 'deviational' behaviours; and the alarm over delinquency, now viewed as a sociological development of intimidating dimensions. Theories on social peril analysed historic developments, which viewed from that perspective were ever more troubling for the authorities and the affluent. Such events included international and even transatlantic scale migratory flows that set off entry control alarms in host countries; the growth of large metropolises, with health- and poverty-related problems festering in worker districts; and intensified political mobilization largely as a result of the inequalities inherent in those two processes. The outcome was an environment favourable to ideas on social peril that took 'Gypsies' as a preferential object of study and regulation.

Identifying 'Gypsies' as vagrants and rogues, categories into which they had been legally pigeonholed in the past, prepared the ground for the term 'asocial', but that depiction was densified when combined with other (dis)qualifiers, particularly those bearing racial connotations justified by ostensibly scientific evidence. The equation identifying 'Gypsy' with nomad-vagabond-pauper-rogue-delinquent and other undesirable social categories ('undesirable class' was the label used on US and Canadian borders) was consolidated where different voices converged in a new discipline that was taking shape in the late nineteenth century: criminology. That science proposed to solve the problems of mass delinquency typical of modern societies by studying the conditions that would explain crime and consequently lead to its prevention.

Drawing from physical anthropology and other disciplines, criminologists as influential as Cesare Lombroso resolutely contended that the genetic inclination to delinquency was recognizable in subjects' physiognomy. Therefore, studying skull and facial measurements and shape would enable experts to distinguish even among different types of delinquents. His classification and establishment of typologies was set out in *L'Uomo delinquente*, a widely disseminated 1876 treatise translated into a number of languages that served as a guide in police stations and immigration posts. The identification of dangerous subjects and even of potential criminals was put forward as the key to national and international security in newly developing mass societies. That equation and its application in scientific-legal-police endeavours furnished new arguments for diluting the barriers between preventive and punitive action where civil defence was concerned. Protecting society against its potential internal enemies was viewed as one of government's primary duties. In such a scenario, Lombroso's assertion that 'Gypsies' were a delinquent race would necessarily have a forceful impact.

Against that backdrop, personal identification understandably became an ever more widespread governmental ambition, to which end modern techniques such as photography, anthropometry, fingerprinting and so on were deployed. Census polling and other tools required to keep registries and control the population for tax, military recruitment and voting rights purposes were developed throughout the nineteenth century in conjunction with the consolidation of nation-states. The turn of the century brought a qualitative leap, with the personalization of registration procedures and the issue of personal ID cards. 'Gypsies' were visibly present in all those innovations, for from the outset they attracted the attention of the authorities in charge of enforcing such new controls. Local anxiety around the presumed social peril inherent in Romani presence was reinforced by a general concern over border control, with the institution of international procedures to hinder transnational movements.

One of the earliest and best known cases was the special 'Gypsy' watch implemented by the Bavarian police corps that set a pattern on which rules were later modelled in Germany as a whole. As early as 1899 a bureau headed by Alfred Dillmann was established in Munich specifically to register and control the people so branded. In addition to descriptions of physical appearance for purposes of identification and genealogical information, Dillmann's unit collected data on the criminality associated with 'Gypsy' lifestyles. Its 1905 *Zigeuner-Buch* held the records and photographs of over 3,000 Romanies.[26] Persuaded of the utility of that effort and of the futility of any attempt to integrate 'Gypsies', Dillmann set out to apply the model to the entire empire. Although such centralization remained elusive prior to Nazi rule, similar registries were set up in other German states, generating a database later used by the Nazi regime. By 1925 Munich's special 'Zigeuner' unit had registered 14,000 Romanies.

Such reactions in legal and police realms were not by any means exclusive to Germany, however. In 1911 the Swiss Government broached France, Italy and Germany itself with a proposal to share information on itinerant populations. In 1912 France introduced an anthropometric ID for nomads that included full face and profile photographs, fingerprints and anthropometric measurements. Requiring their bearers to obtain police visas to enter and leave towns and cities in effect identified them as presumed delinquents.[27] Beginning in 1913 Switzerland undertook identification procedures that involved creating racial profiles and a 'Gypsy' registry. Somewhat later, Hungary and Czechoslovakia also instituted special identification cards. In Austria the photographic identification of Romanies in the Burgenland area (bordering Hungary, where the Romani population was particularly dense) from 1928 on was ideal for police action. The dozens of pictures on

The Roma and Anti-Gypsyism: Parallel Histories

Illustration 10 Romani family at Neudorf bei Landsee, Austria, German General Intelligence Service photo, 1934. As the police used photography in records on population characteristics, families were required to pose alongside their homes [German Federal Archive – Digital Image Archive].

file in regional archives in which Romani families were required to pose at the entrance to their homes and with their work tools constituted a photographic record of individuals, families, lifestyles and possessions highly useful to the police force [Illustration 10].

The 'Gypsy plague' became a matter typical of modern policing in the interwar period, both in terms of the new registration techniques used and the necessary international coordination called for to control the movements of a minority present in nearly all European countries. Very early on Switzerland in particular adopted initiatives to foster inter-country police coordination, an aspiration that met with greater success after the 1924 creation of the International Criminal Police Commission (predecessor of today's Interpol), headquartered at Vienna. Joint action by German and Austrian authorities in 'combating the Gypsy plague' formed part of the infrastructure for such international policing. Proposals were even entertained for establishing a central office for the exchange of specific information to enhance efficacy after the problem was discussed at congresses held in 1931 and 1932. A trial for alleged cannibalism in Czechoslovakia that generated alarm in neighbouring countries was indicative of the clearly biological racialization of the debate on 'Gypsies'. Nourished both by police investigations involving the use of modern criminological techniques and by the opinions of ethnographers and other specialists, such developments were echoed in and amplified by the sensationalist press.

As noted by Celia Donert[28] in connection with Czechoslovakia, such debates were directly influenced by a discourse on social health and eugenics, matters of ever more widespread concern in Europe. America was similarly impacted, for eugenics, which emerged in the latter half of the nineteenth century with the increasing favour accorded scientific methodology, migrated in short order from the academic sphere to police practice on both sides of the Atlantic. Along with the prestige of its advocates, Darwin's progeny among others, in the United States a second fundamental boost came in the form of the early official support afforded theories on selective reproduction and the sterilization of those deemed unfit. A centre established in the 1910s in New York collected and kept information of eugenic interest, feeding a nascent corpus of studies addressing the problems of social health. The factors deemed responsible were all set on an equal footing despite the broad differences among them, with the same importance attached to physical weakness, mental problems, disorderly sexual behaviour, drunkenness, vagrancy and poverty (pathologized as pauperism). In the 1920s contests were called to award and distinguish the most 'apt' families while arguments were wielded to justify sterilization in the event of mental illness, promiscuity and other 'degenerate' behaviours.

Whereas today such studies are generally deemed pseudoscientific, in the early decades of the twentieth century they were highly reputed in academic and political circles. To say that eugenic culture was widespread in American and European societies is no exaggeration. The category 'not worthy of life' extensively used in Nazi Germany to gloss over the murder of all manner of people was already in the air in other countries' interwar science and politics. The 'asociability' attributed to Romanies and specifically to their nomadic lifestyle served eugenicists broaching modern social problems from genetic perspectives to brand 'Gypsies' as inferior beings who constituted a burden on and even a peril to mainstream society.

August Forel, a prominent Swiss psychiatrist, lumped criminals, prostitutes, alcoholics, the mentally ill, tuberculosis patients, drug addicts, 'Gypsies', rogues, Jews, Chinese and Blacks together under a single heading. Switzerland was the first European country to legally perform eugenic sterilization. Other experts such as Eugen Bleuler and Ernst Rüdin concurred that there was no room in perfect social order for anyone 'deviating from normality', a category that included homosexuals, single mothers, Jews and 'Gypsies'. Concern around the supposedly errant and asocial lifestyle of Swiss 'Yeniches' induced medical doctor and psychiatrist Josef Jörger to conduct a detailed study of the genetic disaster that befell a family (numbered 'zero' in his sample) after one of its members married a Roma woman. Their lineage was presumably then contaminated with a 'virus' expressed as a series of traits associated with nomadism: crime, immorality, mental weakness and pauperism.

In that context, the fact that Robert Ritter, the scientist primarily responsible for Nazi racial policy in connection with 'Gypsies', trained at Berne where he was introduced to the theories of Jörger and others is particularly meaningful. Many threads can be found that tie the Romani population's pre-Hitlerian legal and social status in Germany to the situation prevailing after the Nazis rose to power in 1933. As appropriately noted by Michael Zimmermann,[29] one of the first historians of the Romani genocide under the Nazi regime, whilst the 1919 Weimar Constitution theoretically awarded Romanies full citizenship, local legal initiatives brazenly overturned that constitutional right. To name one specific instance, the 1926 Bavarian law on 'combating the Gypsy plague', identifying Romanies as people with no known residence or job, ordered their universal registration, prohibited nomadism and threatened transgressors with forced labour.

No less significantly, that regional pattern spread nationally in 1929 or served as a basis for subsequent Nazi legislation, in particular the 1938 decree on 'combating the Gypsy plague', that lumped 'Gypsies' together with other 'asocial' or 'unfit' elements. The economic crisis raging at the time, which was particularly hard on Germans, favoured an environment of social alarm that intensified traditional anti-Gypsy prejudice. In 1929 a municipal initiative obliged Sinti and Roma peoples to vacate the lands where they normally camped and relocate on grounds on the outskirts of Frankfurt. That facility, Friedberger Landstrasse, closed in 1935 to give way to a more efficient concentration camp system.

Although many such precedents can be cited, Hitler's ascent to power added new and decisive elements that sealed the fate of European Romani people. The genocidal programme was not defined or implemented in unwavering terms at the outset, however, but underwent steady evolution throughout the Third Reich, as discussed in a later chapter. That the Nazi regime organized the collective murder of Romanies into virtual disappearance in some areas of Europe is nonetheless a proven fact. As pointed out by Mark Levene, Germans would in all likelihood have deemed the attack against 'Gypsies' justified even in the absence of the Nazi racial apparatus.[30] That notwithstanding, the regime's racial science undeniably put forward arguments and methods that acquired the same genocidal bias as was applied to the Jewish population. In combination with political machinery and police practice it made new resources accessible to the perpetrators of the Romani Holocaust. Just as the assimilation of liberal tenets gave way in the nineteenth century to disciplinary prevention, the Nazi regime paved the way to direct physical extermination of a group it defined in racial terms.

CHAPTER 2
THE ROMANI GENOCIDE UNDER NAZISM

Labelling a series of events as 'genocide', a word charged with political and moral innuendos, must be justified. Irresponsible or indiscriminate use of the term must be avoided lest it be worn thin or divested of its critical and incriminatory power, as well, of course, as for reasons of linguistic rigour. In keeping with that criterion, in the first few pages of this book the word 'genocide' is applied in its historic context and in Chapter 3 (which deals with the legal, social and cultural reaction to the Romani Holocaust after the collapse of the Nazi regime) it is set into the context of the fate inflicted on European Romanies. It is not a particularly original word choice, inasmuch as historiography has been resorting to the term in the most recent studies on the matter. Nonetheless, the reasoning underlying that choice must be discussed explicitly, for the persecution, torture and attempted annihilation of Romanies in the territories under Nazi police and military control described here can only be so categorized.

Numbers and intentions

The severity of the damage inflicted on a given community tends to be determined on the grounds of the number of victims. In the case of the Roma people, however, no absolutely reliable figure has yet been established on the number who perished under Nazi persecution. Although the initial estimates varied widely (with a minimum of 90,000 and a maximum of 1 million), with the advance of scientific research specialists have narrowed the range, to around 250,000–500,000 people. At this writing, however, the most recent studies persistently lean towards the high end of that range and do not rule out future upward amendment. The ongoing discovery in the former Soviet Union, in Ukraine in particular, of collective graves resulting from the massacres perpetrated by the *Einsatzgruppen* (killing units) and their collaborators may raise the figure significantly. Nonetheless, the conclusion ultimately reached may well be that no statistic can be reliably defined due to the lack of pre-existing records in many cases and the subsequent destruction of many of these graves.

Anyone familiar with the overwhelming figures on Nazi victims can readily set that half million people murdered merely because they were 'Gypsies' against the backdrop of the destruction of other groups affected by Nazi racial policy and military practice: from 5 million to 6 million Jews, 3 million to 4 million Soviet prisoners, nearly 2 million non-Jewish Poles, 80,000–100,000 'unworthy lives' (the mentally and physically ill), around 5,000 Jehovah's Witnesses, an unknown number of homosexuals, and so on. It is frankly hard to count the dead by thousands and millions without being repelled by the sort of logic that quantifies a group's suffering on the grounds of the larger or smaller number of victims, an approach informed by political interests and with questionable scientific effect. In contrast, this book attempts to give people a face and a name by using their own words as the basis for the historical narrative and introducing the unquantifiable value of its impact on individual lives. The numbers nonetheless also support the view that the collective European Romani experience in the Second World War qualifies as genocide, more obviously when expressed in relative terms. Whilst approximately 65 per cent of Europe's pre-1933 Jewish population had disappeared by 1945 as an outcome of the Holocaust, a mean figure is very hard to calculate for the Roma people, given how widely it varied region by region. In any event, the estimates are indicative of human, material and cultural destruction that can be compared (unfortunately for them) to Jewish losses. 'More than two-thirds of the Sinti and Romanies living in the German Reich and the territories annexed to it perished in the Nazi Camps,'[1] according to Kay. That percentage was even greater in some cases, most notably in Third Reich Germany and its sphere of influence, where 70 per cent of pre-Nazi German, 80 per cent of Austrian and 90 per cent of Czechian Romanies had died by 1945 as a result of persecution. Very high percentages were also recorded in other regions occupied by Nazi Germany: 45 per cent in Poland, 75 per cent in Ukraine, 90 per cent in Estonia, 60 per cent in Lithuania and so on according to the most updated estimates.[2]

A second consideration, beyond statistics, normally addressed in the discussion around the Holocaust should likewise be mentioned before introducing the history of the Romani genocide, for it also affects its denomination as such: intention. Was it in the Nazi animus to eliminate the Roma people as a whole out of racial prejudice and perpetrate what today we deem genocide? Was that the intention from the outset or was it an option stemming from and related to the course of the war? Can responsibility be attributed to Hitler or were other links in the chain of command instrumental to Roma people's fate? In light of these and other questions related to the genocidal intentions of the authors of these mass murders Romani historiography can be seen to have inherited some of the premises that informed scientific study and public discussion of the Jewish case. 'Intentionalism' and 'functionalism' lie at the core of extensive and decisive debate on Holocaust historiography, although those notions may also on occasion be eclipsed (but not obviated) by the logic supporting the attempts to build a new approach to the history of Nazi persecution of the Roma people.

A number of essential traits characterizing the process should be introduced from the outset. First, the measures to control and persecute the Romani population were not the outcome of a single, consistent line of action, but constituted a legal, political and scientific jumble of overlapping ideas characterized by ambiguities, contradictions and voids. As Zimmermann noted, that was because centrally adopted decisions and instructions were very variably and arbitrarily enforced and interpreted by different local and regional (police, municipal, party) authorities. Regional initiatives in particular intensified the effect of such measures when applied to the local Romani population: authorities in the Austrian Burgenland, for instance, pressured very early on for more radical enforcement of repressive directives to eradicate any 'Gypsies' in their region. Action at this second and decisive level splintered the effect of nationwide rules into a very complex scenario of diverse local realities. Rosa Mettbach's attempt to seek refuge in Munich in 1942 (a story told at the beginning of this book) can only be understood against that backdrop.

Whereas some historians such as Guenter Lewy have attempted to interpret that as evidence of less severe anti-Gypsy than anti-Semitic aggression at the hands of the Nazis, alluding to the possibility of escape afforded by such inconsistencies in some cases, as a rule local enforcement intensified the destructive effect of national racial persecutory measures. Proof that the local desire to be rid of 'Gypsies' raised the intensity of national rules can be found in the fact that those entrusted with Romani families' arrest and deportation failed to distinguish between sedentary and nomadic groups, between those known to engage in a trade and others with no economic resources, between 'pure' and 'mixed' race and so on, contravening national instructions. A further outcome of that situation, to cite an extreme example, was the incarceration of Romani soldiers serving in the German army in concentration and extermination camps [Illustration 11]. As mentioned later, some of those sent to Auschwitz had even won medals for their battlefront valour.

Illustration 11 Karl Heilig, soldier in Rommel's Afrika-Korps. One of the many Romani soldiers in the German army distinguished in the First and Second World Wars whose lives ended at the Auschwitz-Birkenau extermination camp [Dokumentation und Kulturzentrum, Deutscher Sinti und Roma, Heidelberg].

The Roma and the Holocaust

Above and beyond the precise legal conceit 'intention', there was an 'awareness that the acts committed will lead to the destruction of the targeted group'.[3] A number of occasions and decisions denote the destructive intention of those responsible for Nazi anti-Gypsy policy. Pursuit of those aims was implicit in a number of cases: the early 1940 conversations around the 'Gypsy plague', in which Heydrich and Himmler famously participated; the action against Roma peoples by the special forces that occupied the Soviet Union beginning in 1941 and the so-called Auschwitz Decree that in late 1942 ordered the deportation of all the Reich's 'Zigeuner' ('Gypsies'). The intention to annihilate the Roma people was in place even before the war. Clearly, however, for Romanies, like Jews, the Second World War constituted a point of no return with measures that sought to exterminate both the people and their culture.

With the territorial expansion of the hostilities, and especially after the invasion of the Soviet Union, the Nazi police and military apparatus used an anything but innocent argument against Romanies: they were collectively accused of threatening Reich security because they were presumed to be spies and saboteurs serving the enemy. That drew from a commonplace that had circulated in earlier times. According to it the nomadic lifestyle and lack of national roots attributed to Romanies should be viewed as treason and anti-patriotism, further to which the term 'Gypsy' was identified with nomad and enemy. That accusation served as an excuse for the hasty elimination of whole Romani communities after 1941, as discussed later. The inclusion of women and children with adult men in the mass murders was justified by military logic in a context of out-and-out battle with the partisans.

That specific argument might initially seem to have set measures against the 'Gypsies' in a dimension based more on social and political (nomadism, delinquency, lack of national roots) than racial premises. Nonetheless, the generic attribution to a whole community of people of non-sedentary, non-legalized and antipatriotic lifestyles is an anthropological conceit rooted in racial prejudice, as Henry Friedlander was quick to point out.[4] The collective inferiority assigned to 'Gypsies' as a (sub)human group in Nazi racial cosmovision was what determined the fate of the Romani families who fell in the hands of German troops and their collaborators as more and more terrain was occupied. Universally applied, the accusation of espionage served as grounds for general extermination. Quite beyond specific arguments, the underlying racial discourse with stigmatizing and punitive intentions made Roma (for the mere fact of birth as such) police and military targets, as proven by Sevasti Trubeta in connection with the Balkans and Martin Holler with the territories occupied in the Soviet Union.[5]

According to research conducted by David Motadel also in the Balkans, Muslim Roma residing residing there were accorded different treatment more out of political expedience than of nuances in Nazi racial precepts.[6] Viewing Islam as a potentially useful military ally (a Muslim military unit serving Hitler had recruited some Romani soldiers), the Nazi regime temporarily tolerated the protection afforded Muslim Romani communities by a number of Muslim religious authorities in Crimea and the Balkans. In Croatia the Ustacha, the ultra-nationalist militia controlled by Ante Palevic's collaborationist regime, even agreed to refrain from deporting so-called 'White

Gypsies' (sedentary Romanies who had long been living in Bosnia and Herzegovina). According to Motadel, Nazi interest in Islam may have lowered the number of Romani victims in a region with a Muslim majority. Nonetheless, at around 30 per cent the survival rate attests to mass murder because in addition to the subsequent change in Nazi authorities' attitude, their Romanian and Bulgarian allies remained absolutely impervious to arguments of political-religious desirability in their respective areas of influence.

The measures adopted in the latter regard by German military and political authorities ran counter to the practice implemented by the authorities in Nazi satellite states, creating differences in the fate of the various Romani communities. As discussed later, these groups' destiny varied with local circumstances, although, as Weiss-Wendt noted, as a rule Nazi doctrine on biological purity drove racial cleansing in collaborating States.[7] Empowering and endorsing pre-existing prejudice, Nazi racial ideology amplified the traditional anti-Gypsyism extant in both official policy and civil society through a number of nationalist projects aiming to cleanse the social body and purge 'undesirable' elements. The massive deportation of Romanian Roma to Transnistria (Soviet region occupied by Romanian troops in parallel with German advances) by Antonescu's phyllo-Nazi regime is a paradigmatic example, for it did not except even the families of military personnel in active service. Whilst prior to the Nazis rise to power anti-Gypsyism existed not only in Germany itself but throughout Europe, after 1933 it took a new turn with the application of measures that collectively defined Roma as a racially inferior community presumed to constitute a threat to society in need of speedy eradication.

The pathway to genocide was charted very early on. As discussed below, before the war began Romanies' fate under the Nazi regime was characterized by imprisonment, forced labour and sterilization. Historian Ludwig Eiber invoked a memorandum prepared in March 1936 for Hans Pfundtner, Secretary of State in the Reich's Ministry of the Interior and one of the authors of the Nuremgerg laws. That memorandum, which included a proposal 'introducing the total solution to the "Gypsy plague" on either a national or international level', is clearly relevant to any interpretation of the early stages of 'Gypsy' persecution at the hands of the Nazis.[8]

Nazi rise to power: Discrimination, sterilization and imprisonment

The Nazi regime established the grounds for its anti-Gypsy policy in the period running from 1933, when the party came into power, to 1938 immediately prior to the onset of the Second World War. New rules were decreed and the procedures for 'combating the Gypsy plague' reorganized, as summarized in the title of the decisive December 1938 decree. It was the first stage in ever more intensive harassment and persecution of the Romani community, carried to even greater heights during the war years.

The measures forced on Sinti and Roma communities are reminiscent of the Nazi anti-Semitism described by Raul Hilberg in his classic study of the decimation of European

Jews.[9] An initial phase to determine who was Jewish was followed by the revocation of their civil and political rights and ultimately by pillage, deportation and extermination. Anti-Romani policy differed in that two of the stages delimited by Hilberg were combined. The definition and classification of 'Gypsies' was a task entrusted to a unit explicitly created for that purpose. Headed by Dr Robert Ritter, the unit benefitted from official support and extensive police backing. At the same time, police action involving the arrest and imprisonment of Roma classified as 'asocial' was intended to cleanse German cities of elements deemed undesirable. The outcome was the establishment of municipal internment camps for Roma, symbolized by Marzahn. What was officially known as Rastplatz Marzahn (literally, 'Marzahn resting place') was created on the occasion of the 1936 Berlin Olympic Games, themselves designed to be a showroom for Nazism [Illustration 12].

Such police action was not new, of course, nor were other forms of harassment implemented earlier (closure of campgrounds, raising of rent, exhaustive police control, etc.). But under Nazi rule they became more frequent and in some cases systematic, particularly in Bavaria, cradle of Nazi police anti-Gypsyism. As noted by another key Holocaust scholar, that line of action was undertaken without waiting to have the findings of the research conducted by Ritter and his team to define and locate the 'Zigeuner' population living in Germany.[10] Dachau had Romani prisoners as early as 1933. As discussed below, such initial German camps played a significant role in applying scientific theory to police practice. That approach proved to be decisive for

Illustration 12 Marzahn internment camp for Roma outside Berlin established on the occasion of the 1936 Olympic Games. Two men in front of caravan No. 5; photo by Racial Hygiene Unit, division headed by R. Ritter [German Federal Archive – Digital image archive.]

crystallizing the so-called 'Gypsy plague', the view of Romani presence as a social and political problem in drastic need of solution.

In addition to action specifically targeting Romani communities, the Nazi regime enacted laws embodying the movement's general racial architecture that affected all deemed inferior and consequently detrimental to a society based on the purity of the Aryan race. In July 1933 the *Gesetz zur Verhütung erbkranken Nachwuchses* (law for the prevention of hereditarily diseased offspring) authorized the forced sterilization of Romanies. Deemed to be 'asocial elements', they shared that fate with Afro-Germans, people with physical or mental incapacities and so on. In 1934 around 500 Romanies were sterilized, although the practice continued uninterruptedly throughout the Third Reich, ever more extensively and fiercely. Initially free subjects were required to submit to it as a precautionary measure to presumably elude deportation, although that ultimately proved to be a false guarantee. Later at the concentration camps themselves sterilization continued to be practised until the end of the war, with increasingly unsafe and painful methods, a form of collective torture dealt with in greater detail later.

Sterilization had in fact already been forced on communities whose reproduction was deemed a social problem in places such as the United States, Switzerland and the Nordic countries in keeping with the eugenic principles so in vogue at the time (and which continued to be applied to Romani women in Czechoslovakia up until as late as 1970). The fact that in Nazi Germany mandatory sterilization was imposed on the Roma beginning in 1933 and continued until 1945 attests to the intended biological annihilation of a whole people, while also standing as proof of the early racial bias inherent in such persecution.

Legislation that would come to be known as the Nuremberg laws, a body of regulations designed to limit civil rights and protect 'German blood and German honour', was enacted in 1935. That set of laws was progressively rolled out to deprive Jews of citizenship, along with other groups that presumably endangered the conservation of German racial purity. A complex system of racial discrimination was instituted to establish different categories of subjects: Germans, Germans with different degrees of mixed blood, and on the lowest rung Jews and other communities deemed inferior. The brief introduction to these laws, drawn from the Nazi party's 1935 congress, did not explicitly mention 'Gypsies', although subsequent legislation positioned them with Jews and Blacks among the racial groups affected by the revocation of civil rights.

The gradual, fragmented implementation of this legal device is significant, for it meant the target populations were not suddenly deprived of all their rights, but discriminated against little by little and ultimately imprisoned. They were not allowed to marry or have sexual relations with Aryans, employ Germans, hold public office, engage in certain trades, purchase goods, attend school and so on. Such atomization had a numbing effect. Disbelief, certainty that the measures were temporary or the hope that the latest legal deprival would be the last conditioned many families' ability to react. Such circumstances are known to have affected Jewish people as well as Sinti families who, like the Winters, had been settled in Germany for generations, as can be gleaned from the memoirs authored by Walter Winter, a Holocaust survivor.[11] Their relations with their neighbours, one of the brothers' successful career as a member of the local football team or Walter's own enrolment in the navy supported Walter's belief that he would be acknowledged as a member of the national community. He clung to that certainty until 1941 when he was expelled from the navy, obliged to engage in forced labour and ultimately deported to Auschwitz.

Along with laws affecting groups deemed racially inferior or biologically impaired, so characteristic of Nazi concern over the 'new man' and racial purity, Romanies were the target of measures specifically intended for them as early as the pre-war period. Such measures made them a prototype and primary component of a group branded as delinquent, indolent and undesirable, who would have to be eradicated from a new and healthier German nation. The institution of the first internment camps for them was instrumental in that regard. Such developments are even less extensively known than subsequent Romani deportation and death in the infamous camps established in third countries. From 1935 to 1939 German municipal authorities took the initiative, requiring the local Romani communities to live in enclosed and policed areas specifically established outside their cities for that purpose. Such places, half-ghetto, half-concentration camp, became veritable jails housing whole families. They were built outside Cologne, Düsseldorf, Essen, Frankfurt, Hamburg and many other German and Austrian cities. In places such as Königsberg the facilities previously built for the homeless were reused for these camps, in keeping with the contradictions in pre-Nazi anti-Gypsy policy on which National-Syndicalism rested. Theoretically seeking to settle Romanies, deemed innate nomads, such measures and places actually served to evict Sinti and Roma peoples from their places of abode, expelling them from their homes in many German towns as part of racial cleansing operations.[12]

Custodied by the SS or local police in uniform, they also constituted a convenient source from which to build genealogical registries used for policing and scientific purposes, while also constituting recruitment centres for forced labour or sites where sterilization was practised. Their inhabitants were at times the involuntary subjects of Nazi propaganda photographs [Illustration 13]. At first Romani families living in these camps were allowed to leave during the day to work and required return at night, as Otto Rosenberg remembers in connection with Marzahn (Berlin), where he was a childhood recluse.[13] Although the Roma at the Maxglan Camp outside Salzburg were initially permitted to leave the grounds, they were eventually allowed to work only as slave labourers. Internment and concentration camp inhabitants were visited by Ritter's scientific teams, who registered them, took samples of their blood and asked about their genealogy and other matters. The Roma imprisoned at those two camps were also used by Leni Riefenstahl as extras in her film *Tiefland* (although she later denied any involvement).[14]

Camp living conditions were inhumane and not only for want of basic infrastructure and freedom. According to Rosenberg, hunger was an everyday sensation at Marzahn, along with the fear instilled in them there.[15] The guards at Höherweg Camp outside Düsseldorf engaged in particularly cruel practices, using dogs against prisoners and after curfew locking the doors to the barracks from the outside. Such mandatory municipal settlements afforded the infrastructure which, remodelled after 1939, was used to house the continuous flow of people who were to be massively deported to faraway ghettos and concentration camps. In

Illustration 13 Family caravan at Halle camp. Racial Hygiene Unit photos served both research and propaganda purposes, illustrating Roma people's 'good' living conditions in camps built specifically for them. [German Federal Archive – Digital image archive.]

1943 all the prisoners still at Maxglan near Salzburg, including seventeen children who had been born in the enclave since its institution, were deported to Auschwitz-Birkenau.

Every single person imprisoned in those facilities built before the war has their own individual story. Johann Trollmann, nicknamed Rukeli, is the main character in one of the few known today, an impactful life history that has inspired both research and novels.[16] Before entering Ahlem Camp outside Hannover in 1938, Trollmann was a successful and popular German boxer [Illustration 14]. He was too successful and popular for the Nazis not to set its sights on his Romani origin, especially since Hitler himself deemed boxing to be a genuinely virile and German sport. Consequently the Nazi press and judges with similar leanings took it upon themselves to topple Trollmann. This idolized athlete never stepped up to the ring without smiling and blowing kisses to the unprecedented number of women spectators in a sport that had traditionally drawn an overwhelming majority of men. His boxing style, nimble, fast, well-sparred and skilful in the study of the opponent's weak points, was disqualified as being scantly virile and very un-German, 'like a Jew'. The trophy he won in 1933 was requisitioned after he was involved in a notorious show of resistance, appearing in the ring with dyed blonde hair and body doused in talcum powder to caricaturize the Aryan model. Thereafter he had to eke out a precarious living in lower category sports events and fairs. Ultimately arrested, he was taken to one of the camps for

Illustration 14 Sparta Boxing Club, 1929. Johann Trollmann, Rukeli, third from right, was a champion who defied Nazi rule [US Holocaust Memorial Museum, Washington, courtesy of Hans Firzlaff].

'undesirable Gypsies'. In his short, but intense, life he was to be recruited to the army by the country that had deprived him of all his rights and in the end sent to the camp system where he perished, but not before being forced to box for the guards as revengeful entertainment.

Two synergetic forces in place prior to the outbreak of war played a decisive role in the organization of a national system to capture and deport Roma and Sinti peoples from such local spaces: the racial scientific apparatus applied to 'Gypsies' and the Nazi regime's police (especially criminal police). The pioneering Bavarian system for addressing the 'Gypsy plague', efficiently rolled out by a diligent Dillmann whose records book was mentioned in the preceding chapter, would serve as a model for the rest of Germany after 1936. That was the year Himmler, who had seen how the system operated in person when in Munich, brought a large group of Bavarian policemen to Gestapo headquarters and the Reich Criminal Police Department (RKPA). As discussed below, from 1938 to 1939 the trap on which Romani genocide was based was dually baited with racial scientific 'evidence' and criminal police action.

Scientific theory, police application: A crucial tandem

The RKPA was one of the institutions primarily responsible for persecuting Romani and Sinti peoples, first in Germany and later in the rest of Europe. Created in 1936 and like others of the regime's police forces placed under the direct command of Reinhard Heydrich, its management was entrusted to Arthur Nebe, who later ordered the mass murder of Romanies in the USSR, according to Gilad Margalit.[17] In addition to its nationwide squads specializing in drugs, pornography and gambling, it had a team specifically devoted to 'Gypsies'. The general philosophy informing its action was wholly in line with the ideas on crime prevention in vogue at the time, whereby delinquents were viewed as subjects with a socially and biologically determined criminal personality. Identification and preventive measures would consequently be the key principles for ensuring law and order.

The qualitative leap in the 'preventive' effort that came in late 1938 largely determined the fate of the Reich's Romani population. The aforementioned decree on 'combating the Gypsy plague' signed by Himmler in December that year was drafted by the RKPA itself. It aimed to solve the so-called 'Gypsy plague' on the grounds of 'their racial character'. The issue was addressed from a racial perspective and not only because the measures stipulated identified the Romanies as a race based on their characteristics, but also because it drew a distinction between different categories of 'Zigeuner' depending on their racial purity. Significantly, the post-Nazi German justice system chose January 1943 (date of enactment of another decree discussed later) as the date after which Romani survivors of Nazi persecution would be allowed (although not encouraged) to claim indemnity. According to that post-war jurisprudence, persecution prior to 1943 was not racially inspired. That assertion is dually surprising because not only the 1938 decree and police action stemming from it deemed delinquency a collective racial characteristic of 'Gypsies', but also given the extensive scientific endeavour undertaken in parallel to categorize and label the Romani population in eminently racial terms.

The work performed by the regime's racial scientists was, alongside criminal police action, the source of the essential materials for organizing the Romani genocide. The responsibility for racially defining 'Gypsies' was attributed to the Centre for Research on Racial Hygiene and Demographic Biology, headed from the time of its institution by psychiatrist and neurologist Robert Ritter. The specific (although not rigorous) arguments resulting from the research conducted by Ritter and colleagues were instrumental in formulating the idea that 'Gypsies' would contaminate the Aryan people from within and had consequently to be treated as a racial problem. Although they did not constitute a peril as serious as the Jewish 'race', 'Gypsies' were deemed a primitive, socially inadaptable people. Their collective nature, according to that discourse, tended toward delinquency, a reluctance to work and the rejection of any social discipline or law.

One of the foremost outcomes of this scientific team's research was the creation of a corpus of individualized racial reports for approximately 24,000 people examined in Germany, home to an estimated 30,000 Romanies and Sinti before the war. Although they drew from police and administrative documents to which they were given access by the respective institutions, they relied primarily on the data collected by a series of studies conducted by record-gathering groups sent to internment camps created for German and Austrian Romanies. Families were interviewed and examined in the field, often under coercion. Blood tests were performed and anthropometric measurements taken,

Illustration 15 Dr Robert Ritter in 1938 at Stein in der Pfalz, Germany. Drawing blood from a Sinto for his racial studies, assisted by Eva Justin [German Federal Archive – Digital image archive.]

facial moulds and craniometric models were made and genealogical maps of the Reich's Romani population were drawn [Illustrations 15 and 16]. Holocaust survivor Philomena Franz recalled that 'the criminal police measured our noses and ears, recorded our hair colour and many other things. They said I was a pure race Indian. Others were classified as mixed race, even though their parents were both genuine Sinti'.[18]

Building on the data gathered and the results of such studies, Ritter and his team classified the Romani population into the categories used in Himmler's 1938 decree. The categories of 'Gypsies' living in Germany who were to be provided with identity cards in keeping with the respective racial report were: pure 'Zigeuner', whose brown cards were to bear the initial Z and mixed blood or 'Zigeuner Mischlinge' (ZM, mixed, mixed blood, mixed race or half-cast 'Gypsies'), whose brown cards were to bear a diagonal blue line. That latter main category was divided into sub-categories depending on the greater or lesser percentage of 'German' mixed with Romani blood. Anyone with a Romani grandparent or two partially Romani grandparents would be deemed 'mixed'. Depending on their forebears, all individuals branded as 'Z' or 'ZM' would be given a police ID card that would determine their fate. The primary conclusion drawn from these studies was that 90 per cent of the Reich's 'Gypsies' bore mixed blood as a result of

Illustration 16 Craniometric studies and racial science. Eva Justin [?] and Dr Adolf Würth measuring the head of a young Sinto, 1938. Establishing Sinti and Roma genealogies to distinguish between 'pure' and 'mixed' 'Gypsies'. [German Federal Archive – Digital image archive.]

their centenary interbreeding with the lowest rungs of the local population, deemed to be an asocial and criminal sub-proletariat. The sole solution to such a genetic combination would be sterilization and imprisonment, as proposed by Ritter in a scientific paper published in 1938. His work was essential to the formulation of the aforementioned decree enacted in December of that year, in terms of both the classification and identification of Romanies. It was equally instrumental to establishing the racial grounds underlying the basic premise on how to address this 'plague'.[19]

One example of the outcome of his work for the Nazi system can be found in Erna Laubinger, Unku in the Romani language. Born in 1920 to a German family engaging in horse trading, Unku is better known for having inspired a children's story published in 1920 about the friendship between a working-class child and a Romani girl. Its Jewish communist author, Grete Weiskopf, used the pseudonym Alex Weiskopf. That book, which has a story of its own, is dealt with in greater detail in Chapter 3. Its editorial success outlived Unku, who had a tragic end. In 1939 her family was imprisoned in an internment camp for 'Gypsies' built on the outskirts of Magdeburg where they were subject to racial research [Illustrations 17 and 18]. The report signed by Ritter classified

Illustration 17 *Unku*, **Ena Laubinger in 1936 at Dessau-Rosslau, Germany.** Sixteen-year-old Unku smiling for photographer Hans Weltzel shortly before her family was decimated under Nazi racial persecution [Courtesy of the University of Liverpool Library - Special Collections.]

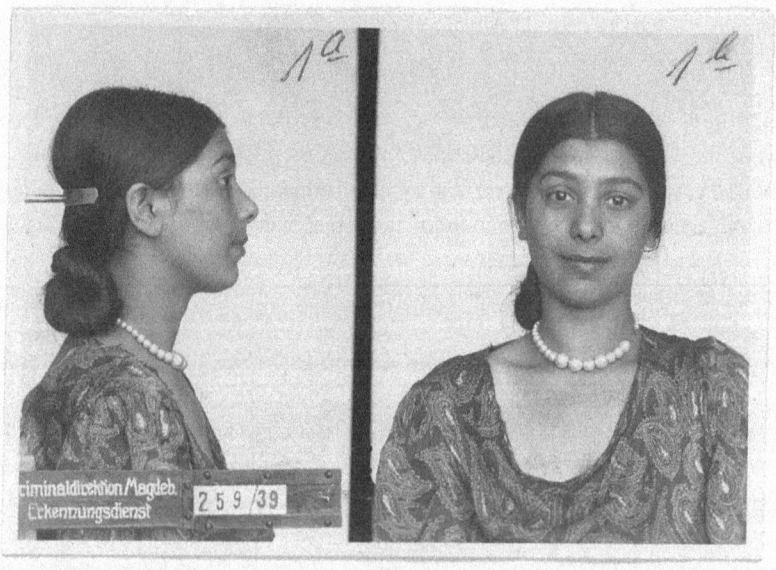

Illustration 18 Magdeburg criminal police photos of Ena Laubinger, 1939. The descent into Nazi camp hell mirrored in her gaze [Landersarchiv Sachsen-Anhalt, Magdeburg].

Unku as a 'mixed Gypsy'. In early March 1943, further to the instructions in the so-called Auschwitz Decree (to be discussed later), she and her two small children and the rest of her family were sent to the *Zigeunerlager* or 'Gypsy' camp at Auschwitz-Birkenau. She died there a few months after being tattooed with prisoner number Z-633.[20] Many other Romanies whose stories have not been recorded followed a similar route from municipal internment to extermination camps.

Ritter did not work alone. He headed a team of collaborators who shared the responsibility for examining, classifying and proposing measures against the Romani population. His innermost circle included anthropologist Adolf Wurth, zoologist and anthropologist Sophie Ehrhardt and nurse Eva Justin, an especially close collaborator. She later earned a PhD. in anthropology with a study she had conducted to analyse Romani children's behaviour. Justin used a group of minors separated from their parents, who had been taken to internment camps. Grouped in special 'homes' where they were visited, examined and interviewed by Justin for years, they constituted the empirical basis for the premise put forward in her thesis that 'Gypsy' children were genetically criminal, for not even being raised outside their families and in keeping with strictly German criteria sufficed to modify their tendency to defy the law. Sterilization was the only scientific solution to the problem. Once the study was concluded, most of the children were sent to camps such as Auschwitz-Birkenau.

Ritter and his team helped drive the transition of racial ideas about 'Gypsies' from the academic and scientific to the political arena of laws and police measures. They collaborated closely with the Reichskriminallpolizeiamt, RKPA (Criminal Police Department), signing reports that led to the arrest, sterilization and deportation of many Romanies. In short, they advanced key ideas for the design of the Nazi regime's anti-Gypsy policy. And yet their accountability to the German judicial system after Hitler was defeated was anything but exemplary. These scientists not only continued in public office, but the outcome of the trials to which they were (with great difficulty) brought was frustrating for those demanding justice. Such was the treatment dispensed to the aforementioned, who are only the most prominent and well-known of a very large group of collaborators. The Nazi system's expert network was extensive and over time integrated scientists from other countries, as Viorel Achim showed for those involved in Romania. To assess the effects of Ritter and team's pre-deportation identification and classification tasks, they should be viewed in connection with the medical experiments undertaken later by Nazi racial scientists in the concentration and extermination camps. Doctor Josef Mengele was not the only one to use Romani prisoners as subjects of laboratory experiments, as discussed later.

To return to key year 1938, clearly the route to deportation was charted with the December decree on 'combating the Gypsy plague' or even before. Between mid-year and throughout 1939 around 2,000 Romani males, accused of vagrancy and indolence, were detained in Germany and Austria and sent first to camps at Buchenwald, Dachau, Sachsenhausen and Lichtenburg and subsequently to Mauthausen and Ravensbrück. There, Nazi enthusiasm for classification marked them with the respective, although variable symbol: a triangle, if black meaning asocial and if green, criminal, sometimes with a Z in the middle. That was only the beginning of a process that was intensified in all respects by war.

The Roma and the Holocaust

With the war: Deportation, forced labour and confiscation

With the 1939 onset of what would become the Second World War Nazi discrimination against the Romani population, like the regime's anti-Semitic policy, deepened. Starting with the invasion of Poland and the parallel expulsion of Jews from territories reserved for pure Germans, the Reichssicherheitshauptamt (RSHA, Central Reich Security Bureau), to which the Criminal Police was subordinate, issued a warrant (October 1939) calling for the arrest and subsequent deportation to Poland of 30,000 German Romanies and Sinti. Heydrich clearly equated Jewish and Romani fates in those instructions, a principle confirmed by Himmler in a meeting held in 1940: 'the Gypsies are a question in their own right. If possible, I want to get rid of them this year. They are 30,000 in the whole Reich, but they nonetheless cause very substantial racial damage.'[21]

Although such mass deportation was not implemented on the spot, the invasion of France, Belgium and the Netherlands constituted a decisive step in that direction. In May 1940 around 2,400 Romanies living in the western Reich were deported, in a single operation, to occupied Poland on the grounds that as enemy spies their presence in Germany constituted a peril. As Wolfgang Benz notes, that was a dress rehearsal for subsequent genocide.[22] Himmler ordered Criminal Police headquarters in Hamburg, Bremen, Cologne, Düsseldorf, Hannover, Frankfurt and Stuttgart to arrest the Sinti and Roma in their respective regions and send them to camps in occupied Poland. The Reich's expert racial biologists personally aided in the selection. In November of that year a similar number of Roma were deported from Alsace. Due to the non-existent hygiene at the final destination 80 per cent of the German Sinti and Romanies deported to Poland in May 1940 perished. The reluctance of the German authorities in Nazi-occupied Poland's General Government to admit new groups of Romani prisoners, which momentarily curbed further deportations, attests quite obviously to the inclusion of 'Gypsies' in the racial cleansing hastened by the outbreak of war.

After annexation into the German Reich in 1938, in Austria that ambition had a decisive impact on the substantial Romani population long settled in Burgenland, a region bordering Hungary. Lackenbach, one of the municipal internment camps discussed in the preceding section, witnessed a qualitative leap. Operative after November 1940, the camp had been instituted by Vienna's Criminal Police to comply with a decree ordering the mandatory resettlement of around 6,000 Austrian 'Gypsies', who began to arrive in droves. Some, such as Rosa Mettbach's family, had already been living under police control in semi-freedom. At Lackenbach they were registered and engaged in forced labour and from there were sent to ghettos or concentration and extermination camps in occupied Poland. The camp also served as a way station on the route to deportation for Romanies who had been previously grouped in smaller camps. The St Pantaleon-Weyer Camp in Upper Austria, for instance, closed in 1941 after sending its 301 Romani prisoners still living there to Lackenbach as an intermediate step on the journey to Łódź ghetto.

Both camps bear witness to the realities of the slave labour performed by Romanies, along with Jews and other groups of prisoners. Paradoxically, however, the offence most frequently attributed to Romanies was indolence. Weyer had in fact been instituted in 1940 as a camp to re-educate asocial and work-shy elements 'through work'. Most of the prisoners there, outside of a few of varying origin, had been branded 'Gypsies'. Whole families were subjected to forced labour and abuse. Working-age men were employed in hard manual construction and drainage jobs in the area, but they were not alone. Women, children and the elderly literally gave their lives performing a variable suite of tasks.

Forced labour was practised not only in the camps, but also in some cases in policed spaces where Sinti and Romani families lived briefly in semi-freedom thanks to their 'good behaviour' (generally army-related), which saved them from the first wave of deportations [Illustration 19]. As Walter Winter recalls in his survivor's memoirs, after he had to leave the navy in 1941 and before ending up at Auschwitz in 1943, both he and his siblings Erich and María were forced to work at Damme Airport, near Vechta.[23] They were obliged to adapt their own vehicle for freight to deliver stone tiling for a local

Illustration 19 Walter Winter in German Navy uniform, 1942. In 1943 Winter was deported to Auschwitz-Birkenau and, other concentration camps, from where was sent to fight on the Soviet front [Dokumentation und Kulturzentrum, Deutscher Sinti und Roma, Heidelberg].

shop. Renowned companies such as Bayer, Krupp, Siemens, AEG and arms, aircraft, automobile and chemical factories as well as electric power plants used Romani forced labour during the Third Reich.

Prisoners' forced labour, known to have been standard Nazi practice, bore much of the burden involved in the war economy and effort. In that Romanies shared the fate of Jews and other groups deemed Germany's enemies. The Nazi camp system was the embodiment par excellence of the 'work to death' premise that combined military and racial logic. Preliminary documents had been forthcoming for the Nuremberg trials held immediately after the war. Used to try some of those responsible for the crimes perpetrated against whole communities on the grounds of race, nationality or other grounds, they acknowledged the efficacy of the formula (slave labour-induced extermination), intensified by abuse. The reams of information gathered by the US government for the Nuremberg trials cited the opinion of Reich Propaganda Minister Joseph Goebbels on the best way to deal with asocial elements. Referring to Jews and 'Gypsies' he contended that 'the idea of exterminating them by labour is the best'. According to a 14 September 1942 conversation with Minister of Justice Thierack, he believed they should be exterminated in general and unconditionally, along with Poles serving three- to four-year sentences and Czechs and Germans sentenced to death or life imprisonment.[24]

Regime machinery also capitalized on other benefits to be drawn from the mass deportation of subjects previously deprived of their rights on racial grounds. The voracity with which Jewish property and assets were seized by the Nazis is well documented, but little has been written about the pillage of the Romani population's worldly possessions. The amount and type of goods confiscated unquestionably varied, given the two groups' sociological characteristics. Nonetheless, the volume of looting of Romani property should not be underestimated, for that would entail ignoring a very significant fact: many deported families (whose property was immediately seized) did not fit the cliché tiresomely invoked by the regime's 'anti-Gypsy' propaganda, depicting Roma as necessarily nomadic and impoverished.

Some Romanies were prosperous businesspeople who, with persecution, lost their means to make a living along with their freedom. Ludwig Eiber collected stories of families in Munich who, having engaged in transport, were deported and the children sterilized, with no regard for the fact that some of the family members had served in the army.[25] Luthiers, public officials, bakers, owners of stage shows and so on, not all the Reich's Romanies wandered nomadically from one place to another to eke out a subsistence living [Illustration 20]. As the Mettbach family recalled in their interviews with Toby Sonneman,[26] some deliberately converted to nomadic life in pursuit of refuge from Nazi persecution, for their traditional sedentary lifestyle proved less secure in the new scenario. Many more or less well-to-do Romanies and Sinti were sent directly to Auschwitz from the relative comfort of their everyday lives. Viennese Romani Franz Rosenbach, for instance, recalled: 'I was in a suit, wearing white shoes, a hat and a tie. We had to go into some kind of room where they took everything away from us. When I protested, I was immediately hit for the first time. We had to strip naked, women too,

Illustration 20 Rosa Lehmann (maiden name, Höllenreiner) in the 1920s at her house at Munich with her father and nephew. Rosa was deported to Auschwitz with her husband and children in 1943 [Dokumentation und Kulturzentrum, Deutscher Sinti und Roma, Heidelberg].

and they cut off our hair.'[27] Although little is known about most confiscations, including the seizure of artistic objects such as recorded by Jonathan Petropoulos, looting of the Romani population's property could be materially tracked in some cases.[28] Documents in custody at the United States Holocaust Memorial Museum, which bears an account of the confiscation of the properties of 250 Romanies deported from Berlin, attest to such injustice.

The pillage to which German and European Romanies in general were subjected was characterized by a second particular that should not be overlooked. The hybridization between genocidal policies and sheer greed exhibited by the attachment procedures in place under the Nazi regime led to an 'anything goes' philosophy: from kitchen utensils to shoes, toys and paintings, including glasses, watches, new or used clothing mended by other prisoners and so on. Everything taken from the deportees was stored in warehouses and sent from one end of Nazi-occupied Europe to another as required. The procedures involved in that apparatus and its bureaucracy are known for Jewish prisoners, but they were in all likelihood also used against other groups such as the Romanies. According to Jud Nirenberg, the same forms designed for confiscating Jewish property were used for 'Gypsies', simply crossing out the word 'Jew'.[29] The thoroughness of that looting was the outcome of practical as well as genocidal intention. On the one hand, anything of value or second- or third-hand benefit in a war economy was put to good use. And on the other, that practice erased all trace of an internal enemy who had to be eliminated. A case recorded by Jiří Lípa in a report on the attachment of a series of Romani properties in Czechoslovakia in 1943 illustrates the voracity involved. The list of confiscated items includes furniture, goats, beehives, potatoes, farming and other tools, and so on that were to be sold in public auction.[30]

Logically, Nazi-occupied and -fragmented Czechoslovakia was one of the first countries where the local Romani population's fate resembled that of German Sinti and Romani peoples. In Slovakia the orders to eliminate 'Gypsies' were applied somewhat more indulgently than in the Czech area in the Bohemia-Moravia Protectorate. Even so, the general trend was to imprison Czech Romanies in forced labour camps. The living conditions in those camps were so precarious that even voices initially favourable to using such facilities to re-educate 'asocial' elements questioned the practice. One Slovakian MP contended: 'The camps were established in order to re-educate the asocial elements, not in order to torture people and bring them into an even worse moral degradation.'[31] Lety, the site of one such camp, initially organized by the local police bureau as a forced labour centre for men only, gradually became a concentration camp where women and children also lived and died. Josef Seryneck, one of the prisoners who managed to escape, joined the partisans who combated the German army in Bohemia-Moravia. None of the thirty children who were born in the camp survived, and the group of prisoners still living there in late 1942 was sent to Auschwitz as part of a general deportation policy discussed later. Czech Romanies are still struggling today to have the camp, used in the post-war period to raise livestock, converted into a space to pay tribute to the victims.

As in Czechoslovakia, developments in Nazi-occupied France mirrored both the regime's racial cleansing intentions and pre-existing anti-Roma prejudice, widespread throughout Europe. In France, the Nazi administration's instructions were enforced over a layer of previous abuse. Since 1912 French law linked nomadism to vagrancy and criminal conduct, while personifying the concomitant threat 'Gypsies' posed to societal security. Such obligatory assimilation had been the pattern in place since the turn of the century, along with stigmatization that adopted the form of anthropometric ID cards, as mentioned in Chapter 1 [Illustration 21]. By 1924 around 30,000 people were attributed the legal status *nomade*. Very similar legislative and police conditions were in place in nearby Belgium, whilst an agreement signed in 1936 coordinated border controls between the two countries. Nazi authorities were indisputably able to draw widely from such anti-Gypsy laws to the benefit of Third Reich racial policy.

In France more specifically, there is a clear link between anti-Gypsy policies before and after German occupation, as revealed by studies authored by Filhol and Hubert and Foisneau,[32] among others. Before surrendering to Germany, the Third Republic's Government decreed the incarceration of all so-called *nomades* on the grounds of their potential peril as enemy spies (April 1940). That same policy was later implemented in both the area occupied directly by Hitler's army and in theoretically independent France governed by the collaborationist Vichy regime. In the latter the legal and police resources deployed for that purpose were modified by defining the term

The Romani Genocide under Nazism

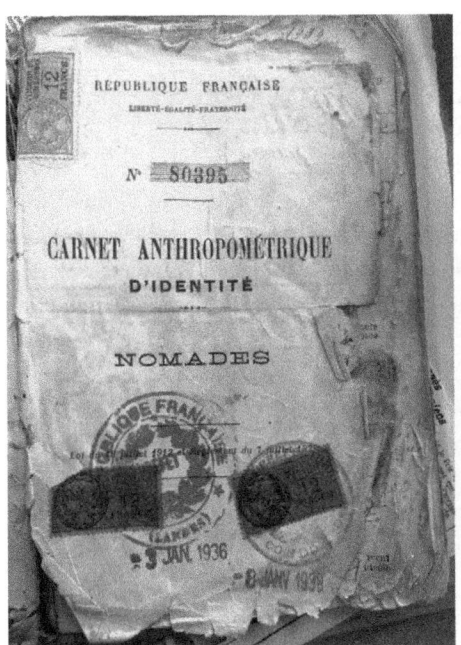
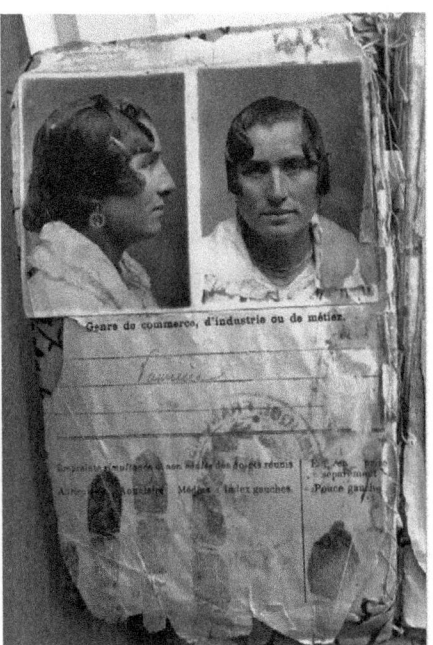

Illustration 21 Anthropometric ID used to control 'nomad' peoples in France. Front side of document and full-face and profile photos of Teresa Gabarre, 1936–9 [Médiathèque Mateo Maximoff, Paris].

nomade more broadly. On those grounds, many Romani families were imprisoned in internment camps while others were obliged to camp in specific areas they were not allowed to leave even to seek ways to make a living. In addition, couples unable to prove they were legally married were physically separated.

The 140 or so internment camps built in the two parts of France took in approximately 6,000 Romanies, imprisoned in shameful conditions, pillaged and obliged to work. Some children were separated from their parents and given over to religious institutions. This chapter of recent French history only began to be publicly acknowledged in the 1980s. Saliers, one such camp in the Vichy zone, was established to 're-educate through work'. In 2015 photographer Mathieu Pernot, looking through departmental archives, discovered hundreds of anthropometric ID cards borne by camp prisoners, most of whom were Romanies from the Camargue, and told their story in an exhibition that included some of the survivors' testimonies.[33]

Whereas most of these French camps were not used for intermediate detention prior to deportation and extermination, they nonetheless caused the suffering and death of many *Manouches* (French Romani) families and Roma people more generally. Django Reindhardt is the object of a number of biographies that afford ample information on the special and representative case of this famous musician. A foremost member of France's successful *Quintette du Hot Club*, he initially believed the Second World War was no business of his, given that it involved a clash between *non-Gadjés* (non-Romanies).

63

Nonetheless, an awareness of the suffering of other *Manouches* and his own efforts to escape from Nazi-occupied France prompted him to compose *Requiem pour les frères tsiganes* (requiem for my Gypsy brothers and sisters), a testimony of the Romani genocide interpreted only once after the country was liberated.

One incident in France related to collective deportation and extermination was especially significant: the so-called Convoy Z that carried 352 Romanies to Auschwitz in cattle cars. The point of departure was the camp at Malines, Belgium, a place used primarily to regroup deported Jews but also 'Gypsies' as needed. Convoy Z carried only Romanies who had been arrested either in northern France (mostly in the area in and around Nord-Pas-de-Calais, included by the Nazis in the so-called 'German military administration zone in Belgium') or in Belgium itself. As late as 1944, they were all sent in that convoy to Auschwitz-Birkenau, where 90 per cent of them perished. According to a study by Mónica Heddebaut, some of the families involved were horse traders, professional musicians, circus performers, basket weavers and so on. The youngest of the prisoners was just thirty-eight days old, whilst the oldest was eighty-five; three-quarters of the Convoy Z passengers were women and children under fifteen. One of the French families, the Vadoches, had been incarcerated at the Montreuil-Bellay Camp. The sole Auschwitz survivor was Victor Vadoche, nine years old at the time.[34]

The Montreuil-Bellay Camp serves as an example of the symbiosis between Nazi instructions and local policies long in effect in France. Like others reserved for the internment of '*tsiganes nomades*', this camp continued to be used after the Allied forces liberated the country from German occupation. Whilst in August 1944 the French Republic's provisional government ordered freedom for all Nazi prisoners, shortly thereafter Minister of the Interior Adrien Tixier revoked application of that measure to '*nomades*', whose release from such camps was to be studied case by case. Consequently, in 1945 and as late as 1946 some Romanies were still living in the Second World War camps in France. The perception of 'Gypsies' as a national problem persisted in official policy more or less generally and was extended with measures such as the mandate to carry an anthropometric identity document, as discussed by Ilsen About.

Such stigmatization of an entire community, depicted (and treated) as the anti-model of good citizenship, was the view of Romanies that also prevailed in other European countries before and after Nazism. The authors of Third Reich racial policy put that premise to the test and used it and all it implied ever more extensively as the war progressed.

Ghettos and executions: The war spreads eastwards

After 1941 the Third Reich scaled up its anti-Gypsy measures, while also preparing to invade the Soviet Union. The establishment of that eastern front, preceded by intervention in Greece and the Balkans, intensified the racial cleansing campaign in the German rear guard. Jews and Romanies, already targeted by Nazi discourse (and concomitant measures) on racial inferiority, were drawn into the rabid wave of anti-Slavic racism that fuelled German military operations in Soviet Russia. Attributing them 'sub-human' status inspired mass killings of unprecedented dimensions.

A circular dated in Berlin on 5 November 1942 on 'Criminal Procedure against Poles and Members of the Eastern Peoples' addressed to chiefs of police equated Jews and 'Gypsies'. The respective instructions ordered the abolition of their legal rights and placed both communities directly in police hands on the premise that their racial inferiority threatened German security. The measures adopted against Romanies in 1941 and 1942, like those affecting Jews, were implemented in essentially two dimensions of a single process of collective extermination. On the one hand, the exponential rise in deportations to ghettos and various types of camps built preferably in Poland entailed the speedy or slow death, depending on the case, of thousands of Roma people. And on the other, firing squads, normally drawn from among the *Einsatzgruppen* (killing units), executed whole groups of people more immediately and no less massively.

Most of the camps and ghettos for Romanies from countries under one degree or another or Nazi domination were located in occupied Poland. In some cases these ghettos are well known as places for Jewish imprisonment and death. The one in Warsaw was the destination for Hungarian, Romanian and Bulgarian Romanies, as Adam Czerniaków, president of the *Judenrat* (Jewish council established under German law) noted in his diary before committing suicide.[35] Nor did their presence go unnoticed by Emmanuel Ringelblum, insightful chronicler of life in the ghetto who in the 17 June 1942 entry in his diary recorded the arrival of what he called a 'new blight – the Gypsies'. The 240 families at issue wore a white arm band bearing a red Z. Steeped in prejudice, he described the fear of pillaging their presence inspired in Jews: 'they will rob, steal, break window panes and pinch bread out of shop-windows. They will not quietly starve to death as Jews do.'[36]

It is hard to say whether that observation perceived greater Romani than Jewish ability to resist and rebel. What the author of the diary explicitly says is that he knew that other Romanies had been sent to gas chambers. That was also the fate of the Romani families reaching the Warsaw ghetto, from where they were taken to the Treblinka extermination camp in early 1943, along with thousands of Jews [Illustration 22]. Other similar ghettos where German Romanies were sent included Białystok, Krakow and Radom, all in Poland and all torn down one or two years later after their residents were taken to extermination camps or exterminated directly when the ghetto was shut down. Sambor, where Romanies were housed with the Jewish majority according to Tyaglyy,[37] is a case in point.

One of the better known cases relating to Romani genocide is the ghetto at Łódź (or Lizmannstadt in German). Five thousand Romanies from Austria's Burgenland region were taken there in 1941. The Austrian authorities had insisted on being relieved of the inmates formerly at Lackenbach Camp to free their country of 'Gypsies', confirming a prior anti-Gypsy tradition of 'genocidal trajectory' to use Florian Freund's apt description.[38] At Łódź, the Austrian Romanies were crowded into a specific area of the ghetto denominated the 'Gypsy' camp. Most, from 4,400 to 4,600, died there in a few months' time, largely due to an outbreak of typhus attributable to the dreadful living conditions that prevailed.

The Roma and the Holocaust

Illustration 22 Polish Romani women. Lublin ghetto, 1940 [photograph by Max Kirnberger, material in the public domain].

Conditions in that overpopulated ghetto prompted a complaint even by the official in charge of its administration, who protested to Himmler, accusing Eichmann himself, as organizer of the deportation system, of cramming more prisoners into the place than it could handle. This circumstance is mentioned in Hannah Arendt's indispensable account of the Eichmann trial in Jerusalem. According to the ghetto administrator, Eichmann 'had deceived him and his men with "horsetrading tricks learnt from Gypsies"'.[39] The many Romani victims who at Łódź had to bear the stereotype of 'Gypsies' as cheats included several members of the family of the young woman whose story is told in the opening pages of this book: Rosa Mettbach lost her mother, sister, nieces and nephews at the camp. When the ghetto was torn down in 1943, the survivors, along with the remains of its Jewish population, were sent to the Chelmo extermination camp. During the trip a new method of mass assassination was tested on them, death by gas, using lorries in which engine combustion gases were pumped back into the body of the vehicle. According to Saul Friendländer, very few witnesses later mentioned the presence of Romanies at Łódź, despite the number and fate of those imprisoned there.[40]

In countries allied with the Third Reich Romani communities were an increasingly common target for internment and deportation. Research to explore Giovanna Boursier's[41] pioneering study on such persecution in fascist Italy in greater depth is still outstanding, although the victims' voices have been heard thanks to a number of papers attempting to recover lost memory. For many years the existence of racial persecution against Romanies in fascist Italy was denied, for they were not explicitly mentioned in the racial laws that deprived Jews of their rights beginning in 1938. Nonetheless, 'Gypsies' had long been depicted as a national problem in which political policy spilled over into police practice, confirming that the underlying anti-Gypsyism so common throughout Europe was also present in Italy. That translated, under the contention that they endangered national security, into imprisonment in policed internment camps in a series of pre-established towns. Alternatively, especially after an internment order issued in 1940, they were sent to concentration camps, either specifically for 'Gypsies' or shared with other types of prisoners. A recent study by Paola Trevisan on the northern border provinces contains information on the contradictory combination of categories applied to them as both 'undesirable foreigners' and 'dangerous Italians'.[42] Romanies under Italian rule experienced a variety of fates. Some were deported to the heart of the German Reich, while others were able to escape and even join the partisan Resistance after the armistice signed in the wake of Allied disembarkation in the south in 1943. Until that time, it was not in vain that Mussolini controlled areas such as Albania, where Romanies were imprisoned together with Jews in nearby concentration camps or deported to Buchenwald and Mauthausen.

Ion Antonescu's phyllo-Nazi regime in power in Romania heightened the impact of traditional Romani persecution, particularly after Germany invaded the Soviet Union. Acting on a nationalistic and eugenic discourse that called for the segregation and internment of 'Gypsies', Antonescu's May 1942 decision to deport them to Transnistria induced the death of 14,000 to 25,000 Romanies, according to Achim.[43] The order presumably was to oblige them to camp in areas set aside for them where they would organize around one elder who in each community would be accountable for the work of all its able-bodied members (anyone between twelve and sixty years old). Nomadic and sedentary Roma peoples alike, poor families and those in possession of means to earn a living, even Romani families with members serving in the army, were branded as stereotypically indolent. The operation was concomitantly orchestrated under conditions that more than mere expulsion and resettlement resembled an attempted final solution to the 'Gypsy plague'. The families arrested were deported in cattle cars where many died of starvation and cold. On arrival, the survivors found their new settlements absolutely wanting in any means of subsistence. Malnutrition and disease, particularly a typhus epidemic, were the primary causes of the death of thousands of people. According to Vladimir Solonari, such deaths could be directly attributed to a deportation policy in which 'crime prevention' was the excuse invoked to justify an attempt at racial cleansing. The rest of the Romanian population, scantly protesting the fate of the country's Roma peoples, adopted an indifferent attitude towards developments very descriptively narrated in a novel by Ioan T. Morar, *Negru și Roșu* (Black and Red).

The fate of all Romani communities soured throughout Nazi-occupied or fascist-controlled or -leaning Europe. As in Romania, in the new independent, phyllo-Nazi state of Croatia governed by Ante Pavelic, 'Gypsies' were in the crosshairs of demands for the racial cleansing characteristic of the resulting nationalistic discourse. Here other elements came into play, such as the prioritization of defining Serbs as Croatia's 'internal enemies'. Romanies were nonetheless accused of being spies who threatened

Illustration 23 Romani prisoners taken to Jasenovac camp in Croatia, 1942–3. Under the surveillance of the Ustasha, the ultra-right-leaning Croatian police force, they shared the fate of Serbian prisoners [US Holocaust Memorial Museum; courtesy of Muzej Revolucije Narodnosti Jugoslavije].

national security and sent en masse to the Jasenovac extermination camp, where they were the second most numerous community after Serbs [Illustration 23]. Between 16,000 and 24,000 Romanies lost their lives in that *Ustasha* (Croatian fascist)-run camp, characterized by less industrialized but no less cruel extermination methods than in place in other Nazi facilities. 'The most mechanized form of killing, aside from deliberate starvation and disease, was throwing live victims into the huge furnace at the brick factory.' According to a study by Alexander Korb, 75 per cent of the Romani population in Croatia were victims of *Ustasha* violence.[44]

Regional variations denote the extent of local discretionary manoeuvring. In Bulgaria legislation providing for racial discrimination characteristic of Nazi Germany limited Romani mobility, prohibited mixed marriages and ordered imprisonment in camps on Bulgarian soil. Local political and religious representatives, however, with the support of public opinion, resisted complying with the orders to deport Jews and Romanies to German-controlled concentration and extermination camps. Even though the Jews and Romanies living in regions occupied by Bulgaria during the war were not afforded the same treatment, that country's Romani population was indisputably the one least affected by Nazi genocide in Eastern Europe.[45]

The Romani Genocide under Nazism

Illustration 24 Roma on their way to execution, photo taken between 1941 and 1943. Here in Serbia, under the watch of Milan Nedic's phyllo-Nazi Government police [US Holocaust Memorial Museum; courtesy of Muzej Revolucije Narodnosti Jugoslavije].

In the Balkans, in contrast, deportation to concentration and extermination camps was supplemented by collective killings of Romani prisoners [Illustration 24]. In Serbia in autumn 1941 the Wehrmacht and Security Police executed groups of adult males in operations theoretically targeting local partisans, while women and children were imprisoned in the concentration camp at Sajmište. There, as Kay noted, 'Jews and Roma were convenient and supposedly expendable groups whose execution could satisfy the required reprisal quotas without producing undesired political repercussions and aggravating the anti-partisan struggle'.[46] That pattern of genocidal violence was standard practice on the eastern front and affected regions in the former Soviet Union, where 'Gypsies' were grouped together with other dangerous subjects (communists, partisans, Jews) targeted for hasty elimination by the German army as it advanced.

Only sporadic traces of collective Romani torture and murder in those regions are known today, and the incidents for which there is evidence have not been systematized space- or time-wise. Nonetheless, a few sporadic studies, drawing from unpublished Soviet State records, attest to widespread genocidal intentions. Although the German occupation army came with no explicit instructions for Russian Romanies, the military operations undertaken and squadron head officers' initiatives made 'Gypsy'

69

annihilation such systematic practice that it is comparable to the Holocaust by Bullets inflicted on the Jews.

Martin Holler researched the German army's behaviour in a number of former Soviet regions.[47] Based on the dossiers generated by the Soviet Extraordinary State Commission on Crimes Committed by Germans and Collaborators (Russian initials, ChGK) created in 1942, Holler reconstructed *Einsatzgruppe* (killing unit) practice in operations conducted in northern Russia, documenting a number of specific episodes of collective executions. In February 1942, more than twenty Romani families who had been sent to Filippovshchina in 1941 to work as farmhands were taken from their homes and executed by an assault force comprising Germans, Finns and Estonians, who later forced other locals to burn the dead bodies. According to one witness, a German officer had a ten-year-old boy, who had managed to escape with local assistance, thrown onto the funeral pyre. There are also records of two episodes that took place shortly thereafter in which 'Gypsies' and Jews shared the same fate: mass murder. The witnesses to one, which took place at Moglino, narrated the special cruelty with which twenty-one Romanies were killed. To save on bullets, children were torn from their mothers' arms and stunned by hitting them on the head before being thrown into the common grave. The same records give an account of four other mass executions perpetrated in April 1942. At Krivitsy, fifteen Romani prisoners, including several children, were lined up before being riddled with bullets. The same procedure was used against twenty-five Romanies in nearby Savinovshchina. In Oredezh seventy-two were murdered and a further 120 later deported to a neighbouring district.

Further evidence for this case study invokes the May 1942 murder of thirty-eight Romanies in a prisoner of war camp in the Novgorod region. There children were executed on planks covering the pit so their execution could be witnessed by their parents, prior to their own death at the hands of a firing squad. Any survivors were burnt alive with the corpses. In this case the record includes the name of a sedentary eight-member Romani family, the Massalskys, who had steady jobs (one as a railroad engineer) and were well known to their neighbours. Nonetheless, the persecution and murder of Russia's Romani population was often justified by the accusation that they constituted a peril due to their itinerant lifestyle, which presumably made them innate spies in times of war. Whole families were even incriminated as suspected rear guard enemies. The Novorzhev massacre, which took place in May 1942, serves as an example. There between 128 (according to German sources) and 330 (according to Russian sources) Romanies were tortured and executed. The families in question had repaired, with all their belongings, to the place designated in a call from a German military authority who promised to resettle them in a region where they would supposedly be able to live and work.[48] Similar episodes in other regions such as Smolensk, controlled by *Einsatzgruppe* B, have been reported.

More than a chain of specific episodes documented more or less randomly, the pattern describing the practice of the German occupation army and its collaborators denotes a deliberate policy to eradicate a whole community. The accusation of espionage and the application of the same treatment as inflicted on the partisans who combatted Nazism were mere excuses to conduct summary executions and exterminate Romanies, like Jews and Serbs, on racial grounds. In some cases responsibility for the killings was later acknowledged by those involved, such as an SS officer who headed a unit against Russian resistance in 1943 (confession by Bach-Zelewsk).[49]

In fact, 'Gypsies' were ever more often subjected to the same measures as the partisans, although Resistance fighters affected by this form of violence were in general adult males, whereas among Romanies the victims were whole families. As Holler concludes, Romanies were murdered simply because they were deemed to be 'Gypsies'.[50] The details of the killing at Filippovshchina are particularly eloquent in that respect. Obliged to walk through the streets half naked at temperatures of 30°C below zero, Romanies were ordered to dance on a bridge before being executed. Like shaving the beards of Orthodox Jews, the use of stereotypical 'Gypsy' dancing as part of a macabre ritual is indicative not only of dehumanizing intentions but also of the deliberate symbolic annihilation of a whole culture.

Although only a small portion of what happened to the Romani population on the eastern front is known today, the dimensions of that form of genocide that may be revealed in the years to come will more than likely exceed the established number of dead in camps and ghettos. The data available suggest that such collective killings were widespread in both space and time. Using the same Soviet source as Holler, Tyaglyy documented another series of episodes in Ukraine where Romanies were victims of collective murder, alone or together with Jews, such as in the infamous case of Babi Yar, near Kyiv.[51] In Crimea, the meticulously organized execution of Romani residents in Simferopol by *Einsatzgruppe* D has been deemed an example of the 'most radical approach' by the German occupation army to the 'Gypsy plague' on Soviet soil. Around 200 massacres have also been documented in Poland. One took place at Szczurowa, a city where for generations the Romani population had lived harmoniously (and inter-married) with non-Roma families. There, on 3 July 1943 the German police had ninety-four 'Gypsy' men, women and children taken from their homes to the cemetery in lorries, where they were executed and their bodies cremated in a collective grave.[52]

This form of widespread violence was intensified over time. In April 1945 at Hrastina, near Zagreb, with the war nearly over, an SS unit withdrawing from combat captured a group of forty-three German Sinti who had fled to Croatia, torturing men, women and children before murdering them all. Quite obviously, then, along with Jews and Serbs, on the eastern front the Holocaust by Bullets was also inflicted on Romani victims, whose number may never be accurately known. The cases documented put the scope of the various forms of collective killing driven by German military presence into perspective. Such violence affected Romani populations trapped in what Mark Levene has called the European 'rimlands', multi-ethnic regions where Nation-State confrontations were particularly deadly throughout the twentieth century, from the Balkans to the Caucasian, from Crimea to Poland.[53]

The Roma and the Holocaust

In addition to and in parallel with the executions and other mass murders in which Romanies shared the same fate as Jews, partisans and Soviet prisoners of war, the Nazis applied other measures to Roma peoples that reveal the incongruous persistence of anti-Gypsyism in Third Reich racial policy. That is discussed under the following heading.

From fantasies around a 'Gypsy' reservation to the extermination order

In the scant four months between September and December 1942, the instructions on the fate of 'Gypsies' issued by the official ultimately responsible for the regime's racial policy, Himmler, changed from protecting part of the Romani population, those deemed 'pure' or uncontaminated by mixing with other races, to the Auschwitz Decree. The latter laid down measures for the 'final solution' to the co-called 'Gypsy plague' comparable to the solution prescribed for Jews at the Wannsee Conference held in January that same year.

One of the most intriguing episodes of Nazi policy in connection with the Roma peoples was Himmler's personal proposal to create a reservation in a natural environment where a series of nomadic clans deemed to be racially pure could live in keeping with what was presumed to be ancestral tradition. According to the memoirs authored by Rudolf Höss, Auschwitz commander, the reservation would be located around Lake Neusiedl between Hungary and Austria, although that fact has never been confirmed by any other source. The project actually got underway in September 1942, although it was shelved shortly thereafter in the wake of heated debate among Nazi leaders. The most detailed study of the initiative is described in an article by Lewy, source of most of the facts set out here.[54] The same objections may be raised to his interpretation of those facts, however, as discussed in connection with his monograph on the Romani people. The fact that Nazi racial policy as applied to 'Gypsies' was inconsistent, enabling a few to sporadically escape persecution, does not mean that Romanies were not victims of genocide nor that the regime posed the 'Gypsy plague' more from a social than a racial perspective.

Himmler's fantasies around a 'Gypsy' reservation were couched in eminently racial terms. On the one hand, interest in presumably pure 'Gypsies' was rooted in the effort to rebuild the historic and demographic Indo-European substrate attributed to the Aryan race. On the other, the instruction on distinguishing pure from mixed blood Romanies, in keeping with Ritter's premises on the degenerate status of the latter (most of Germany's Romani population, as noted earlier), was included in the decree on 'combating the Gypsy plague' which from December 1938 established differential treatment for the two groups.

Ritter, however, felt slighted by Himmler with the proposal for a natural reservation, not unreasonably, for the head of the Security Bureau had entrusted his *Ahnenerbe* (bureau for the study of ancestral heritage) with the preliminary research. The bureau's lodestar was the Nazi obsession with deciphering the most cryptic keys to the Aryan condition. As such it sponsored archaeological and ethnographic explorations around the world, in addition to its legendary expedition to Tibet. Paradoxically, Roma people's

Indian origin made them remote but direct bearers of 'Aryaneity' and hence worthy of study and perhaps Nazi protection. Such an incoherent conclusion was closely aligned with the reasoning typical of any racist-inspired operation designed to feed content into supposedly natural but in fact culturally fabricated categories.

For that reason, for some time *Ahnenerbe* researchers and criminal policemen collaborated in compliance with Himmler's instructions to selectively save a sample of Germany's Romani population. Whilst Walter Wüst, vice-chancellor of the University of Munich and distinguished Indo-European scholar, posed his theory that 'Gypsy' fairy tales haled back to an original 'Indo-Aryan' language and philosophy, Arthur Nebe, chief of the Criminal Police, received (much to his disliking) instructions to contact Romani groups to enable researchers to study their language and culture. Those scientists had no qualms about doing just that, even though the 'objects' of their research were imprisoned at internment camps such as Lackenbach.

An instruction signed by Nebe in October 1942 specified the procedure to be followed to implement Himmler's order on the establishment of a 'Gypsy' reservation. Nine leaders were to be appointed, one per tribe identified as pure (eight representing German groups and a ninth, the Lalleri tribe, from the Bohemia and Moravia Protectorate). Their role would be to put Himmler's special policy for pure 'Gypsies' into practice while also serving as intermediaries for conveying information. On the one hand they would provide the police with lists of racially pure Romanies in their respective regions to be sent to these reservations, while on the other they would inform those concerned of the Government's intentions and assume accountability for their conduct. That obviously vested them with responsibilities and some power in a manner similar (but not identical) to the standard modus operandi defined for Jews. These 'Gypsy' leaders, issued a special ID card, would be afforded freedom of movement and could also apply to have some 'mixed-blood Gypsies' of proven good behaviour assigned to their group.

The instruction was only partially applied. Of the nine leaders appointed, five sent in lists. Some attempted to include the names of mixed-blood Romanies, requesting police permission to do so. That obviously opened up a narrow space where power could be exercised. After the war some were accused of extortion or collaboration under circumstances difficult to clarify bearing in mind that the source would necessarily be Criminal Police records. Other leaders, such as Heinrich Steinbach in Berlin-Breslau, were praised for their integrity. In any event, there was no time to broaden that margin for manoeuvre in any direction. Many objections were immediately raised from within the Nazi regime and Himmler had to forego the plan, deemed by Nebe himself to be an unworkable fantasy. Ritter, as noted, was also displeased with the interference. The primary objection, however, came from higher up: from leaders such as Martin Bormann, head of the Nazi Party Chancellery and de facto secretary to the Führer, as well as Minister of Justice Thierack and very likely Hitler himself.

A meeting held on 6 December 1942 was instrumental in permanently shelving the proposed 'Gypsy' reservation. Himmler's argument, backed by the data for 1,000 pure and a further 3,000 well-behaved mixed-blood 'Gypsies' as possible beneficiaries of selective salvation, was countered by Bormann, who defended the thesis representative of the more widely extended view within the Nazi Party. Any exception would jeopardize the struggle against the 'Gypsy plague' and manipulate public opinion. Hitler himself, he added, did not agree with the plan. That put a conclusive end to Himmler's racial fantasy, the idea of isolating a 'Gypsy' group of pure Indo-European origin as a sort of 'historic monument' (to use Höss's words) of cultural interest. That does not mean that the head of the Reich's Security Bureau ceased to encourage research on the issue that had prompted him to imagine the possibility of a reservation. As late as January 1945, with the Nazi regime on the verge of collapse, a young *Ahnenerbe* researcher was issued a special pass for an 'urgent cultural task': to study Romanies in Finland, Latvia and other regions. As Paul Weindling showed in his study on experiments with human beings under the Nazis, Himmler still wanted to determine whether pure 'Gypsies' were actually Aryans.[55] Georg Wagner, the researcher at issue, had been trained in Ritter's team and earned his doctorate in 1943 with a thesis on racial biology based on 490 Romani twins imprisoned at camps such as Mauthausen.

As discussed later, making Romanies a key object of study did not prevent their deportation to concentration and extermination camps nor afford them any special protection. On the contrary, the Nazi camp system operated like a vast laboratory of human experimental subjects where Romanies received treatment informed by biological-racial interests similar to those that inspired Himmler. So viewed, the turnaround in just a few months from creating a reservation to the Auschwitz Decree is less contradictory than might initially be thought. The same infrahuman status assigned to 'Gypsies', formulated in terms of racial discourse with scientifically respectable premises (further to the criteria prevailing at the time), served as the grounds for the two alternatives: lodging Romanies in a reservation like anthropological fossils or working them to death in concentration camps.

The Auschwitz Decree

The Nazis' 'final solution' for Romanies was in fact conceived in parallel with Himmler's idea for a reservation. After preliminary conversations with the regime's highest-ranking leaders, on 16 December 1942 Himmler issued an order for which the procedural details were published on 29 January 1943. Known as the Auschwitz Decree, it determined the deportation in general of the Third Reich's Romanies to the Auschwitz-Birkenau extermination camp.[56] Although whole countries and large regions were explicitly mentioned (Germany, Austria, Bohemia, Moravia, the Netherlands, Belgium and the French departments of Nord and Pas-de-Calais, including the area in Belgium under German administration) while others were not, in practice it was also applied to other areas [Illustration 25]. The instructions were precise, although the discrepancy between the legislation and its application in practice was the most prominent characteristic of the persecution it triggered. The Security Bureau's decree determined the fate of Romanies along the same lines as the categories defined by the Centre for Research on Racial Hygiene and Demographic Biology referred to earlier. Initially it saved the 'racially

The Romani Genocide under Nazism

Illustration 25 'Gypsy' camp at Haarlem, the Netherlands, 1940. Romani communities living in the Netherlands such as the one portrayed here were among the European Roma designated for persecution under the Auschwitz Decree [NIOD, Institute for War, Holocaust and Genocide Studies, Amsterdam].

pure' from deportation, required sterilization of the scant number of demonstrably well-behaved mixed-blood 'Gypsies' as a condition for freedom and ordered all others to be deported to Auschwitz-Birkenau.

In practice no such distinctions were drawn. The deportations conducted between spring 1943 and summer 1944 actually had a substantial impact on Sinti families, long settled on German soil. Contrary to the stereotypical nomadic 'Gypsy' with neither financial nor cultural resources nor any patriotic attachment, many of those swept away by the Auschwitz Decree were members of the Romani middle class present in Germany. Others were artists and army officers in a country that drastically deprived them of their right to exist. The book by Kapralski, Martyniak and Talewicz-Kwiatkowska contains essential information in that regard, in the form of survivors' and witnesses' testimony, in addition to camp records.[57]

Military staff with medals were not infrequently sent to Auschwitz. Some had even been arrested while still in service and bearing their distinctions for military merit. One surviving Polish prisoner recalls seeing several Romani officials in German army uniform in a group of prisoners being taken to the gas chamber. The SS guiding them tore a *Ritterkreuz* (Knight's Cross, earned for valour in combat) off the chest of one of them to keep for himself. In another case, according to an August 1943 report that camp Resistance managed to smuggle out, one such Romani prisoner confronted the SS who abused them saying: 'You coward, you're here fighting against women and children instead of at the front. I was wounded at Stalingrad, I have medals, I outrank you, and you dare to offend me!'[58]

But the decree plucked the life not only out of men physically and mentally able to resist. Whole families, including pregnant women, children and the elderly, were torn from their homes in one and the same operation. Maria Peter recalls how her family was deported to Auschwitz-Birkenau in its entirety in March 1943: her parents, two brothers whose service with the Wehrmacht had been suspended, three sisters with their husbands and children and so on. But in some cases families were also separated, leading to suffering difficult to fathom outside survivor circles. A Czech prisoner remembered a German Romani who was at the camp with his small son while his non-Roma wife and older children were allowed to stay in the family home. Or the 'very elegant, lovely young woman' recalled by another prisoner, who had been deported with her two children. By the time her husband, a high-ranking army officer, was able to come to the camp with the papers needed to demand their freedom, one of the children had died. Just nine years old when arrested, Else Baker survived to tell her own story. Since she had some Romani ancestry, she was separated from the family that had adopted her in Hamburg and sent to Auschwitz-Birkenau. She arrived alone, with her tiny suitcase, wholly bewildered about why she was there, a blow only softened by the protection dispensed to her by another prisoner.[59]

But perhaps the most conclusive testimony in terms of acknowledgement of the perpetrator's intentions was furnished by Pery Broad, an *SS-Rottenführer* (section leader, a Nazi paramilitary rank) who served at Auschwitz. After admitting that persons with orderly social behaviour as measured by the Nazi regime's own parameters had been deported to the camp, he explained that the instruction to respect Romanies who had assimilated the same lifestyles as mainstream society had not been honoured. According to his memoirs,

> girls employed in the Wehrmacht as stenographers, OT [Organization Todt, an organization under the aegis of the Ministry of Arms engaging in civil and military engineering] workers, conservatory students, and other people leading a solid existence and having worked honestly for long years suddenly found themselves in the concentration camp with their hair cut, prisoner number tattooed on them [...]. Hundreds of soldiers were brought straight from the front who had not even been aware that they were mixed-blood Gypsies, and they were ordered to take off their uniforms [...]. From one day to the next holders of the Iron Cross and other awards for valour were regarded as 'asocial' and imprisoned behind the barbed wire of Auschwitz.[60]

One of the reasons for that straightened application of the law to the detriment of settled Romanies was that those who were known to their neighbours, had steady jobs and married to non-Romanies were the ones easiest to locate and arrest. Such reasons, related to the uneven implementation of the decree in practice and in the absence of

The Romani Genocide under Nazism

Illustration 26 Two Romani children at Haarlem, the Netherlands, 1940. The vast photographic material on file is assumed to have formed part of an unfinished study intended to classify Dutch Romanies [NIOD, Institute for War, Holocaust and Genocide Studies, Amsterdam].

any further detailed instructions from Himmler, are a particular not to be overlooked. The lack of racial classifications in the occupied zones also prevented distinctions of any manner to be drawn [Illustration 26]. Nonetheless, there are deeper reasons that explain why the decree on deportation to Auschwitz was extended to apply to such families as well. On the one hand, pressure was brought to bear by local citizens and authorities to be wholly freed of the Romani families living in their midst, who had come to be deemed a racial-social problem. And, on the other, most of the members of the law and order corps involved in arresting and deporting Romanies eluded a distinction they felt questionable or in which they simply did not believe, for it somehow implied the existence of 'good Gypsies'.

As pointed out by Levene[61] and others, the conversion of social-cultural prejudice against 'Gypsies' into racial categories was never free of contradiction and doubt. In the effort to separate 'good' from 'bad' further to Ritter's scientific classification, the doubt that arose was who was 'bad': those who had settled and mixed with the rest of the population, spreading their presumed genetic criminal tendencies? or the racially pure nomads, who resisted all assimilation? The former included the Reich's Romanies who most resembled 'good' German citizens and had contributed to the war effort as members of the armed forces, as noted above. In any event, the confusion among those who had to conduct persecution and the ambiguity of the regulatory and enforcement infrastructure they used did not by any means benefit the victims. Quite the contrary. The traditional prejudice against 'Gypsies', reformulated in scientific jargon that referred to genetic criminality, was internalized by the majority, even among those not of Nazi persuasion. According to anti-Semitic specialist Wolfgang Benz, Romanies may have found even less solidarity than Jews in the social circles opposing or resisting the regime.[62] National-Socialist authorities and their allies knew they could count on majority support when they harassed and imprisoned 'Gypsies', with no need even for euphemisms or pretexts justifying such action. The cause was understood and assumed naturally as progress in the struggle against delinquency.

In that cultural context, the intention to destroy the Romanies, identified as a racial community, was backed by a decisive instrument as well as firm foundations: the Auschwitz Decree. From the date it was enacted that text furnished the legal grounds for the campaign conducted by the police that kept a steady flow of families arriving at the *Zigeunerlager* ('Gypsy' camp). For Romanies, it opened up the Auschwitz hell, a metaphor often used by camp survivors. Some families arrived there together, others after endless and agonizing serial arrests. Philomena Franz describes how hers was affected in the following words.

> Four weeks later, it was my turn. I was sent to Auschwitz. Of the ten members of my family, only four of us were left [at home]. In the end, my mother was left alone. Then they went for her too. They sealed off our apartment, which was destroyed by aerial mines and fire bombs. With that, our whole past was erased forever: photos, paintings, papers, letters, notes, my diary ... everything was destroyed.[63]

The Auschwitz *Zigeunerlager*

The January 1943 decree stipulated that a special 'Gypsy' camp was to be set aside in the sprawling Auschwitz complex, which comprised a large number of subunits of different sizes and purposes. The *Zigeunerlager* ('Gypsy' camp) was fenced off from the rest of Auschwitz II or Auschwitz-Birkenau, the extermination camp forming part of the extensive prison system located in Poland. That area, which had a close-up view of the crematory chimneys, was reserved for deported Romani families. Its thirty-two barracks, all with timber walls, earthen floors and a few ventilation skylights instead of windows, were arranged around a main street. Each could house around 200 people, but ultimately up to 800 were crowded into them. That in itself was torture, as recalled by Elisabeth Guttenberger, deported there with her entire family in March 1943.[64] The first prisoners arrived in February 1943, when the camp was still under construction and lacking the minimal infrastructure with which it was ultimately fitted: an infirmary-hospital, 'sauna'-baths for disinfection, offices, a canteen and a 'nursery'. Some Romani prisoners who had been sent to other areas of the Auschwitz complex prior to Himmler's decree (there are records of arrivals beginning in 1941) were transferred to the *Zigeunerlager* after it was built. By July 1943 it had housed 23,000 prisoners.

The *Zigeunerlager* was a family camp where, contrary to standard Nazi practice, the sexes were not segregated. Romanies were also allowed to keep their own clothes, to which a triangular patch bearing the letter Z against a dark background was sewn, and at first at least their hair (although that soon changed). Those deviations from standard camp policy and the often successful attempts by families or even just acquaintances arriving together to bunk in the same barracks afforded them a certain aura of exception for some Jewish prisoners observing them from the selection ramp that opened onto the southern end of the *Zigeunerlager*. Imre Kertész mentions such impressions in *Fateless*, in a description not devoid of the exotism with which non-Roma eyes viewed 'Gypsies', even under such circumstances.[65] Outside that peculiarity, the *Zigeunerlager* shared many features with other Auschwitz-Birkenau subunits: electrified fences, SS policing, forced labour, hunger, brutality, medical experiments, gas chambers and so on. Zimmermann estimates that 19,300 of the 22,600 prisoners incarcerated in the 'Gypsy' camp died.[66] Some of those brought there from other camps, after being classified for work, lost their lives in other places in the camp system such as Buchenwald and Ravensbrück.

In a way Auschwitz began for Romanies before they arrived. It started at home with the fear of being arrested, knowing some relatives had already been deported there. It began in jails and intermediate detention camps where they were often threatened by Gestapo officers with Auschwitz as a destination, described as a large, hot oven, as recalled by Philomena Franz. But above all it began in the cattle cars into which prisoners were crammed and transported under conditions that often led to death en route. According to a few survivors, for those who endured the trip, the fear of Auschwitz may well have been one of the heaviest burdens carried on the train. In memoirs written years after her deportation Rosa Mettbach explains that when the train stopped for more prisoners in Vienna where she had lived as a child, a policeman who knew the family told her sadly: 'I can do nothing for you more. I can do nothing for you – you're going to Auschwitz.' Elisabeth Guttenberger, in turn, recalls that her cousin asked the engine driver on another train that had stopped alongside their car, what was Auschwitz. 'I'll never forget the engineer's eyes. He stared at us and could not say a word (…), he stared straight through us, not daring to look us in the face. Only when we arrived in Auschwitz did I understand why this man could not give us an answer.' Irrespective of subsequent memory-based reformulations, for many the pre-Auschwitz experience was riddled with fear.[67]

That notwithstanding, arrival at the complex was always a shock with significant consequences for prisoners' later lives, as highlighted in the second half of this book. The scant words with which Antonin Absolon-Růžička relates his arrival at the camp provide a more eloquent description than any report of what entering the Auschwitz-Birkenau *Zigeunerlager* entailed. Thrust out of the train amidst loudly voiced threats, terrified by a landscape bristling with barbed wire and guards, they were all (he had arrived with his parents and siblings) lined up to have their arms tattooed with their respective prisoner number (the youngest had his leg tattooed, for reasons of space), required to strip naked in a room that afforded no privacy and shaved. Only then, when 'we couldn't recognize each other' were they taken to the barracks where his eight-member family was assigned a single lower bunk.[68] From that moment on, the harsh conditions prevailing in everyday camp life logically took their toll among the weakest.

Endless inspections and prisoner counts were conducted both inside the barracks and on the central outdoor grounds. At Auschwitz's 'Gypsy' camp, this second type of inspection was performed in the morning, alongside the barracks, where prisoners were forced to stand for hours, irrespective of their physical condition and the weather.[69] That was standard practice in the Nazi camp system, recalled with horror by all survivors. Nor were the many children who lived with these families in the *Zigeunerlager* (sons, daughters, nieces, nephews, other relatives) spared that suffering. According to survivor Hermine Horvath, the smallest children who had to stand with them 'dropped like flies' when prisoners were forced to stand at attention in the rain, wind or snow. 'The children suffered terribly. If there was anything like human feeling left, it really did upset you.'[70]

The ability to work, the condition theoretically most likely to favour prisoners' slim chances of survival, was inaccessible to the weakest. Being classified as apt for work useful to the Reich economy could free prisoners from being sent to the gas chamber or other expeditive forms of collective annihilation applied to the least fit, deemed an unnecessary burden on the system. Rudolf Höss, in connection with one of Himmler's visits to Auschwitz, describes that situation in the following words. 'He saw the emaciated victims of disease (the causes of which were bluntly explained by the doctors), he saw the crowded hospital block, he learned of the mortality among the children in the "Gypsy" camp, and he saw children there suffering from the terrible disease called "noma". He also saw the overcrowded huts and the primitive and insufficient latrines.' After witnessing such horrors and just before seeing how incoming Jews were classified, separating those apt for work from those to be sent to the gas chamber, Himmler, according to Höss, ordered an SS officer to solve the problem on the spot. He instructed the officer to act as expected of someone in his position, that is, without objecting for want of means. Höss cites him as saying, 'How this is to be done is your worry and not mine.'[71] Against the backdrop of the self-excuses given by the official primarily responsible for the Auschwitz Camp complex in memoirs written as he awaited his post-war trial, the testimony of Czech doctor Jan Češpiva is easier to understand. Forced to serve at the *Zigeunerlager*, he narrates the selections periodically conducted to carry whole barracks full of prisoners to the gas chamber, recalling his personal contribution to saving a group of around eighty teenagers. Knowing there was a workshop at Auschwitz I to learn to make bricks, he managed to convince one of the *Lager* (camp) officers that it would be a good place to send thirteen- and fourteen-year-olds who had not been assigned jobs in the 'Gypsy' camp.[72]

Aptness for work could help a prisoner save his/her life, but it often simply translated into a slower death. As noted earlier, 'working to death' was a racial policy prioritized by National Socialism. As a rule *Zigeunerlager* prisoners were not assigned any specific long-lasting task, but odd jobs in camp construction and maintenance. Elisabeth Guttenberger recalls the hard work, such as carrying heavy stones, required of her family on arrival, when the camp was nearly fully built. Both her 61-year-old father and she herself, seventeen at the time, were deemed apt for the same task. In her case, having finished school afforded her an escape route. After half a year of hard outdoor labour, she was assigned to the camp office, which she herself claimed was the key to her survival. Such less physically demanding work, in conjunction with the possibility of slightly larger rations, kept some prisoners from dying of sheer exhaustion, the more common fate.

Hunger was in fact the most prominent feature of imprisonment for Auschwitz *Zigeunerlager* residents. As discussed later in connection with survivors' experiences and memories, the entire Nazi camp system has been clearly shown to be characterized by malnourishment: the effect of meagre meals on bodies transformed to the point of being unrecognizable by the subjects themselves, the constant obsession with eating both when asleep and when awake, the resources brought into play in practice to find something to chew on and briefly calm hunger pangs, survivors' awareness that much of their fate was owing to the ability to find some extra food, the cruel use by guards of those circumstances as a tool for humiliation and submission, and so on. Everyday life in the Nazi camps cannot be understood outside that foremost characteristic, dehumanizing famine, escape from which became an absolute priority. In the words of the author of the most powerful account of the subversion of humanity practised at Auschwitz, Primo Levi, the word 'hunger' as normally used is not applicable to hunger at the camp, able to consume the physiological reserves of any human being in two or three months and reduce them to animals in the struggle for survival.[73]

The Auschwitz *Zigeunerlager* was no stranger to the epidemics that razed the camp in general. Typhus for instance, although a genuine disease, also served as the excuse for the mass elimination of those presumably infected.[74] It was likewise the reason some never actually reached the *Zigeunerlager*. In March 1943, around 1,700 Romanies sent from Białystok to the main Auschwitz Camp were gassed on arrival, before being registered. The testimony of doctors, themselves prisoners of different nationalities forced to work in the 'Gypsy' camp, is an invaluable source of information about the conditions prevailing. Alfred Galewski, a Belgian Jew forced to serve as a doctor in the infirmary from September 1943 until the camp was closed, is a case in point.[75] The infirmary housed patients of all kinds, bedded in three-tier bunks with around ten people per tier. Those with diarrhoea were placed on the lowest rung and those with diseases such as malaria, typhus or noma on the top. The infirmary had no clothing or even clean bandages. Nor was any medication available beyond the occasional anti-diarrhoetic.

Further to such testimonies the hospital-infirmary clearly operated not as a place to care for the ill, but in fact to implement radical disinfection methods that prompted the death of twenty to sixty patients per day. Some of these diseases, such as scabies, were by no means fatal. But the treatment designed, consisting in repeated immersion in different disinfectant solutions, not only caused 'colossal pain' in the most advanced cases, but also often provoked patient death.[76] The connection between the infirmary and the instructions issued by camp chief physician Dr Josef Mengele, who used it as a laboratory of privilege where he could experiment with human beings, is discussed later.

Under such conditions, *Zigeunerlager* mortality rates were very high. Malnutrition, disease and exhaustion killed most of the 19,300 prisoners who perished there, whilst

5,600 were murdered in gas chambers.⁷⁷ Recent figures propose even larger numbers: Kay contends that 'More than 20,000 Roma in total perished in Auschwitz-Birkenau. At least 7,735 were gassed'.⁷⁸ One of the most difficult experiences survivors had to confront was as witnesses to the endless chain of deaths of loved ones.

> My sister-in-law and her three children fell ill with typhus and died in the sick bay. My sister in-law was the first of our family to die in Auschwitz-Birkenau. Then my sister Josefine's husband died of a serious lung infection which he caught in camp mainly as result of the heavy work he did. Then my sister's first born child died, and, one after another, more members of our family died. My sister Josefine Steinbach has nine children, only one of them died in the camp. Today I still can't believe that the other eight children survived everything until they were gassed in August 1944. My sister could have survived. But when she was supposed to be taken away with me to Ravensbrück before the destruction of the 'Gypsy' camp in Auschwitz-Birkenau, she refused to go because of the children.⁷⁹

In the preceding passage, Maria Peter resorts to chronological memory in her narrative: who perished before, who after, who after having endured to the end.

The camp system allowed no mourning for the deaths it induced. The abuse and contempt it dispensed to dead bodies (compatible with their utilization for other purposes), the mortal remains of the deceased that all cultures in any number of historic contexts have ritualized, is well known. Camp language, which referred to corpses as *Stücken* (kindling or logs), attests succinctly to the intention to deprive these 'others' of the human condition, even after death. The imposed repression of any outward sign of sorrow for the loss of loved ones in the *Zigeunerlager* was a further example of the dehumanization pursued by the system. Elisabeth Guttenberger recalls that just eight days after being assigned a job in the records office, she had to enter her own father's death in the registry, along with that of all the other men who died at the camp. 'I was paralysed, and the tears just rolled down my face. At that moment, the door swung open and *Oberscharführer* (chief sniper) Plagge stormed in and yelled, "Why is she blubbering over there in the corner?"' When informed of the reason, his answer was, 'We all have to die.'⁸⁰

Along with hunger, physical and mental torture was the most effective dehumanizing device around which the camp system revolved. The *Zigeunerlager* was no exception in that regard, although Höss wrote about his 'cordial relationship' with prisoners 'by nature as trusting as children', simple and joyful who in his view harboured no grudge against their captors. 'They were my best loved prisoners'.⁸¹ He nonetheless specified that he was referring to nomadic 'Bohemian', not sedentary 'Gypsies', who he contended had acquired urban vices. With his acritical acceptance of the Ritter-inspired scientific categories applied by the police he was able to ignore his own contradictions. In an earlier passage he contended that certain individuals of Romani origin fully integrated into the social body should not have been deported, whilst his feigned affection for Romani prisoners was entirely compatible with all the abuse inflicted on them at the camp under his direct command.

As noted, the dehumanization of prisoners, designed to induce the loss of any sense of individual or collective identity, was standard procedure in the *Lager* in this respect also. The fact that the area was specifically created for Romani families does not mean they were necessarily grouped as such, nor that families were not separated in the selection process. The methods used to erode stamina and destroy resistance were the same as in camps housing other prisoners, recognizable in the following examples by any reader familiar with Holocaust literature. Assignment of a prisoner number and shaving were among the camp entry rituals that pursued dehumanization and its effect: from then the new arrival had but one identity: that of an Auschwitz prisoner. As Primo Levi notes, tattooing was an unnecessary (prisoners' numbers could be otherwise printed on their clothing, as in other camps) but highly and symbolically significant affront: the numbers assigned prisoners (to replace names) by the system was indelibly printed on their own flesh and could only be erased after leaving the camp. The initial orders called out in a loud voice, the first gratuitous blows ('how can one hit a man without anger?', Levi wondered), deprivation of any personal possession or bond with pre-camp life and of course the outdoor inspections were informed by the same purpose, to isolate, cripple and nullify.[82]

With that domestication programme for new arrivals as the point of departure, punishment and abuse spread in a number of directions. Joanna Talewicz-Kwiatkowska's reconstruction of camp records shows that so-called 'sports' activities were also conducted. These included the obligation to exercise to exhaustion (racing, jumping, rolling on the ground) while suffering physical abuse at the hands of the guards.[83] Other practices included public beatings with the victim braced to a frame and solitary confinement in special cells with standing room only, which almost always ended in death. A similar outcome was sought by assigning prisoners to the *Strafkompanie* (punishment company or penal unit where they were isolated from the rest of the camp, obliged to perform particularly hard work and subjected to even more intense SS violence). In November 1943, for instance, a group of thirty-five Romanies were assigned to that unit. Only five returned in May 1944.[84]

Attempted escape was cause for even harsher and particularly cruel violence, a hardly unexpected development since for camp guards the will to live and resist exemplified by such action was a sign of system failure. Punishment was consequently inflicted on escapees' families and close circles and of course on the person who escaped if later captured. In such cases public punishment was ritualized with macabre ceremonies. Jan Češpiva, the Czech doctor mentioned earlier, recalls that when a prisoner was captured after escaping from the *Zigeunerlager*, the SS took the dead body to each barrack so the bullet wounds and dog bites could serve as a lesson to everyone else.[85]

That regime of everyday terror included an additional component of sexual abuse, inflicted primarily but not solely on female prisoners. Although such memories are difficult to reconstruct, as noted in a later section, survivors' memoirs narrate episodes of aggression in which women's bodies were viewed as just one more element on which *Zigeunerlager* guards could exercise their authority. Philomena Franz recalls being selected for the brothel as soon as she arrived at Auschwitz on the grounds of her appearance. Organizing houses of ill repute outside the camp was standard system practice. But beyond overseeing abusive or forbidden sexual relations described by Fabrice D'Almeida to comprise part of camp guards' everyday lives, such violence had a more general gender dimension that should not be overlooked. Physical violence often materialized in practices that entailed sexually connotated aggression where young women were concerned. An example can be found in the punishment sometimes exerted in special scenarios, such as prepared by SS König when whipping Maria Peter. 'He ordered me to strip naked and to put on a wet men's swimsuit which I had to take out of a tube filled with a black liquid. I was told to lie on a sawhorse and count.'[86]

What had apparently prompted the ire of the SS who whipped Maria was her complaint to his superiors about how food was distributed, in a desperate attempt to acquire more for her sister's children. Nonetheless, the strength of inter-family relations at the *Zigeunerlager* and the protection afforded those nearest and dearest should not lead to the conclusion that because this was a 'Gypsy' camp it comprised a natural, internally close-knit community. On the contrary, the prisoners came from different countries, spoke different languages and had different cultural traditions. Some arrived as a family while others had been separated from their loved ones. Some were sedentary Sinti who had been living in Germany for centuries, where they engaged in different occupations, such as Elisabeth Guttenberger's father, a luthier specializing in antique musical instruments. Others were nomadic Romanies whose lives were spent crossing national borders, such as one of the few prisoners born in Spain and registered in the Auschwitz *Zigeunerlager* records. Palise Taicon, tattooed with the number Z-9115, was born in Barcelona in 1876, although he was deported from Belgium in 1944. German prisoners at least had the advantage of speaking the same language as camp guards, which entailed a number of benefits and saved them from some beatings. 'I remember that I was beaten especially often because I could not learn my prisoner number in German fast enough,' recalls Edward Paczkowski. A Polish Romani sent to Auschwitz before the *Zigeunerlager* was built, he describes the hierarchized Tower of Babel prevailing in the camps.[87]

The natural fragmentation of a population with widely differing origins and crowded into a narrow space was deliberately fuelled by Nazi camp system officials. The system rested on imposing internal hierarchies among prisoners. Appointment to prominent positions (block elders, work supervisors and so on) entailed responsibilities (and punishment in the event of error) but also privileges imperative to survival. Such designations, intentionally used to fracture possible inter-prisoner solidarity, are known to have often been awarded to the strongest or least scrupulous inmates. Measures as apparently simple as appointing young men and vesting them with authority over their elders violated Romani tradition.[88]

The ability to speak the guards' language was a significant item on prisoners' very short roster of useful skills. In the *Zigeunerlager*, German Romanies were usually assigned the role of block elder with authority over all the others, which entailed benefits that necessarily included abuse of the least advantaged. Antonin Absolon-Růžička, who had arrived with his whole family from Moravia, recalls his mother, who spoke some German, complaining because the block supervisor and other German prisoners stole food from her family, which led to a beating inflicted on her father.[89] The narratives contained in survivors' memoirs, a selection of which is discussed in the second half of this book, would help any reader resist the temptation to pass quick judgement on those who lived (and were consequently more likely to survive) in what Primo Levi called the *Lager*'s 'grey zone'. The prisoners who obtained privileges in the camp system were in fact characterized by a wide variety of behaviours. They ranged from those who used their position to organize internal resistance and contact with allied governments or who tried to influence camp officials to help others, to those who capitalized on the minor privilege their position entailed or even those who used it to stomp on the prisoners beneath them, deemed trampolines for survival.

The nature and effect of that 'grey zone' is addressed later, for it lies at the base of a conviction shared by many of those 'saved' who felt their mere salvation distinguished them dramatically from most of the others, the 'drowned', to use Primo Levi's terms. The feelings of guilt so generated were the longest-lasting punishment imposed by the camp system, post-collapse revenge. Among other such feelings, Levi stresses his failure to help other prisoners, something only conceivable after leaving the *Lager*. As he explains in the chapter titled 'The Drowned and the Saved' in *If This Is a Man* (initially published in Italian in 1946 and in English in 1960), the concentration camp was the closest thing to a laboratory to put the human condition to the test, 'to establish what is essential and what adventitious to the conduct of the human animal in the struggle for life'.[90]

In that context, the will of those who tended to solidarity could be readily sapped, as Otto Rosenberg recalls in connection with the beating he received for having allowed a woman living in the block where he was sentinel to leave it to take her son to the latrines. 'They came for me, the SS man and the block elder. They gave me at least twenty or twenty five blows with a stick for that. I had to count along and just couldn't take any more. They hit me between pelvis and back. Afterwards I could neither lie down nor sit nor stand.'[91]

Putting an end to even the slightest hint of resistance and thereby nullifying prisoners' humanity was a camp system modus operandi. That universe cannot be understood without the power to annihilate. To that purpose, even something so intrinsically human as music was a tool for dehumanization. Some accounts of the camps have attributed music a salvational role, a resource prisoners could use to help one another bear their everyday existence, as a way to remember their homes or country or create social bonds. The extent of that presence is hard to determine, particularly in individuals' most mental and silent practice, but in the public space in the *Lager* and in system officials' hands, music was primarily one of a number of means to ensure domination. As described in the memoirs published by Simon Laks, conductor of an official camp orchestra, at Auschwitz more than as an emotional refuge for prisoners music served jailers' own purposes.[92]

Although the *Zigeunerlager* followed the same pattern, in some cases prisoners were allowed to keep their instruments, making non-regulated use at least possible. Marian Perski, a Polish woman who worked in the canteen, remembers some instances.[93] That laxity was more than likely related to the fact that one of the uses made of Romani prisoners' musical skills was for Auschwitz guards' private entertainment. For personal pleasure, birthday parties or other celebrations, the SS resorted to Romani musicians to brighten up their off-duty hours. 'Gypsy' violins and songs were just one more consumer item traded in the peculiar market that developed in the camps. They constitute a further example of how admiration for an element characteristic of a certain culture can be mentally dissociated from respect for the subjects that bring it to life. In connection with that paradox, the question of the Germans' general love for music and its place in the camp system has been widely discussed. Simon Laks himself reflects on the fact that SS who were relentless in their guardians' task could be moved and their behaviour softened when listening to good music. He also recalls the case of a young high-ranking officer who enjoyed playing with the prisoners when off duty. He even played jazz on an accordion perfected by the orchestra's luthier. 'Recently Broad had disappeared from our horizon for much longer than previously. It concerned a trifle: the burning of a few thousand Gypsies and then the same number of Czechs.'[94]

The 'paradox of entertainment' as noted by David Pike[95] with regard to Mauthausen (where there was more than one orchestra, but Spanish prisoners were not allowed to even hum the melodies of Civil War songs) afforded very few opportunities for Romani musicians imprisoned in the camps. Such skills could, however, be one of the resources that could help a prisoner stand out above the rest. Simon Laks, who was Jewish, attributed his own survival to that talent. Being called to camp guards' parties and celebrations entailed some 'benefits' in the form of extra food or cigarettes.[96]

But that paradox was particularly complex for Romani musicians, for in addition to a consumer item for guards' leisure and enjoyment, musicianship was inherent in the creation of official camp orchestras. Many had such a *Lagerkapella* whose raison d'être was its inclusion in the general disciplinary apparatus on which the whole camp system rested. Such orchestras had to play at specific times of day, constituting the audio component of a series of everyday rituals with military connotations intended to instil obedience: music was played to form the task forces when setting up and finishing the days' assignments, during inspections or to enliven work. Orchestras played the same role as popular German or other types of songs that prisoners were forced to sing when performing other tasks, as Rosa Mettbach recalls in the case of Auschwitz-Birkenau. According to Levi, those songs and marches, lying 'engraven on our minds', were the voice of the *Lager* and embodied the intention to annihilate prisoners' humanity before killing them slowly.[97]

Orchestras also formed an essential part of different types of ceremonies, from receptions for visiting hierarchs or Christmas concerts to prisoner punishment rituals. Although Laks contends they were not used in executions at Auschwitz, in other places orchestras were obliged to play in such circumstances. Mauthausen had a *Zigeunerkapelle* ('Gypsy' orchestra, so branded even though not all its members were Romanies).[98] Spanish survivors recall one occasion when the orchestra was forced to play a festive march as it paraded alongside a carriage adorned with satiny bows and the message, 'Hooray! We're back home again!' Its passengers, three recaptured escapees, were subsequently hanged in plain sight of their co-prisoners as the orchestra was obliged to play on.[99] There are records of similar instances in other camps such as Buchenwald.[100]

As discussed later, the presence of Romanies in camps' official musical scenario entailed abuse with a significant component of symbolic, in addition to directly physical, violence. It was not just that these prisoners who, like non-Roma musicians, living in inhumane conditions and subjected to arbitrary high command decisions, were obliged to play in orchestras that formed part of camp system dominance. Of greater significance was camp system cannibalization of such a characteristic and highly valued component of Romani culture and its use as entertainment for the SS, or in death orchestras. The case of a Polish virtuoso violinist imprisoned at Auschwitz who had no formal musical training but was able to play by ear may serve as illustration. No record remains of his name, but the account of another non-Roma prisoner who worked in the room where all new arrivals were subjected to the confiscation and tattooing protocol has been conserved. According to that testimony, the Romani musician from Breslavia, standing naked in front of the guards, begged them to allow him to keep his violin. He would not have forfeited his instrument for anything in the world. By way of sole explanation, even under such circumstances, he played a piece, brilliantly and concentrating deeply on the task. He was immediately assigned to the camp orchestra.[101] Although that position afforded certain benefits that would help him survive for some time, the violinist's experience differs scantly from the fate of a group of Romanies who, before being executed in Russia, were forced to dance, semi-naked, in the snow: the two are interconnected by a racial programme that in addition to taking lives set out to destroy victims' cultural footprint.

The last circle: Children and racial medicine

That National-Socialist cosmovision logically affected children and adults alike. One of the features of the Jewish and Romani Holocausts was the breadth of their reach among the youngest members of those two European communities. Children of the occupied nations deemed to be racially inferior, such as Russians or Poles, were hurled into that same spiral of violence. In contrast, other groups of prisoners who fed the camp system were by definition adult men, political and military prisoners. What distinguished Romanies was that whole families were targeted for deportation to ghettos and Nazi camps. As mentioned earlier, the *Zigeunerlager* at Auschwitz-Birkenau was specifically designed as a 'family' camp. The presence of children (either deported or born there) was consequently a key feature of this *Lager*, that even had a nursery. Nonetheless, the existence of Romani children in concentration camps was actually a much more widespread development, whose dimensions stretched amply beyond the Auschwitz perimeter. Minors could be found in internment and forced labour camps such as Lannemezan in France or Lety in Czechia, at Ravensbrück with their mothers, at Buchenwald as if they were adult workers, at Bergen-Belsen, the end of the road for many, and in the 'death marches' when those or other camps were closed.

Children were not only taken with their parents for family deportation. The rigidity of the racial classifications applied to 'Gypsies' on the grounds of the categories designed by the Racial Hygiene and Criminal Police Unit created situations such as Else Baker's, the aforementioned child of Romani ancestry adopted by a family at Hamburg. In 1943 when she was eight years old she was sent to Auschwitz all by herself, surviving the experience thanks to the help of another prisoner [Illustration 27]. Her questions mirror the shock endured when confronted with harsh camp reality. While her father fought for her liberation and until he succeeded in 1944 Else (Schmidt) Baker recalls her attempts to discover the reason for the smoke constantly belching out of the crematory ovens and the replies she received. 'I was told that they were burning people'. She also remembers her reply: 'But you can't burn people. You burn wood and coal, but not people.'[102] Her incredulity denotes the irreparable theft of that vital fatherland, childhood, inflicted on many Romanies during the Nazi Holocaust.

For most of those who were children at the time, such deprival was the outcome of persecution more long-lasting than in Else's and entailed a fuller invasion of their

Illustration 27 Else Schmidt (centre) with her two older sisters. Due to her blood line, she was deported to Auschwitz in 1943. Her adopted father was eventually able to arrange for her release from Ravensbrück in 1944 [Dokumentation und Kulturzentrum, Deutscher Sinti und Roma, Heidelberg].

social-family and affective fabric. For some, such as Otto Rosenberg, it began when the family was forced to live in the Marzahn Camp outside Berlin. There, when he was nine years old he was studied by Eva Justin, whose self-serving kindness tricked and hurt him. ('It would have been better if I had been given a beating. I could have stood that better than this. I still ask myself today: how could she do something like that when she was so nice and kind?').[103] Later, at age thirteen, he was recruited for forced labour at an arms factory, an experience he recalls as being particularly distressing because he was not allowed to socialize with other workers due to his racial stigma.

For others, such as Reili Mettbach, it started when her family decided to flee Germany amid ever more intense aggression in a journey that took them through Italy, Yugoslavia and Romania. Nine years old at the time, she would still remember much later the voice of her elders handing out constant precautionary instructions, whose urgency was incompatible with childhood behaviour. Hush now, hide quickly, don't do this or that, and so on.[104] For Ceija and Karl Stojka the process began with their father's arrest and deportation to Dachau. It continued irreversibly when they themselves were taken from school and deported with their mother and other siblings to Auschwitz, where they arrived at the ages of ten and twelve, respectively. In addition to her memoirs and paintings, Ceija Stojka left a legacy of interviews with writer and film director Karin Berger that affords fuller insight into the meaning of the alienation involved in the loss of childhood in a concentration camp. Ceija remembers her mother's constant recommendations to refrain from drawing the SS guards' attention, to attempt to go as unnoticed as possible. Don't look them in the eyes, don't misbehave, don't cry, or laugh, and so on. Ceija also recalls her mother's concern over the fact that as she was more venturesome than other girls she did not cling to the maternal skirt tails. Her account of the games she played and talking to herself alongside stacks of corpses, the sole secluded place where she could be 'in peace' at the Bergen-Belsen Camp, is hair-raising. But it also constitutes an eloquent explanation of what Nazism did to many children who, like Ceija, after liberation would come to miss the stench of decomposing bodies.[105]

Some of the Romani Holocaust survivors who later wrote memoirs were children at the time. The second part of this book addresses those literary exercises. But no similarly detailed accounts are available of the experiences undergone by many others who lived and died in the camp system [Illustration 28]. A total of thirty-nine were sent directly to Auschwitz from the St Joseph orphanage at Mulfingen. Those twenty boys and nineteen girls had been separated from their families and forced to live in that institution in 1938, at the orders of the Wutemberg State doctor. There they were studied by the aforementioned Eva Justin. Under the January 1943 Auschwitz Decree they should have been sent directly to the *Zigeunerlager*, but Ritter postponed their deportation to give Justin time to conclude the research for her doctoral thesis, designed to prove 'Gypsy' incapacity for social integration. She ceased to need them shortly before the war ended: the entry date on the camp registry is 12 May 1944.[106]

Disease – or malnutrition-induced death was the fate of most of those children, both at Auschwitz and other camps. At the Auschwitz-Birkenau *Zigeunerlager* the creation of a nursery barracks for the smallest children during the day, which actually served

Illustration 28 Sinti and Roma child genocide victims. In the photo (1936–37) Agnes Stein is holding her daughter Inge. In 1938 her husband was imprisoned at Buchenwald while they were at the internment camp at Holzweg, where many children died due to the harsh living conditions [Courtesy of University of Liverpool Library - Special Collections].

the purposes of Dr Josef Mengele, should not confound the reader about the harsh everyday reality children had to confront. The testimony of František Janouch, a Czech survivor assigned to the camp as paediatrician, describes Dantesque circumstances in the infirmary, where 100 to 150 children were crammed into a barracks also used as a delivery room. They were all naked and bedded on straw mats. 'The children were always crying. At least a hundred children were crying at the same time.'[107]

There was no medicine or hygiene, only an uncontrolled combination of endemic diseases: typhus, diphtheria, gangrene, tuberculosis. Janouch describes how he and a Polish Jew likewise assigned to the infirmary managed to 'organize' (steal) some clothes for them and how they attempted to keep the place clean. Even with that, ten to fifteen children died every day. He recalls that just as some mothers, in tears, were bringing their children to the entrance at one end of the barracks, others were looking for theirs among the stacks of corpses at the other. 'For me those were the most difficult moments I experienced in the camp. Not the beating, not the interrogation, but those children.'[108]

The Romani Genocide under Nazism

Infirmary and nursery were the areas in the *Zigeunerlager* under the direct supervision of Dr Josef Mengele, medical doctor and racial anthropologist who used prisoners as laboratory subjects for his research. That practice is known to have affected many different groups of prisoners throughout the system. In addition to a source of forced labour and a mass murder machine, the camps served as a vast laboratory for purposes deemed scientific, in which Nazi racial medicine used human beings with no regard for the suffering inflicted.[109] Many prisoners were tortured to test human and material resistance for military purposes. Romanies were also so used. At Natzweiler-Struthof, a camp located 60 kilometres outside of Strassburg, Dr Otto Bickenbach tested the sequelae of phosgene, a toxic gas, in a group of fifty Romanies transferred there from Auschwitz. In addition to such experiments directly related to the war, others aimed to determine the utility of certain medical, surgical and pharmacological procedures by cruel and hazardous testing in the prison population. The third and most ambitious general objective was to use prisoners' bodies to advance in physiological and anatomic knowledge and specifically to decipher human genetics to the benefit of the Aryan race.

Such research was conducted extensively at Auschwitz, where Romani children were some of the favourite subjects for the experiments and studies designed by Dr Josef Mengele, head doctor at the *Zigeunerlager*. He was a member of the largest group of camp physicians, responsible among others for guiding the selections that periodically classified prisoners as apt for work or to be sent to death in the gas chamber [Illustration 29]. But Mengele's foremost duty at Auschwitz was research, a task pursued

Illustration 29 Josef Mengele, head physician at the Auschwitz *Zigeunerlager*, 1944. In the centre of the picture, flanked on the left by camp commander Richard Baer and on the right by Rudolf "Höss, former Commander". [US Holocaust Museum, public domain material.]

as unscrupulously as ambitiously. His work was directly associated with the programme defined by one of Germany's most prestigious scientific institutions, the Kaiser Wilhelm Institute of Anthropology, Human Heredity and Eugenics at Berlin. There his mentor Otmar von Verschuer, among the most reputed geneticists of the time, reported on his progress and received some of his experimental materials. Mengele used his post at Auschwitz to create exceptional conditions for analysing the medical treatment for a number of diseases. At the same time, however, he sought the genetic clues to certain issues that had attracted his interest for some time, such as twin reproduction and heterochromia (different colour irises in one and the same person). He chose Romanies as preferred subjects of study, perhaps under the assumption that such characteristics were particularly common in that community. He enlisted Jewish inmates who were physicians, along with other prisoners as mandatory assistants. Czech Jew Dinah Babbitt, who was forced to paint a series of portraits of Romani prisoners as part of the study materials collected by Mengele, remembers his particular interest in subjects with heterochromia. Ludwika Wierzbicka, in turn, a Polish prisoner working as a nurse at the *Zigeunerlager*, also remembers Mengele in detail and in particular his habit of broaching Romani children with candy and kind gestures. 'They trusted him and called him "Uncle".[110]

Kindness, candy and nursery were merely the outcome of Mengele's direct interest in keeping his test bench, his experimental materials, healthy. Ludwika Wierzbicka also reports on the autopsies performed on children who had been the object of research and describes how their organs were preserved in formaldehyde and sent to the Anthropology Institute in Berlin for subsequent study. Unquestionably, however, Miklós Nyiszli gives the fullest account of Mengele's practices at Auschwitz. That Hungarian pathologist, Mengele's direct assistant, published his memoirs immediately after the war in 1946 (*I was Dr Josef Mengele's Autopsy Doctor at the Auschwitz Crematorium* is the original title, modified in subsequent editions to *Auschwitz: A Doctor's Eyewitness Account* and *Auschwitz: A Doctor's Eyewitness Account of Mengele's Infamous Death Camp* and translated to other languages.) The two lines of experimental research that were ongoing at the *Zigeunerlager*, according to Nyiszli, were the study of noma (a gangrenous buccal infection related to severe malnutrition), widespread among the 'Gypsy' camp children, and the analysis of twins to decipher the clues and characteristics of that development.[111]

The cruelty of these tests has been described by a number of witnesses, whose narratives necessarily inspire existential anguish. Mengele's obsession with twins is among the most prominent examples. According to Nyiszli, autopsies were conducted on 'several hundred sets of twins', forcing simultaneous death to capitalize on the opportunity that afforded to compare their organs. In the Hungarian's opinion, Mengele's aim was to control twin reproduction to the benefit of the Aryan race, although his motivation might also have been determined by the desire to prove the prevalence of genetics over other forces, such as the environment.[112] The tentative application of medication and drugs, cross-transfusions, viral injections, the imposition of special diets, experimental surgery and murder via lethal substances were practices

Illustration 30 Theresia Seibel acting in a stage play before the war at Würzburg, Germany. During her twin pregnancy she was placed in the care of University of Würzburg professor Heyde. After her daughters Rolanda and Rita were born they were made the subjects of medical experiment and she was sterilized [US Holocaust Memorial Museum, Washington, courtesy of Rita Prigmore].

undertaken with no deontological constraints whatsoever in respect of beings deemed infrahuman. Auschwitz provided exceptionally favourable laboratory conditions, although the same research programme was conducted not only in other camps, but also in the rear guard [Illustration 30]. In keeping with the dehumanizing criterion that prevailed throughout the system, Romani boys and girls were sterilized en masse with unsafe procedures that often induced their death. The obvious contradiction in preventing the future reproduction of subjects presently earmarked for annihilation formed part of the endless spiral of violence inherent in the bureaucratization of Nazi genocidal policy.

Further to that logic, the time came to liquidate the Auschwitz *Zigeunerlager*. Following Himmler's orders, the 2,900 prisoners still incarcerated there (after those apt for work had been sent to other camps) were all taken to the gas chamber on the night of 2 August 1944. Most, who had been weeded out as not apt for work, were elderly, women and children. Those who were ill in the infirmary were also crammed into the lorries. Mengele was present throughout the entire operation, issuing instructions to ensure order. That was no vain concern. Although the Romani prisoners remaining in the camp could hardly oppose the SS who led them to the slaughterhouse, a few weeks earlier the *Zigeunerlager* guards had been obliged to surrender in an episode of Romani resistance that was to become an emblematic event in post-war memory.

The Roma and the Holocaust

The Resistance, resistance and women's role

The most detailed account of that episode is provided by Tadeusz Joachimowski, a non-Roma Polish prisoner employed in the camp offices. In collaboration with other prisoners, in July 1944 he smuggled the *Zigeunerlager* registry book out of the office and hid it so it might serve as historic testimony, as it in fact did when it reappeared in 1949. According to Joachimowski, one of the camp's officials, *Lagerführer* Bonigut, attempted to obstruct the total liquidation order that was to be carried through on 16 May 1944. That determination led him to advise Joachimowski in advance, knowing he in turn would let the other prisoners know so they would 'not [...] go like lambs to the slaughter'.[113] When the SS arrived on the sixteenth with lorries and ordered the 'Gypsies' to leave their barracks, they were met with disobedience from some of the prisoners, entrenched in one of the barracks and armed with pickaxes, shovels, stones and similar. That reaction delayed the liquidation plan. Faced with a peril they had not foreseen that day, the SS withdrew.

Further to Joachimowski's testimony, Bonigut spoke to him again later to ask him for a list of Romani families who had members serving in the German army to spare them the gas chamber and send them to other destinations. The resulting list contained 3,200 names. Bonigut confronted Mengele and other camp officials to ensure those selected could leave the camp before the liquidation order was reactivated, now irreversibly. Some scholars have questioned certain particulars of this remarkable resistance at Auschwitz, pointing to the difference in time between the events and other narratives (such as Walter Winter's or Otto Rosenberg's[114]) that might serve to support Joachimowski's testimony. Nonetheless, indirect evidence corroborates the latter's account and nothing contradicts it. That collective rebellion has been pivotal to the construction of Romani memory. As the post-war attempts initiated by associations to demand recognition for Holocaust victims pressed forward, 16 May became a symbolic date for Romani activism.

The meaning of the foregoing and other less well-known episodes addressed here must be understood in the context of the great difficulty encountered by the prisoners described by Primo Levi as Nazi system 'pariahs' not only to engage in such action, but even to imagine it. Racial prisoners such as Jews and Romanies, physically and psychically abused more harshly than others, were weaker and more demoralized.[115] Unlike political and military prisoners, in general they lacked the physical training that helped some attempt a getaway, the relatively better nourishment that enabled others to resist, or the cohesive internal hierarchies or outside support from resistance networks, to implement escape plans, for instance.

That notwithstanding and despite the punishment inflicted not only on those who tried to escape but their inner circles or families, some of the Auschwitz *Zigeunerlager* prisoners also attempted to flee, in what was normally their last show of defiance. According to camp records, there were thirty-eight attempted evasions between 1941 when it was created and its 1944 liquidation. Whereas the fate of seven of the escapees is unknown, none of the other thirty-one survived. Once recaptured, their punished bodies were exhibited to the other prisoners by way of warning. On occasion the records reveal additional details, such as the fact that Höss awarded three extra days off to any SS thwarting escape attempts by Romani prisoners, who were subsequently executed.[116]

Evasions were also attempted in other camps, not only at Auschwitz. Two women previously introduced in this book whose voices will continue to be heard in Part II, expressed their insistently rebellious instincts in that manner. Philomena Franz attempted to escape from Ravensbrück, for which she was harshly punished, and in 1945 ultimately managed a successful escape from a smaller camp in Germany near Wittenberg, thanks to a local resident. Rosa Mettbach escaped from the train that was carrying her to the Łódź ghetto and again from Lakenbach in Austria, only to be caught and sent to Auschwitz-Birkenau. The latter was a compound perhaps even more strictly policed than others, where opportunities for escape were minimal. But the Nazi system was unquestionably diversiform and in other camps Romani defiance may have had a greater likelihood of success. French detainment camp records, for instance, show a fair number of escapes, and even of a few involving whole families, that ended in success.[117]

Other forms of resistance in French camps have also been documented: rioting, protests, confrontation with guards and so on, inconceivable at Auschwitz but possible there. Angèle Siegler, jailed at Choisel, is one such case. This twenty-year-old woman, after waiting in line for a ration of sugar for her baby, cast the tiny amount she was given to the ground and confronted the guards, protesting and threatening to organize collective disturbance. Another is the Adam family arrested at Rennes, who created such chaos at the camp that it led to a power outage. Other Romanies imprisoned at Poitiers helped a clergyman contact Jewish prisoners in their camp. In light of all these episodes in France, studied by Foisneau and Merlin, Romani participation in the anti-fascist Resistance must be revisited. Those two historians have documented the participation by French Romanies outside the camps in the struggle against German occupation and the collaborationist authorities, providing shelter for partisans, engaging with them in the Resistance and even enlisting directly as armed Resistance fighters [Illustration 31].

Romanies participated in the anti-fascist Resistance throughout Europe, although their contribution has been scantly studied, with only a few documented cases. One exception can be found in Josef Serynek, a Czech Romani deported with his family to Lety, from where he escaped in 1943 to join the local partisans. Known as the Black Partisan, he headed a group of fighters primarily comprising likewise escapee Russian prisoners of war who attacked the German army, a feat for which he was later distinguished in his country. In Yugoslavia Stevan Djordjevic Novak was also deemed a national hero for fighting Fascism.[118] Belgian artist Jan Yoors, in turn, describes in his memoirs how the British Government contacted him in France to request the support of the Romani Lovara group with whom he had been in close relations since childhood.[119] He reports on Resistance activities in which he participated and the involvement of his friends the Pulikas and other Romani families [Illustration 32].

The Soviet Union is a special case, for there Romani participation in the struggle against the Nazis and German occupation ranged from enlistment in the Red Army to different forms of civil resistance. Since most of the country was not occupied, the experience and memories of Soviet Romanies in connection with the German invasion

The Roma and the Holocaust

Illustration 31 Marion Kaufmann (centre), Jewish girl given refuge by a Romani family in 1944, the Netherlands. Solidary resistance: the help afforded Marion's parents to hide their daughter outside Amsterdam included support from this family, whose name went unrecorded [US Holocaust Museum, Washington].

Illustration 32 Jan Yoors and Pulika family members. Member of the anti-Fascist resistance, Yoors worked for the British government and involved his Romani friends in the struggle against the German army [US Holocaust Memorial Museum, Washington, courtesy of Kore Yoors].

is less one of persecution than of national pride for forming part of the Resistance as soldiers, partisans or workers, according to Martin Holler's research. Thousands of Romanies served in the Soviet army and dozens were awarded medals. One, Aleksandr Baurov (mentioned in Chapter 1), was a member of a family of musicians who trained as a military engineer and participated in the defence of Leningrad. But he was not alone in the Red Army. Other Romanies were soldiers, pilots, tank commanders and so on. Whilst they were not in the military, on occasion the members of the (likewise cited in Chapter 1) Teatr Romen contributed to the war effort. A company founded in Moscow in 1931 at the initiative of Ivan Rom-Lebedev, a Romani associated with the Bolshevik cause, they provided entertainment and encouragement for Soviet troops.[120]

The valour and defiance inherent in other apparently less heroic acts that may receive less attention than such daring forms of resistance and rebellion should not go without mention. Revisiting such instances is tantamount to redefining the term 'resistance' itself, normally capitalized and masculinized in its narrowest interpretation given its semantic association with armed action, physical strength or assumption of military risk. Taking a close look at everyday life in the Nazi camps and women's role there may prove enlightening in that regard, for it reveals a series of 'minor' actions ultimately instrumental to the fate of some survivors that broaden the definition of resistance. According to the memoirs of several, mothers and even grandmothers played an essential role in family cohesion and nourishment. Ceija Stojka describes intense memories of her mother, a widow deported with her children first to Auschwitz and then to other camps. Her untiring efforts to find food for them earned her beatings deemed deserved. And she could be as insistent on reusing remnants of fabric no matter how tattered as on encouraging her daughter to eat newly sprouting grass. Ceija remembers her aiding and being aided by other women with whom she networked in solidarity at Ravensbrück and Bergen-Belsen, and affording protection for children with no families.[121]

According to Otto Rosenberg, his grandmother, who had raised him from early childhood and whom he called 'mama', adopted a mother's role. In his memoirs he remembers her caring for himself and other children in the family. Although they were initially separated into different sections of the camp, his grandmother managed to get her ration of bread to him, for which both were beaten. When the *Zigeunerlager* was liquidated, she kept the younger grandchildren ('so many grandchildren … who all clung to granny') at her side while pushing him forward to be selected for Buchenwald with others deemed apt to work. When Otto insisted she should step forward also, she replied, 'No, I cannot leave the children on their own here. It is impossible for me to leave the children. Their fear – no, I will stay here my boy and you go.'[122]

Memory indisputably seeks a safe haven and idealizes reminiscence as a way to give vent to traumatic past experience, as noted by Zoe Waxman in connection with narratives describing mutual inter-prisoner caring.[123] Behaviours based on the traditional role of Romani women in keeping the family economy healthy (collecting, nourishing, trading), along with the collective upbringing customarily practised by nomadic groups, were capitalized on at the camps. A few studies have shown that

The Roma and the Holocaust

Romani women's ability to establish support networks, even in the form of 'artificial families' such as at Ravensbrück, served as the foundations for a greater capacity to endure harsh camp living conditions.[124] Such resistance, which countered the dehumanization characteristic of the camp system, may possibly explain the fact that women played an essential and even pioneer role in testifying to and vindicating the memory of the Romani Holocaust in their writings, as discussed in Part II of this book.

***

With the gradual defeat of the Third Reich, Allied troops began to liberate prisoners from the concentration camps in the territories progressively conquered. Liberation began in the summer of 1944 when Soviet troops entered Poland. They freed Auschwitz prisoners in January 1945. As camp system officials felt surrounded and withdrew, they attempted to erase any trace of the circumstances that had prevailed there. That entailed not only destroying all the facilities and any incriminating documents but also murdering thousands of prisoners at the last minute, both in the camps and the so-called 'death marches' that led them to areas still under German control. Later, US and British troops, advancing from the west, liberated other camps on German soil, including Bergen-Belsen, where many Romanies ended their days. The conditions there were even more atrocious than those that had horrified liberators in other places. The photos taken and films shot reflected what was found, an experience that changed the life of some of the observers (several of these documents are on display at the United States Holocaust Memorial Museum).

It was the end of a nightmare with which not all who had endured through the onset of liberation were able to cope. 'End' may not be the most suitable word choice in this case. After the war French *nomades* had to stay at the camps to which they had been taken by Nazi and collaborationist authorities. In Germany and Austria many Sinti and Roma peoples found that as the assets that had been confiscated from them were not returned, they had little choice but to live 'provisionally' in the camps where the Nazis had imprisoned them (at Cologne and Düsseldorf). Overall, after the war Romanies across Europe continued to confront the everyday idiosyncratic racism known as anti-Gypsyism. The account of what happened after Nazi defeat, a significant chapter in the Romani Holocaust, is discussed in the following chapter.

CHAPTER 3
THE LONG ROAD FROM DENIAL TO ACKNOWLEDGEMENT

In 1945 Walter and Erich Winter, two Sinti brothers who had been deported to concentration and extermination camps and forced to serve on the Russian front in the last few weeks of war, were finally able to return to their home at Kloppenburg, Germany. In his memoirs, discussed later, Walter Winter describes the painful shock that homecoming was. The brothers had to wage a new battle to recover their confiscated home and firmly resist being recorded in the local registry as non-German residents because their IDs had been seized by the Nazis. 'The lads with whom we had gone to school and played football were now local authority civil servants. They knew precisely who we were. Nevertheless, they wanted to register my brother Erich and myself as being stateless.'[1]

At the time, they still had the strength to react and resist. But they had yet other obstacles to overcome. To set up the circus they decided to found as a way of earning a living (continuing family tradition), they had to navigate de-Nazification bureaucracy in the hands of the British authority in the region and prove they had not cooperated with Hitler's regime. And to obtain their respective ration coupons they had to deal with the mayor of nearby Vechta, who had held the same office under Nazi rule.

Far from exceptional, these two brothers' experience was typical of the ordeal facing all Romani genocide survivors after the Second World War. Exhausted, decimated and traumatized, they had for many years to cope with a type of suffering many described as a second Holocaust. As historians Thomas Neumann and Michael Zimmermann explain in a study published with Winter's memoirs, that was largely because the defeat of the Nazi regime did not entail the subsequent acknowledgement of all its victims.[2] Roma people were denied that status for a very long time, based on the presumption they were not persecuted on strictly racial grounds. Both in Germany and in many other countries, communities branded as 'Gypsies' continued to be subject to legal abuse and social discrimination. It took a persistent struggle on the part of Romani associations, activists and advocates to attain recognition for these victims of Nazi terror for whom refusal meant substantial additional suffering. The community's representatives deemed acknowledgement of Romanies as Holocaust victims to form part of broader demands for the recognition of the civil rights historically denied them. This chapter synopsizes such institutional abuse and the struggle to eliminate it.

The Roma and the Holocaust

'Persecuting the survivors'

Holocaust historian Sybil Milton used that expression in the title of a paper on the fate of the Romani population in German territories after the war and Nazi defeat.[3] Her conclusions are consistent with the claims made by a few earlier scholars. For instance, in his afterword to Philomena Franz's memoirs published in 1985, Wolfgang Benz states that anti-Gypsyism persisted after the war. He contends that the anti-Gypsy prejudice in place in contemporary society was among the primary reasons for not acknowledging Romani Holocaust victims as such and for the refusal to collectively recognize that thousands of people were murdered under Nazi rule simply because they were Roma. According to Benz the problem lay not in the past but in the present, for such bias allowed a self-proclaimed democratic society to ignore the suffering of these victims 'in the tacit understanding that persecuting "Gypsies" was justified'.[4]

Such early studies on the invisibility and denial of the Romani genocide contained data, later supplemented by further research, on what may very likely be deemed the most fallacious case of the generally questionable de-Nazification undertaken in post-war Germany. The legal and administrative identification and trial of Nazi collaborators imposed by the allies were narrow and inconsistent processes, inasmuch as the 8,500,000 German members of the National-Socialist Party could have been indicted. In practice, such accountability was handled differently, with concomitantly uneven results, depending on the authority occupying each zone of a divided Germany, as well on the political priorities in place at any given time. The respective proceedings, in turn, were quite clearly never intended to demand accountability of those who had persecuted people branded as 'Gypsies'.

That became painfully obvious with the rules established to compensate Nazi victims, part of the more general approach to the restitution of the damage caused by Germany during the war that the allies announced would be demanded beginning in 1944. With the war over and the country occupied by Allied forces, the ordinances decreed in the regions governed by United States, English and French troops varied. With the creation of the Federal Republic of Germany in 1949, however, the acknowledgement of the restitution owed to victims was gradually turned over to the new German administration, entrusted with enacting laws and generating jurisprudence on the matter. The World Jewish Congress, an international organization founded in 1936 in response to Nazism that had attempted to persuade the Allies to react to the Holocaust during the war, assumed the defence of the interests of the victims of anti-Semitism in that new political and legal scenario. Its demands for the German government to acknowledge the crimes committed against Jews prevailed and victims were promised reparation, made extensive to the new State of Israel. The German judiciary nonetheless failed to dispense equal treatment to all theoretically eligible for reparation as the object of Nazi persecution on political, racial or religious grounds.

A 1956 German Superior Court of Justice sentence clearly stated that 'Gypsies' could not qualify for inclusion under that category of victims, for their persecution could not be attributed to such causes. As the courts long contended, the treatment accorded Romanies in Nazi Germany and Europe was not the result of a racial programme in which they were deemed inferior human beings, but of legitimate police practice geared to crime prevention. That at least was how the courts interpreted events prior to the issue of the Auschwitz Decree in January 1943, under which thousands of German and other European Romanies were deported en masse to the Auschwitz-Birkenau extermination camp. Nothing that occurred before then qualified for punishment or compensation. By resting their argument on the assertion that the 'Gypsy' community as a whole was known to be asocial and tended to delinquency, post-war German courts endorsed and extended Nazi discourse.

The persistence of anti-Gypsy prejudice in European societies and culture had much to do with the failure to perceive that the Nazis' racial characterization of Roma people was based on attributing genetic criminality to the entire group, merely for having been born into certain families. One fact not to be overlooked is that some jurists contended that not even Himmler's 1943 decree was sufficient grounds to consider Roma as victims. With the persistence of such precepts the persecution that sent thousands of people branded as 'Gypsies' to Polish ghettos and concentration camps beginning in 1940 was deemed for many years to be free of racial overtones. Despite its aforementioned title ('combating the Gypsy plague'), the 1938 decree whereby many other Romanies were taken to detention camps, underwent racial testing and had their possessions confiscated merited the same interpretation, as did the even earlier order mandating the sterilization of Romani men and women.

The treatment dispensed to Dr Robert Ritter, author of the racial categorization applied to Roma people by the Nazi regime, is typical of the contradiction inherent in the mentality of a majority of the post-war German population. After Nazi surrender, Ritter was given a criminology professorship at Tübingen University and in 1947 joined the Frankfurt Health Service, where he worked as child psychologist and hired his former assistant Eva Justin. Two years of investigations of accusations met with failure in 1950 when the prosecutor's office deemed there was insufficient evidence against him. Beyond the outcome, the details of the proceedings attest to the cruelty of the post-war (in)justice dispensed to Roma people. The accused's arguments (that he was unaware of extermination and had confined his advice to sterilization) were accepted. The experts summoned to testify used Ritter's own writings as objective scientific grounds to describe 'Gypsy' nature, whilst the victims' testimonies were not taken into consideration due to their presumably scant evidential power.

On the contrary, however, from the outset information had been forthcoming on the racial and ideological nature of the persecution unleashed on Romanies under the Nazi regime and the harm it caused. Although aware of that situation, when the time came the Americans chose not to remind the German courts accordingly. In a December 1944 document, the American administration charted a map of useful skills with which to handle such labyrinthian judicial proceedings. The section on Roma people (headed 'Gypsies') noted that they were deemed by the Nazis to be an 'inferior race', adding that after the 1938 decree 'the majority were put into concentration camps and their property was confiscated and the ultimate object was undoubtedly to exterminate the species altogether: this aim appears to have been accomplished to a very large extent'.[5]

The trend outside Germany was to look the other way when Romani Holocaust victims were denied justice, whilst the domestic population needed to believe that Nazi regime crimes were attributable only to a small number of rulers with the sole aid of a group of brutal perpetrators. Involvement on the part of civil society as a whole or of professional or expert communities (medical doctors, civil servants, technicians) was unthinkable. Gilad Margalit made that observation in his insightful review of the German judicial system in place at the time.[6] The prevalence of scientific prestige above any other consideration can be gleaned from the Ritter case as well as from the fate of some of his collaborators. Although tried, Justin was acquitted on the grounds that her youth and inexperience at the time (she was thirty-five in 1943!) were attenuating circumstances. For many years Erhardt, another collaborator, continued in the employ of Tübingen University, where she used the data collected during the Nazi regime for her research.

Court cases such as these attest both to the limited extent of de-Nazification and the consolidation in post-war discourse of the stereotyped view of 'Gypsies' as a community characterized by an idle, alienated, wandering lifestyle: in short, a social problem. Such a depiction extended the Nazi viewpoint over time, an unsurprising consequence of the fact that a number of the officials devoted to the 'Gypsy plague' during the Third Reich continued to hold government positions in the Federal Republic of Germany. Cases in point included Joseph Eichberger, formerly in charge of Romani deportation and subsequently head of the Gypsy Department with the Bavarian police force; Leo Karsten, head of the Gypsy Affairs Bureau with the Nazi criminal police and later of the Baden police Migration Department; and Rudolf Uschold, a Bavarian policeman summoned to testify in the Ritter trial, to name a few.[7]

At the same time, the courts were perpetuating the criminalization of the Romani population that preceded Hitler's rise to power, as discussed earlier. They could do so on the grounds of the existing legislation, for laws on 'Gypsies' decreed prior to the Second World War were recovered or maintained in its aftermath, with utter disregard for the suffering inflicted on Romanies by the Nazi regime and the role of such legislation in the legal and cultural structure underlying Nazi racial cleansing policies. In Cologne and Düsseldorf, for instance, provisions drawn from the 1938 act on 'combating the Gypsy plague' remained valid. In 1953 Bavarian Parliament, in turn, enacted a law on vagrancy and indolence patterned on earlier rules. Similar situations can be identified in other countries. After the war Austria kept an 1888 edict on the books that called for special policing of 'Gypsies'. In Spain the regulations governing the Civil Guard, the country's most prominent law enforcement agency since it was founded in the mid-nineteenth century, provided for special measures for 'Gitanos' that were not abolished until 1978. And in France a law dating from 1912 on so-called 'nomads' remained in force until it was amended in 1969.

These were actually not only legal or institutional reactions. The courts and authorities endorsed and represented the attitude towards 'Gypsies' that prevailed in mainstream society. In France, Lise Foisneau, citing archival sources, showed that in addition to extended internment in detention camps after the war, Romanies suffered very violent anti-Gypsyism at the hands of their neighbours. After release some were accused of collaborating with the Germans while others ran up against more general attitudes around the undesirability of their presence. In that context, after release from German occupation Roma people were arrested and murdered by French armed forces and civilians both. Sixty to 100 Romanies were arbitrarily arrested and around thirty executed in the Massif Central region studied by Foisneau.[8] The victims were men, women and children between the ages of two and sixty-five. The French press collaborated by carrying news items with a clearly anti-Gypsy bias. In one case a young man was accused of robbing and killing the crew on an English aeroplane that crashed near Puy-de-Dôme, when the aircraft had actually exploded in mid-air before landing. The youth was later shown to have been simply obeying Maquis orders to collect the weapons from the remains of the accident, that is, collaborating with the French Resistance.

In an environment so imbued with anti-Gypsyism, the possibility that the German courts and administration, the apparatus dispensing restitution, would admit Romani demands for indemnity seemed remote. In addition to allowing many police staffers formerly devoted to 'combating the Gypsy plague' to keep their jobs for many years, that apparatus often denied Romanies restitution of possessions that had been seized. Similarly, those who had lost their IDs under the Nazi regime also found it difficult to exercise their civil rights.[9] In addition, immediately following release from the camps most Romani survivors, rather than seeking refuge at the centres for displaced persons supervised initially by the Allied forces and subsequently by the United Nations Relief and Rehabilitation Organization (UNRRA-IRO), attempted to return directly to their former homes as quickly and directly as possible. As a result they were unable to produce institutional records that could serve as administrative grounds for their claims as victims.

In 1963, however, a court in Cologne returned the country's first verdict in favour of Romani plaintiffs. It found that a group who had fled Germany in 1939 after being subjected to racial testing by Ritter's team was entitled to claim reparation for persecution on racial grounds. A decisive factor in that dramatic turnaround was the attitude adopted by Kurt May, head of the United Restitution Organization office at Frankfurt, an institution that played a key role in bringing action in favour of Jews persecuted by the Nazi regime. May encouraged historian Hans Buchheim to study Roma deportation to Polish ghettos and participated personally in the research. He interviewed judges, officials and policemen and ultimately convinced his friend Franz Calvelli-Adorno to publish an article in 1961. The article questioned the premise according to which since collectively classifying an entire community as 'asocial' was not a racist attitude, any consequential operations could not be penalized. That paper was decisive in introducing the change in judicial practice that established the year 1938 (as opposed to 1943) as the date after which Roma could be regarded as victims of Nazi racial policy.[10] Some of the possible plaintiffs were deceased by that time, whilst those still alive found it difficult to prove their right to indemnity for want of any record of their illegal arrest. Yet others were deprived of reparation for earlier measures such as imprisonment in internment camps (at Marzahn-Berlin, for instance) or sterilizations.

One case mentioned in Chapter 2 illustrates the disregard for and denial of Roma suffering inflicted by the Nazi regime. The episode at issue involved Unku, the girl who inspired the lead character in a tale titled 'Ede und Unku',[11] who was arrested and deported to Auschwitz in her youth. In 1972 the book was decreed required reading in German Democratic Republic schools. Its anti-Fascism was highly valued. The author's profile, the splendid photographs by John Heartfield (photomontage pioneer and 1930s anti-Nazi propagandist) and the fact that it had been one of the books famously burnt with Hitler's rise to power in 1933 made it an exemplary story. But the focus of this curricular requirement was class conflict, not Roma suffering for racial reasons. A 1981 filmed version[12] made no mention of the fate of the Romani characters, most of whom perished at the hands of the Nazi regime. Alerted by a letter to the editor signed by a woman who asked why the suffering of Romanies murdered at Auschwitz and other camps had been overlooked, activist Reimar Gilsenbach undertook research on the exclusion of the Sinti population in the German Democratic Republic and initiated a campaign to build a monument in honour of Romani Holocaust victims. His proposal to remember Unku with a fountain at Magdeburg and similar initiatives were rejected, however. The memorial was not erected in that city until 1998, after the disappearance of the German Democratic Republic's communist regime.

Roma people living in Soviet Union satellite countries may have been even less able to claim restitution after the war. That narrower opportunity could be attributed both to the attempt by the new communist authorities to shirk any responsibility for the measures implemented by the National Socialist Government and its allies and to the strained official relations with the Federal Republic. Although circumstances differed across the anything but monolithic communist bloc, Romania may serve as illustration of what many Romanies encountered. Those who managed to return from the horror of deportation to Transnistria simply moved back to their places of origin or the outskirts of Bucharest. They were not targeted by the new communist regime with any specific policy but rather included, albeit mandatorily, in national unity discourse. A pre-existing General Romani Union was dissolved in 1949. The re-establishment of diplomatic relations between Romania and the Federal Republic of Germany in 1967 finally provided a channel for communities such as the Jewish and Roma peoples to claim compensation. Beginning in 1970 the Romanian Government cooperated in filing claims and supplemented investigations with accounts that laid all the responsibility for the events on Germany, disregarding the collaboration lent at the time by certain sectors of Romanian society.[13]

On the whole the narratives on national unity that prevailed in post-war communist countries, which highlighted the role of the heroic 'people' subjected to such suffering and ignored the racist premises whereby it was inflicted, went hand in hand in the Romani case with policies geared to their assimilation in mainstream society. The procedures and effects of those policies differed widely, from mandatory, albeit subsidized, permanent settlement (in Bulgaria and the Soviet Union) to more repressive measures such as the confiscation of horses and other possessions in Poland and Czechoslovakia.[14] Although in some cases opportunities were afforded for training and social improvement (against a backdrop of general anti-racist discourse that disappeared after 1989), mandatory assimilation came at a high cost, with cases of mandatory sterilization as part of a social integration programme.

Acknowledgement of victims and the right to memory

As inferred by the foregoing, Romani claims to be acknowledged and treated as victims of Nazi violence were met with ongoing resistance. Such claims were in fact systematically rejected for as long as the prevailing criterion was that the measures adopted against 'Gypsies' were not racially motivated but adopted to prevent crime. Those who dared to individually demand acknowledgement and compensation as Nazi victims from the judiciary risked institutional and social derision that intensified their loss of social bearings. But not only individual initiatives ran up against a wall of incomprehension and repudiation. Collectively organized claims were also denied, such as those brought by *Die Vergessenen* (the forgotten ones). An association founded in Munich as early as 1946, it applied for permission to represent all Romani victims at the Nuremberg trials, in addition to demanding official acknowledgement for them. Voices in the Romani community were also raised early on from outside Germany. In 1946 French writer Mateo Maximoff published a text in the *Journal of the Gypsy Lore Society*, in which he criticized not only the persecution but also the disregard for those who, like his family, had participated in combatting Nazism.[15]

Claims were therefore heard from the outset, a fact that counters what some studies purported to see as Romani silence and innate disinterest in commemorative memory. Rather, it was the response to such initiatives that was lacking. As noted, the legal-institutional apparatus and mainstream society alike refused to take Romani claims into consideration. Moreover, Romanies had no organization similar to the one that centralized Jewish survivor claims. Emigration, in turn, was a less feasible option for Romanies than for Jews. Their only safety net was the family,[16] families that had not only been decimated but torn apart: 'sterilization, humiliation, and the insults to their culture made it hard both to share their stories and to communicate their traditions and values'.[17] In that scenario Romani genocide survivors had to wage a dauntless battle for survival practically unaided, often with the added disadvantage of the destruction of their occupational network and disappearance of their property. They had also to bear the pain of the post-traumatic silence that weighed on their experience as survivors, while at the same time concealing their culture and lifestyles, their Romani identity, to elude persistent social stigma and police harassment. Not unsurprisingly, they felt like 'strangers in their own land' in Eve Rosenhaft's words.

It was not until the mid-1960s that a tiny crack opened for Romani claims to prosper in a more general scenario of a maturing social awareness of the scope of the Holocaust. Thanks to the Eichmann trial held in Jerusalem in 1961 and the Auschwitz proceedings in Frankfurt from 1963 to 1965, the racial significance and scope of Nazi barbarism began to penetrate public awareness. Starting at that time, German society undertook to confront its recent past more critically and the implications of the concentration camp system were brought to worldwide public attention by the media. As part of an active research programme and political pressure exerted by Jewish groups on both sides of the Atlantic, academic research on the genocide perpetrated against that community of Europeans was undertaken. In that context, Raul Hilberg published his foundational study in 1961. Attendant upon the expansion of Jewish Holocaust historiography was the emergence of a discourse on the singularity of the racial persecution and concomitant destruction inflicted. And whilst many historians were reluctant to integrate other types of victims in the same narrative, some Jewish scholars also furnished data on the Romani genocide. Simon Wiesenthal, for instance, equated the fates of European Jews and 'Gypsies' on the grounds of records found in Prague in 1963.[18]

Lines connecting the two targets of persecution were also drawn on Romani initiative. In the early 1960s Ionel Rotaru, a Romanian refugee in France whose Romani identity was questioned by his detractors, founded an international association, *Communauté Mondiale Gitane* (world 'Gypsy' community) that, in addition to demanding legal and social changes to improve Romani communities' lives, led initiatives to claim indemnity from the German administration for victims of the Nazi regime. Although he was scantly successful in the latter endeavour, his struggle was decisive for the earliest research on the Romani genocide. He gathered information in Germany, sought attorneys in France and contacted Jewish historian Miriam Novitch, herself a Holocaust survivor and author of a study on the Romani genocide under Nazi rule. Rotaru's initiatives were essential to consolidating Romani international associationism [Illustration 33]. The political nature of his activism included ideas such as the creation of a Romani space or refuge, Romanestan, and the issuance of an international passport for Roma the world over. That, along with the public impact of his activism for the cause (with constant press releases, calls to politicians or the UN, etc.) made his presence awkward for the French government. His association was banned in 1965, and Rotaru himself was the target of an aggressive media campaign designed to discredit him.[19]

Despite that outcome, his demand for the recognition of victims in connection with claims for a broader suite of rights was inherited by the Romani movement that was arising in a number of countries and introduced internationally at the First Romani World Congress held at London in 1971. The same discourse was also logically assimilated by the subsequently founded International Romani Union, an organization consolidated after 1978 in response to demands from a number of quarters. That series of events inspired the first broad-based study on the 'Gypsy' Holocaust, conducted by Puxon and Kenrick and published by the University of Sussex in 1972.[20]

The consolidation of a Romani voice claiming the recognition denied the victims of Nazi persecution was a plural and not consistently coordinated endeavour, with representatives and initiatives in a number of countries. Logically, the issue could be broached most directly in Germany, where a response to what continued to be the deep moral implications of claims deliberately ignored was demanded from the political class

The Long Road from Denial to Acknowledgement

Illustration 33 Ionel Rotaru, activist and Communauté Mondiale Gitane President, *c.* **1965**. Rotaru was among the first to encourage Romani genocide studies and the institution of proceedings to indemnify victims [photo by Jacques Richard, courtesy of Ilsen About].

and public opinion. Conditions favourable to those initiatives materialized in the late 1970s and early 1980s, when the significance of Nazism in German history became the object of intense public debate in which historians played such a leading role that it was christened the *Historikerstreit* (historians' quarrel).

Capitalizing on that scenario, German Romani activists adopted a more publicly visible defence of their cause, moving from judiciary scenarios to the public square, organizing protest marches and undertaking other symbolically charged measures. They enlisted the collaboration of an association devoted to the defence of abused minorities *Gesellschaft für bedrothe Völker* (society for imperilled peoples), founded in 1970 by Tillman Zülch. One determining factor in the movement was the success of a commemorative ceremony on the Holocaust organized at the Bergen-Belsen Camp, attended by 2,500 people. The crowd included representatives from Germany and thirteen other countries, genocide survivors and their descendants, Jewish delegates, German MPs and European Parliament President at the time, Simone Veil, herself a Jewish genocide survivor.

A few months later in April 1980, a group of activists initiated a hunger strike in the Dachau Camp complex to demand recognition of Romani Holocaust victims and protest against police use of Nazi criminal records on German 'Gypsies'. That campaign garnered the support of the Social Democratic Party and secured its commitment to tackle the discrimination dispensed to the country's Romanies. The result was the establishment in 1982 of the *Zentralrat Deutscher Sinti und Roma* (Central Sinti and Roma Council of Germany) inspired in many respects, including its very name, by the Jewish model for defending victims' rights to the authorities (at inception, only the term 'Sinti' appeared in the name; 'Roma' was added later). In his visit to the central council's newly founded Heidelberg office, Helmut Schmidt became the Federal Republic's first Chancellor to officially acknowledge that the Romani genocide had been perpetrated by the Nazi regime out of racial prejudice. Romani Rose, son of a Holocaust survivor and participant at the Dachau event, was elected council president, an office he still holds today.[21]

Inasmuch as the very late date of official acknowledgement of the Romani Holocaust in Germany meant that many of its victims died before receiving reparation, it should come as no surprise that beginning in the latter 1980s one of the central council's most active concerns was memory. Its demands claimed specific acknowledgement of the racially inspired suffering inflicted by the Nazi regime on Romanies in official Holocaust discourse and its significance for German society. In that context, the erection of a memorial in Berlin as a site for remembering and respecting victims (an idea launched in 1988 but only implemented years later) could be understood as an ideal occasion to imbue that endeavour with new impetus. It might also be analysed as a site where different visions of the meaning of the Holocaust in German history and identity clashed, a complex space in light of the diversity of the victims and other actors, particularly after German reunification in 1991. Further to a study by Nadine Blumer, Romani Rose was particularly belligerent in that controversy from the outset, co-authoring a series of articles in the media and participating in protests where victim hierarchy was a key issue.[22] Given that the focus of the original initiative for the memorial was on the Jewish Holocaust, the Romani protest cast light on the existence of a tendency to separate first- from second-class victims in the recognition of the destructive effects of Nazi policy. In his debate with Jewish and other representatives, Rose paradoxically criticized that hierarchization while at the same time demanding a special space for Roma and Sinti people in the memory of German society at large, exclusive of other groups such as Jehovah's Witnesses. The controversy inspired by the memorial was long-lasting and ultimately solved in German Parliament, which in 1999 decreed the erection of different, but interconnected, memorials for the various groups of victims.

The struggle to integrate Nazi-inflicted suffering on Romanies into official accounts of that dark episode of national history and the critical review of its meaning for German identity itself constituted quite an endeavour. It nonetheless made excellent sense at a time when younger generations of Germans could distance themselves from their parents' traumatic past but had yet to acquire any knowledge of the persecution of a people such as the Roma. Philomena Franz, the first Sinti Nazi concentration camp survivor to publish her memoirs, was inspired to write them in part because her son had been insulted in school for being a 'Zigeuner' ('Gypsy').[23] Her recognition in that aggression of the racial prejudice that had driven the wheel of Romani genocide at the hands of the Nazi regime prompted her to speak to the school's teachers and pupils about what had happened to her people, acting on a need to bear witness to those events. After that she began to write. That would not have been possible prior to the change in the cultural and political environment that took place in the 1980s. Like many others Philomena Franz had for decades been obliged to bear the suffering imposed by the silence surrounding Romani Holocaust survivors until she was able to publish her memoirs in 1985.

Such experiences made remembrance of the persecution inflicted by the Nazi regime an essential component of Romanies' collective modern identity, viewed as a space for establishing bonds between cultures with different traditions and histories. That component has been studied in depth by Slawomir Kapralski, who also called into question prior visions of the weakness or non-existence of commemorative memory among Roma peoples.[24] As he noted, commemorative traditions around Nazi persecution have been constructed in many ways. A wide variety of accounts and ceremonies attest to the efficacy of social and political initiatives in creating a sensation of belonging. The Caravan of Memory, for instance, celebrated in Poland since 1996 with the support of the Tarnow Ethnographic Museum, consists in a journey in which victims are remembered with speeches, songs and similar. The caravan makes three stops: at the monument to all Auschwitz victims at Tarnow; at the collective grave at Zabno, where a group of Romanies were shot to death in 1943; and at Szczurowa, where the German police murdered ninety-three townspeople because they were 'Gypsies'.

Remembrance of the Romani genocide under the Nazi regime is multifarious and open and continues to be reformulated today. In Spain for instance, a country where their peculiar historic circumstances saved 'Gitanos' from direct Nazi deportation during the Second World War, Romani associations presently relate commemoration of the Holocaust to the so-called *Gran Redada* (mass raid), an eighteenth-century plan for general imprisonment geared to the biological extinction of all Spanish Romanies. In Germany, in turn, associations competing with the central Sinti and Roma council have linked the historic suffering entailed in Nazi genocide to the more recent suffering borne by Eastern European Romani immigrants deprived of German State protection. None of that is unusual, in light of the enormous symbolic and consequently political power with which that historic development is imbued.

That notwithstanding, the tardy acknowledgement of Romani compared with Jewish entitlement to memory attests to the widely differing fate that has characterized those two groups of victims. It was not until some time after the war that Jews were able to place their cause on the political, legal and moral agendas of Western societies, for racial persecution was initially masked by what were viewed as crimes against humanity in general. After that first hiatus, however, the dates serve as eloquent markers of the difference. In 1982 Dachau became the first concentration camp to bear a commemorative plaque honouring Romani Holocaust victims, whilst it was not until 2005 that European Parliament passed a resolution recommending that such genocide should be officially acknowledged. The Berliner memorial to Sinti and Roma victims of National Socialism,

Illustration 34 **Pond at the memorial monument on Sinti and Roma genocide, Berlin.** Designed by Israeli artist Dani Karava, it was unveiled in 2012 [photo by Mike Peel, material in the public domain].

in turn, was only unveiled in 2012 [Illustration 34]. The final link in the chain of the history of recognition of the Romani Holocaust is the ongoing progress in research on and the transfer of academic knowledge to the public sphere.

Where history stands: Research and dissemination

Studies around a given subject matter always contain information relevant to more than just academic issues, for all research is informed by its social coordinates. The role of investigation in this area is directly related to developments around acknowledgement of the victims. Moreover, research and the dissemination of its results can change the social perception of and institutional approach to academically analysed problems. While dealing with the past, history is a present-day discipline closely related to a society's future projects. Although such a commitment informs the analysis of any historical subject matter, it is particularly pertinent to the study of Nazism and the Holocaust (as illustrated by the aforementioned controversy among German historians). For all those reasons, this final section of Part I contains a brief account of the advances in the understanding of the Romani genocide under the Nazi regime and the analysis of its social implications.

Some approaches to the subject stress the paucity of research on Romani genocide, especially as compared with the Jewish Holocaust. It can no longer be contended, however, that the Romani experience has been scantly addressed, as can be deduced from even a superficial glance at the bibliography included hereunder (a selection of the works most readily accessible to readers that does not aspire to be exhaustive). In addition to the abundance of works already in print, much research is presently underway. Some of those studies will very likely affect the present perception of the scope of the Romani Holocaust in the light of sources newly available, including the records describing events that took place in regions comprising the former Soviet Union.

A comparison between the literature presently in place on the persecution of Romanies and the research on the Jewish Holocaust, beyond the enormous difference in volume, reveals that the former bears much later dates and is greatly fragmented, features charged with both scientific and political significance. As pointed out by About and Abakunova in a comprehensive online review of the literature up through 2016, recognition of the Romani genocide as a subject worthy of study came very late in the day.[25] Consequently, no research programmes as systematic and ambitious as applied to other components of Nazism have been forthcoming. The comparison to the Jewish Holocaust is, of course, mediated by the obvious difference between the two communities' capacity to fund studies and undertake academic initiatives with political support. During a long first initial stage, studies on the Romani Holocaust were largely undertaken in extra-academic spheres with no outside funding, on a local scale and driven by activists intent on demanding acknowledgement for victims. Against that backdrop, Puxon and Kenrick's aforementioned endeavour is even more meritorious.[26]

The year 1996 saw publication of the treatise that initiated sustained academic historiography on the Romani genocide, authored by German historian Michael Zimmermann.[27] The date of that pioneering study compares rather unfavourably with the date of publication (overcoming a series of difficulties), 1961, of Hilberg's well-known treatise that played a similarly foundational role for research on the Jewish Holocaust. Prior to Zimmermann's undertaking, scantly any systematic academic research had been conducted on the Nazi persecution of 'Gypsies'. A few Jewish Holocaust historians such as Henry Friedlander and Sybil Milton[28] might be cited as advocating for broadening the scope of Nazi victims and they themselves made reference to Romanies in their studies. Other examples can be found in Wolfang Benz's[29] brief but powerful study for Philomena Franz's memoirs in 1985 and the multi-volume memorial entitled *The Gypsies at Auschwitz-Birkenau*. Sponsored by the Auschwitz Museum, the latter was published in several languages in 1993, but in an expensive edition with only a short run.

The turning point in any event came with the publication of Zimmermann's aforementioned study, characterized by commendable scientific rigour that combined a wealth of data with a persuasive interpretation thanks to expert contextualization. He carried his research further in other papers published prior to his premature death in 2007. By that time the subject had attracted the interest of other historians who retrieved written records and proposed new interpretations. Lewy and Margalit,[30] referred to in Chapter 2, were among the authors to join those ranks. At around the same time, Hertfordshire University in the UK published a three-volume anthology of research from different sources of variable scope.[31]

The Roma and the Holocaust

Since the turn of the twenty-first century the field of Romani Holocaust research has grown and new courses have been charted. To date the most comprehensive review of the state of the art can be found in a book edited by Anton Weiss-Wendt in 2013 as a tribute to Zimmermann.[32] Many of the authors contributing to that volume have continued to research the area and participate in academic networks and congresses. Celia Donert and Eve Rosenhaft edited a book in 2022 that provides an overview of the most recent research on the implications of and retrospectives around this Holocaust.[33] Nonetheless, many areas have yet to be explored, leaving significant voids. The USC Shoa Foundation created by Steven Spielberg in 1994 keeps records of dozens of interviews with Romani Holocaust survivors that up to now have gone practically unresearched. The sole exception to date is a study underway by Anabel Carballo. A BESTROM Project researcher, she is using those interviews for her PhD thesis, along with others on file at the Heidelberg *Dokumentations und Kulturzentrum Deutscher Sinti und Roma* (Documentation and Cultural Centre of German Sinti and Roma), Washington's Holocaust Memorial Museum and the *Yahad-In Unum* archive in Paris. That no such study has been undertaken until so late in the day is surprising, particularly as compared with the use of such testimony to study the Jewish Holocaust. What all this questions is the legitimacy of continuing to cast the Romani Holocaust in terms of 'other victims', a centre-periphery model rendered obsolete by advances in historiographic research. As Eve Rosenhaft contends, the question now is to reflect on which narrative (language, explanatory paradigm, intention) should be used to do justice to the many elements of a process that will never again be a mere appendix to the account of the (Jewish) Holocaust.[34]

At least, it will no longer be so viewed by researchers engaging in the subject. That can hardly be said about the knowledge within reach of the general public (the suite of data available to society at large that affects its perception of social problems), however. As noted in the introduction to this book, given the nearly negligible visibility of the Romani genocide at the hands of the Nazi regime, recognition of that people's right to a place in history and collective memory still stands today essentially where it stood in the immediate post-war period. Whereas the Jewish Holocaust is a theme familiar to the public at large, having been widely addressed in cinema, literature, the media, memorials and museums, the Romani genocide is a matter of interest to a mere handful of citizens who are hard put to find information on the subject in books or other cultural products. Although there is no lack of historiographic research, dissemination is wanting, at least on a scale that would allow new knowledge to reach beyond the narrow limits of specialized publications and congresses. Much more work is needed to transfer academic expertise to public knowledge, whether in the civic, educational or commemorative dimensions.

That is no easy task, for it involves deploying languages and media formats that call for both effort and imagination. But difficulties also stem from the dimensions at issue. The walls of silence can only be felled by persistent and cumulative discourse on the part of many institutional and individual actors. Be it said that although a number of initiatives have been undertaken and must be acknowledged, many more are needed to successfully transfer the knowledge at hand. This chapter closes with a review of some of these indispensable cultural products, including museums and exhibitions, feature films and documentaries, websites and blogs, along with educational materials that have addressed the Romani Holocaust. As a summary it aspires not to be exhaustive but selective and interpretational. The inference to be drawn is that resources are available for anyone seeking information.

But this summary also highlights how slowly social perception changes around subjects overburdened by a long tradition of simplification and stereotype. As noted above, many more initiatives will be needed to do away with the historic anti-Gypsy prejudice so tightly woven into Western societies. Giving a full account of the cruelty inherent in the Romani genocide may be the first step in questioning stereotypes unconsciously assimilated and still in place today, to warn of the danger they entail. That would enable mainstream society to realize they are essentially the same stereotypes that under given historic circumstances 'justified' the murder of half a million people deemed racially inferior because they were 'Gypsies'.

The purposes of knowledge transfer may be effectively secured through museums and memorials if the materials on display are supplemented with effective communication and discourse expressed in terms sensitive to the fate suffered by victims. The relevance of such cultural products in today's societies has been fuelled by the Central Sinti and Roma Council of Germany's collaboration with the Polish State's symbolic Auschwitz Museum in the form of participation in the section on Romani genocide. Questions might be raised around the accuracy of some details having to do with timing or the nuances in the account chosen, as Van Baar has done by objecting to what he deems an overly uniform sociological depiction of the population at issue.[35] In contrast, no doubts can be harboured around the pertinence of voices such as this to ensuring that memory forms a legitimate part of Europeans' historiographic culture. More generally, in Germany the history of Nazi persecution of Roma people is broached in a number of museums and memorials, from the permanent exhibition on display at the former Gestapo office at Cologne to the biographies illustrating the fate of Sachsenhausen Camp prisoners outside Oranienburg, to cite just two examples.

Nonetheless, including Romani victims among those persecuted by the Nazi regime is not the only objective, for museum discourse, if acritical, may nourish stereotypes and maintain a hierarchy of victims. After studying the depiction of the Romani genocide in three museums in Slovakia, Croatia and Hungary, Ljiljana Radonić identified issues around the depiction of Romani victims, including the occasional but paradoxical use of perpetrator lingo (categories such as 'asocial'), the display of impersonalized or stereotyped photographs (unlike those depicting other victims), the attribution of contentious features (such as nomadism) to a whole social group and others.[36] The discourse used to narrate the history of the Romani genocide in museums is at least as important as its inclusion in such spaces.

A number of temporary exhibitions have also been organized, which on occasion may convey more complex messages with a forceful impact. An example can be found in those displaying plastic art authored by Romani Holocaust survivors. Their paintings and drawings depicting Nazi persecution and family life prior to deportations narrate their personal experience as victims, describing a history of suffering in very personal dimensions that can be individualized, given names and faces. That is one of the reasons underlying the enormous value of the exhibitions of Ceija Stojka's oeuvre, shown in a number of cities (2021 in Sintra, 2020 in Madrid, 2019 in Nijmegen, 2018 in Paris, 2017 in Marseille, etc.). At times displayed with documentary films of the artist's life produced by Karin Berger, Ceija's testimonial paintings are a first-person account of the experience of the Romani genocide, also narrated in her memoirs, discussed later [Illustration 35]. Another member of the Stojka family, Ceija's brother Karl, likewise resorted to painting as a middle road between testimonial and therapy. The United States Holocaust Memorial Museum published a catalogue of his oeuvre on the occasion of an exhibition at the Austrian Embassy in Washington in 1992.[37]

Karl Stojka's is one of the nine biographies of children that served as the leitmotif for another exhibition, the 'Digital Exhibition about Genocide of Sinti and the Roma'. That excellent display was an initiative undertaken by Tweedewereldoorlog, a Dutch platform that engages in disseminating details around the Second World War. Available online, the exhibition is a carefully composed, rigorous and multilingual depiction of the Romani genocide produced in conjunction with the International Holocaust Remembrance Alliance (IHRA), institutions such as the Anne Frank Sichtung and

Illustration 35 Ceija Stojka, one of the Romani Holocaust's most powerful narrators. The artist during a book presentation at the Austrian National Library (Vienna), 2008 [Photo by Manfred Werner].

Illustration 36 Laubinger family, Romanies. Part of the University of Liverpool exhibition *Don't Forget the photos* [courtesy of the University of Liverpool Library - Special Collections].

specialist counsel. It constitutes a highly recommendable resource. Other exhibitions, while not actually online, have websites with substantial information on their content, providing alternative channels for heightening public awareness around the Romani genocide. The main attraction of the travelling exhibition entitled 'Don't Forget the Photos', for instance, is a magnificent collection of black-and-white photographs kept by Liverpool University library. Taken between 1932 and 1939 by Hans Weltzel, they depict the everyday lives of a Sinti family prior to arrest and deportation [Illustration 36]. The complex relationship between photographer and victims has been researched by Eve Rosenhaft, whose contribution to the exhibition and adaptations to different scenarios affords a magnificent example of how academia can contribute to dissemination. The website cited contains a wealth of information and graphic materials.[38]

Photography is indisputably a powerful communication vehicle able to emanate realism that impacts viewers. The fact that such realism is often artificial, that is, the result of staging with decipherable elements, may enhance a picture's narrative capacities. These images, whether the small full-face and profile photographs drawn from police records or of survivors exhibiting their arms tattooed arms with the Auschwitz Z-number, play a substantial role in the dissemination of academic knowledge. A worthy example in this regard can be found in the exhibition organized by the Wiener Holocaust Library titled 'Forgotten Victims: The Nazi Genocide of the Roma and Sinti', an account of the Romani

Holocaust drawn from documents on file in a number of institutions. Held in London in late 2019 and early 2020, it can now be viewed online because the United Nations chose it to illustrate Roma Holocaust Memorial Day 2020.[39]

Motion pictures, of course, are also impactful. Although some cinema has been produced around the Nazi persecution of European Romanies, the genre continues to be underexploited. The earliest films on the Holocaust featured Romani characters sporadically or as a backdrop (such as in *The Last Stage*, the first picture ever on the Holocaust, released in 1948). But the very first feature film in which the plot revolved around the Romani genocide was *And the Violins Stopped Playing*, a US-Polish co-production released in 1988. In recent years a handful of pictures have been filmed that directly or tangentially but very effectively introduce the viewer to the Roma Holocaust. Unfortunately such films, exquisite in a number of respects, have had an overly short run in commercial movie theatres. The one most directly focusing on the subject is a feature by Romani producer Tony Gatlif, *Korkoro* ('freedom' in Romanes), a French film dating from 2008 that narrates the fate of a family afflicted by Nazi persecution. Étienne Comar's 2016 film *Django*, likewise set against the backdrop of occupied or collaborationist France, narrates the life of musician Django Reindhardt and describes the impact of the Nazi regime on life in Romani communities. A few years earlier, in 2013, another biopic directed by Joanna Kos and Krzysztof Krauze titled *Papusza* (doll in Romanes and the poet's nickname) narrated the life of Polish Romani poet Bronislawa Wajs. That film stands as proof that aesthetic refinement can be made compatible with the narration of a story seeped in content. The biographical approach adopted in these films indisputably makes the suite of messages they intend to convey more readily accessible to viewers.[40]

A few documentaries have also been produced, two presently in open access online. Unku's story, mentioned both in this chapter and Chapter 2 of this book, is told in detail in Jana Müller's documentary biopic on the life of young Erna Laubinger, with photographs, interviews and documents. Subtitled in a number of languages, it forms part of the website to the aforementioned exhibition 'Don't Forget the Photos'. Another documentary in open access and subtitled in several languages was recently (2022) produced using interviews conducted in German with Philomena Franz. A similarly named website, in addition to the film itself, contains supplementary information on the life and oeuvre of that Romani genocide survivor.[41] The latter initiative forms part of the BESTROM ('Beyond Stereotypes: Cultural Exchanges and the Romani Contribution to European Public Spaces') research project. That same project has recently sponsored initiatives designed to publicize research findings through theatre, as in *Und wohin jetzt?* [and where to now?], a Bremer Shakespeare Company (BSC) play proposing a new reading of documents. The Sixteenth episode of the BSC and Universität Bremen series 'Aus den Akten auf die Bühne' (AdA, off the record, on stage), it premiered in June 2021.[42]

This brief overview would be incomplete without some mention of the blogs and websites published in open access on the internet for the purposes of education or dissemination. These are particularly important resources, given that in today's societies discourse must be positioned on platforms accessible online to be deemed in the public domain and regarded as raw material suitable for disseminating ideas in social networks. Of particular prominence in that regard is 'The Fate of European Roma and Sinti during the Holocaust', an excellent multilingual website edited by Gerhard Baumgartner, who enlisted other specialists. It is funded by the Austrian Government, the Parisian *Fondation pour la Mémoire de le Shoah* (foundation for remembrance of the Shoah) and IHRA.[43] This site contains rigorous, but synopsized, information on a number of components of the Romani Holocaust, including prior persecution, deportation, the camps and survivors. The project uses photographs not only to document but also to educate in the form of an open-access, online handbook for teachers willing to confront the challenge of telling these stories.

Other initiatives in open-access websites combine research with dissemination, either by summarizing extensive papers for wider dissemination or by providing the public at large with access to written records on Roma persecution by the Nazi regime. Particularly recommendable in that context is a pithy article by Eve Rosenhaft published on the National WWII Museum (headquartered in New Orleans) website. The website published by the aforementioned BESTROM project also carries open-access versions in English and German of a study by the present author, initially intended for publication with the Spanish edition of Philomena Franz's memoirs. One final example is the website published by the *Università Cattolica del Sacro Cuore* (Milan) in conjunction with the USC Shoa Foundation on the Sinti and Roma in Italy. That open-access site carries both interviews with survivors on record at the latter institution and synopses of historic documents on the Romani genocide.[44]

From the standpoint defended here, the many other resources of this nature in place, although of indisputable merit, do not suffice. Denser collaboration between the academy and the media is much needed. Cooperative and imaginative efforts to enhance the flow of knowledge in both directions are wanting. Whilst dissemination should assimilate and reformulate the results of academic research into formats intended for dissemination, research should also bear transfer in mind in the design of scientific projects. That necessarily means careful consideration of the language used, the approach adopted and the stories narrated.

Efforts in that respect may contribute to preventing the repetition of a series of unfortunate circumstances that surrounded one of the most iconic depictions of the Holocaust [Illustration 37]. In it Settela Steinbach, a terrified child, stares out the window of a car brimming with deportees. That image, portraying the face of a frightened little girl framed by a scarf gazing at the viewer and at what she will no longer see during her imprisonment, is actually a photogram of a short film by Rudolf Breslauer, a Jewish prisoner in the camp at Westerbork, the train's point of departure.[45] The film then proceeds to depict the operation to seal the car doors shut before the train leaves the station to carry its freight directly to Auschwitz. For a very long time the child at the window was assumed to be Jewish, and in that understanding, the photograph that showed the live gaze of a death sentence became a symbol of the Holocaust. In the Netherlands, the deportees' point of departure, Stella's picture became as famous as Anne Frank's.

Illustration 37 Settela Steinbach, photogram from the documentary filmed at Westerbock Camp, the Netherlands, 1944. A Romani girl briefly pokes her head outside the car that will carry her to Auschwitz. All the cars were subsequently sealed closed [*Open Beelden*, min 6:21 to 6:24].

In the 1990s, however, journalist Aad Wagenaar[46] researched the story behind the photo and found that it actually portrayed a nine-year-old Romani girl, Settela, one of the members of a Sinti family that was deported in its entirety to Auschwitz-Birkenau in 1944. There she, her siblings and her mother all died. When Wagenaar published a book with the results of her research, most of Dutch society reacted with disbelief and reproof, in all likelihood due not only to the reluctance to afford 'other' victims the same status as Jews, but also to scantly disguised anti-Gypsyism. Settela's story was not over yet, however. After Cherry Duyns filmed a documentary[47] based on Wagenaar's research, the book was re-edited and reached an even broader readership when it was translated into English in 2005. That version carried an afterword by academic and Romani activist Ian Hancock. Hence the disappointment visitors to Amsterdam's *Verzetsmuseum* (resistance museum) may feel when viewing the film on Westerbork in which no mention is made of Settela. The placard identifying the film continues to relate it solely to the suffering inflicted on Jewish people, amply represented in the other documents displayed in the same hall.

Settela Steinbach is the name of one of the Romanies identified by research, an exception to the general rule. The identity of the group of men and boys in the camp at Belzec portrayed in the photograph [Illustration 38] normally used to illustrate the Roma

Illustration 38 Group of Romani men and boys at Belzec Camp, Poland, 1940. There is no record of their fate [US Holocaust Museum, Washington].

genocide is completely unknown, for instance. Stories such as Settela's, once known, should not be ignored in any museum. Her case also sheds light on her mother's story, whom a survivor remembered calling to her daughter to pull away from the window to keep from being hurt, as well as her father's, a violinist who survived the concentration camp but died in 1946. Knowing the names and lives of victims is one of the keys to reparation, restoration and commemoration. Major efforts have in fact been devoted to identifying the victims of the Jewish Holocaust. Part II of this book addresses that sort of knowledge through the memoirs and testimonies of a few Romani genocide survivors afforded the opportunity to tell their stories in their own words.

PART II
MEMOIRS: REMEMBERING EVENTS LONG IGNORED

CHAPTER 4
NEITHER HEARD NOR BELIEVED: SURVIVORS' ACCOUNTS

One of the takeaways from Part I of this book is the wide variety of documentary sources that can be drawn from to study the Holocaust and more specifically to rebuild the history of Nazi persecution of Europe's Roma peoples. Information can be gleaned from legal documents such as the Auschwitz decree, police files holding ID, arrest and confiscation forms or Nazi scientists' reports confirming the Roma to be a separate race; prisoner records and camp officials' correspondence; reports drafted by commissions investigating German army crimes in situ (such as those who gathered eyewitness accounts in the former Soviet Union) and photographs and films made with all manner of intentions (for police records, scientific study or camp management, taken as souvenirs by German soldiers [Illustration 39] or by Allied forces when liberating the concentration and extermination camps). Those and others, broached with the suitable critical tools, afford the means to trace the history of the Holocaust and expose the ideological intention of negationist theories that have attempted to question its existence.

Paradoxically, the documents that contain the most direct information on racial persecution (survivals' accounts) are the ones that have been believed least worthy of recognition as historical sources. Precaution in that respect is imperative, of course, for as Primo Levi himself noted, human memory is a marvellous but flawed instrument. Such critical insight by the author of one of the most powerful descriptions of camp operation is particularly admirable. As he himself notes in the first pages of *The Drowned and the Saved*, memory is subject to the contrarious risks of forgetting some events and reformulating the ones most frequently recollected as stereotypes.[1]

As Levi knew and is common knowledge, memory also depends on the extent to which each individual represses or otherwise deals with traumatic experience. Moreover, memories change, adapt and even falsify events depending on what life thereafter brings. And yet Primo Levi's memoirs are indispensable to understanding the Holocaust. Like his, many other memoirs written by camp survivors contain a type of truth difficult to find in other records.

Any review of these accounts must nonetheless be conducted with the knowledge needed to understand and interpret them. In addition to information on the conditions in which they were written (who, when, with what intention and other questions discussed below), the reader needs to interpret them judiciously. That is something historians must be accustomed to doing with any kind of document. Using survivor memoirs to research Holocaust history involves simply making use of the tools best suited to each case, bearing in mind the nature of these documents and conscientiously choosing

Illustration 39 '**Romani prisoners lined up for execution**'. Note on the back of the photo found in the possession of a German soldier, Soviet Union, undated [NIOD, Institute for War, Holocaust and Genocide Studies, Amsterdam].

the respective analytical bounds. This chapter is consequently devoted entirely to explaining the circumstances surrounding the formulation of such memoirs, along with all their implications for the historical developments narrated. Readers are nonetheless encouraged here to consult any one of these accounts, be carried away by them, embrace what they mean in terms of human suffering and be receptive to their transparent intelligibility. Although written from the distance and prudence recommended by academic endeavour, the present study was prompted by the non-academic sentiment experienced when reading one such narrative.

What do Holocaust survivors' memoirs have to say?

The accounts written by Roma men and women who survived Nazi persecution form part of an extensive group of personal documents authored by those who witnessed the Holocaust. Given their nature and scope, the events involved have logically generated a vast corpus of testimonial literature. Different types of personal documents written during what Wieviorka called the 'era of the witness' have been progressively discovered, assessed, published and used in research.[2] Some are real-time testimonies set on paper as the events narrated were happening, such as in Anne Frank's or Victor Klemperer's famous diaries or in chronicles from ghettos in Warsaw or elsewhere. Most, however, bear retrospective witness drafted after the defeat of the Nazi regime and release of its prisoners. Some such accounts were composed very soon after the fact, such as Miklós Nyiszli's memoirs or the first volume of Primo Levi's. More often, however, they were written and published decades later, particularly in the case of Romani survivors. The second part of this book is based on a short number of memoirs published after 1985. Other series of personal documents, including letters, photos and oral testimonies also on record, are not discussed at any length here, although they are used sporadically as background for the autobiographical accounts on which these pages focus.

Memoirs are a special way of attempting to explain what the Holocaust was. Such narratives rest on the eyewitness status claimed by the author-victims, who nonetheless often lacked the energy and resources needed to record their experience until after Hitler's defeat put an (at least theoretical) end to their suffering. The authors adopt their own biographies as a guide to narrate the stories they want to tell. Although their primary objective is to bear witness to a regime of terror and death which very few survived, these narrators tend to include events in their pre- and post-Nazi life, introduced as what in their view are elements relevant to the core of their chronicle, the Holocaust.

And they are in fact relevant, even more than might initially be thought. One of the most important keys to interpreting survivors' memoirs lies in time management: their narratives move back and forth along the timeline defined by past, present and future. They describe their authors' lives, although not linearly but rather persistently revisiting one or another episode. Hence the need to bear in mind that they are formulated from 'their' respective presents, from the 'moments' when they were written and consequently to realize that they are affected by the conditions prevailing when the authors raised their voices. As Jewish Austrian psychiatrist and Holocaust survivor Viktor Frankl wrote, both the need to speak out and the difficulty to do so felt by those who came out of that infra-world alive have to do not only with the concentration camp experience per se, but also with 'how we feel now'.[3]

That keen insight was provided by someone who had to filter what he saw through professional observation to establish sufficient distance to structure his traumatic memories. 'Prisoner 119,104's Report: A Psychological Essay' was the tentative initial title of his text, whose editorial vicissitudes are discussed below. Holocaust scholars who have drawn from memoirs and more generally survival testimony as an historic source are bound to share the impression that the events recalled have been filtered. As Dominick LaCapra points out, remembrance consists not of 'pure' facts only but is influenced and altered by the subject's subsequent life, while it draws as well from collective memory.[4] As one of the few researchers who use Roma survivors' memoirs as a source, Eve Rosenhaft ponders the conditions under which these accounts were written, believing them to be closely related to their authors' life experience in post-war Germany. Another researcher, Julia von dem Knesebeck, in fact uses such documents in her study of Romani survivors' and their families' struggle in post-Hitler Germany to be officially recognized as victims. Taking Rosenhaft's approach as a guide, Knesebeck contends that just as the narratives of events in the camps are modulated by the post-war present, recollection of life prior to the genocide as described in these memoirs is formulated from the standpoint of subsequent persecution.[5]

Along those same lines, readers are forewarned that the documents inspiring the second part of this book are accounts written from the authors' respective presents, narratives that refer to a current time (and the time lapsing between the Holocaust and when the text was penned) even more directly than to Nazi persecution. That does not mean, however, that their validity as sources for learning about the past or their credibility should be questioned. Nor should they be deemed accounts that distort reality. For a very long time Holocaust historians were particularly sceptical of eyewitness narratives. The tendency to omit testimony difficult to prove in the awareness that it could potentially prompt legal action (such as the famous *Irving vs Lipstadt* case) was less the fruit of scientific uncertainty about how to broach the objectivity/subjectivity dilemma than of the priority lent to challenging denial. That meant, however, that historic research denied itself a wealth of information, while at the same time shattering Primo Levi's hope[6] that the ever wider gap between survivors' suffering and subsequent generations' comprehension would be bridged by future historians.

The foregoing is not to deny the voids, inconsistencies, contradictions or idealization present in these narratives or the fact that they are guided by specific intentions (like any other historic document, be it added). Rather, the idea is to recognize that memory is selective and even volatile, as many of the survivors explicitly state in their accounts. Paul Steinberg, for instance, author of another book essential to understanding the camp system, explains how unsettling it was to doubt the veracity of his own recollections when giving a written description of a traumatic past. He wonders why he is unable to remember the facial features of a dear friend and fellow in captivity who died at Auschwitz, but has vivid memories of the scene in which Mengele selected his victims upon arrival at the camp. When exchanging memories with another survivor, Steinberg notes, 'He's mentioned names and details I don't recall at all, just as certain people who mean something to me have left no trace in his memory.'[7]

Historians must be alert to the selective nature of memory, adjust for it with other documents, investigate gaps. But above all, they must attempt to capitalize on the density of historical material accumulated in the successive layers comprising these accounts. An event lived in 1943 and revisited in 1985 reflects the conditions prevailing in the narrator's present, in 1985, as well as those in place in 1943 (deportation to and arrival at Auschwitz, for instance). It also bears witness to what was experienced in the time between those two years (how events in 1943 marked survivors' subsequent lives and the way they lived their post-camp experience). These memoirs are a genuine historical black box. When broaching them, historians must make the effort to constantly contextualize, setting accounts against their many historical and biographical timeframes. The rewards are substantial, for they enable researchers to weave personal histories into their own explicative narratives.

Memories, then, deal with the past and present, a past formulated on the grounds of the events experienced through the time when they are recalled and mediated by the conditions under which that series of experiences can be expressed. One of the characteristics of the genre is the issue of whether writing such accounts is favoured (or obstructed) by the conditions prevailing. As a rule, Holocaust survivors cannot

Neither Heard nor Believed: Survivors' Accounts

readily find the means and time to raise their voices as witnesses. First, they have to wait some time to be able to confront an experience that was devastating in itself before starting to describe it in writing or other media. In that respect several became narrators more easily and earlier than others. As Primo Levi notes, political prisoners had a few advantages: their own ideological conscience, the objective of combating fascism, the access to positions that afforded them more information and an overview of the camp system, compared to the camp '*pariahs*', Jews and 'Gypsies'.[8] The latter, persecuted for racial reasons, were not part of a uniform, previously defined community, nor did they rally around a shared sense of combating Nazism. Some of them actually discovered their racial status when punished for it. Moreover, Jews and Romanies experienced even greater abuse than political prisoners within the multiform Nazi camp universe, which sought to erase the human condition most vigorously in the case of camp 'rubble', to borrow the term used by Simon Laks in *Music of Another World*.[9] In other words, the camp experience could not be recorded in writing at Auschwitz-Birkenau as Nico Rost did at Dachau. A Dutch anti-fascist, Rost resolved to honour the memory of his fellow combatants ('put all my might behind bringing back to life all the fallen with what I write'). He devoted his efforts in that regard to writing a marvellous diary initially as a series of scattered notes, later published in more structured form under a number of titles (the quote is translated from the Spanish edition of *Goethe en Dachau*, used here for the reasons explained in the annotated bibliography at the end of this book).[10]

Most of the survivors had to wait longer to gather the strength to face the empty page, for writing about traumatic memories reopened unhealed wounds. Many were even hard put to verbally express their experience and its impact on their later life. In the late twentieth century Reili Mettbach, a Sintizza who was a child during the Nazi persecution, told her interviewer Toby Sonneman: 'Fifteen, twenty years ago, I couldn't have talked about it. I would have got too angry and upset. I was hateful. Bitter.' Her aunt Rosa Mettbach was still unable to find the words that described her memories: 'I cannot explain how that was.'[11] Although Rosa began to overcome that mental block with Sonneman's prompting, others were never able to. One, a third member of the large Mettbach-Höllenreiner family, had lost his daughter at the Maribor Camp, after having been beaten away while trying to rescue her, still alive, from a heap of corpses. Throughout his post-war life, his mental health and social behaviour were irremediably shattered.

The sorrow inherent in remembering their own and their loved ones' suffering was intensified by the guilt collectively felt by those who ultimately became witnesses. That stemmed primarily from the very fact of survival: the weight of the thought 'why me and not them' was one of the heaviest burdens imposed by the camp system. Touched on earlier, this subject will be taken up again when voiced by the survivors. But it should be discussed here also in the context of the enormous difficulty faced by those who attempted to use their memories productively by putting together a coherent account of their experience.

The external obstacles that stood in the way of that endeavour were even greater. As many survivors discovered on their return from the camps, those who had not been involved in the system appeared to be unable or unwilling to listen to them. Steinberg expressed it in a nutshell: 'The family and friends I came home to stopped up their ears. Those who could avoid me fled.'[12]

Many found that their (according to Primo Levi, 'violent') need to tell their story ran up against a wall of incomprehension, incredulity, excuses and disinterest. Immediate post-war European societies are known to have failed to confront the Holocaust or assume the profound cultural and moral crisis it implied. In some cases the reasons were psychosocial: the troublesome acceptance of the horror personified by the survivors, the feeling of guilt around possible complicity or at least non-resistance, the need to put an end to the war. Political motivations were present in others, such as the weight and extended duration of the lack of heed to the accusations around the Holocaust raised by the Jewish community to the Allies during the war or international balance of power-related interests during the Cold War. The editorial incidents surrounding Viktor Frankl's memoirs referred to above constitute a significant example of the disinterest that prevailed for some time. Written in 1945 as a result of the author's need to relate his experience, they were published in Vienna in 1946 and translated into English in the 1950s.[13] They nonetheless made little to no impact on the book market until they were revived by a glowing review published in the early 1960s, when they became a worldwide bestseller. As noted, a number of 1960s court cases with extensive media coverage prompted Western societies to lend an earnest ear to those who talked about Nazi genocide.

Until then, survivors felt isolated and unable to communicate. It is hardly surprising that they could only broach their memories when conversing with other survivors, a community that shared the justifiable sensation that the language that served mainstream society so well as a communication tool was utterly useless to them when attempting to verbalize their experience. The threat of incredulity cast over the prisoners at the time by camp guards (who, according to some survivors, tortured them with the idea that there would be no way to prove what had happened there and that no one would grant them any credibility) became a daily nightmare that could only be banished by structured written testimony and public recognition.

Although Jewish survivors had to wait some time to be heard, Roma ex-prisoners were faced with a much longer-lasting blockade. The anti-Gypsyism legally and culturally persisting in German post-war society prevented 'Zigeuner' who had lost their families, health and possessions from demanding recognition as victims of Nazi racial policy. As explained in Chapter 3, the post-war judicial opinion that actions against the Roma people (until 1943 at least) constituted legitimate police practice not only ignored the suffering endured by many Romani victims. More significantly, it also criminalized an entire community defined in racial terms, thereby clearly prolonging Nazi discourse. The German judiciary confided more in the perpetrators than in the Roma survivors who pressed charges. That bias is clearly visible in cases such as Eva Justin's, who was acquitted on the grounds of her justification of her recommendation to sterilize a young Sintizza. She claimed to have acted out of good faith, for as the girl wanted to marry an Aryan, her sterilization would circumvent Nuremberg law provisions prohibiting mixed marriages. She contended further that the girl would be unable to return to her Romani origins because she had been raised among 'good' Germans, whereas her hypothetical descendants would inherit her biological family's asocial status. The prosecutor consequently deemed that Justin's 'preventive measure' helped the girl, whose future would have been at greater risk if she had not been sterilized.[14]

Post-war anti-Gypsyism was not only legal but obviously drew from and nourished a sociocultural bias widely extended in German society. Ceija Stojka recalls in her memoirs being the object of a racial slur hurled at her by a man in a market who, seeing her Auschwitz tattoo, called her a 'dirty Gypsy' and wondered out loud how Hitler could have allowed her to survive.[15] While such sentiments were widespread throughout Europe, they were particularly intense in Germany. Otto Rosenberg wrote that he, like many others, was obliged to work to rebuild Berlin shortly after his release from Auschwitz ('Berlin is our city too' he chose to think), while also recalling how his entitlement to German nationality was denied to him by post-war German justice. 'They said I was not a true German (…) "Gypsy. Wanderlust. Has no ties to the city of Berlin".'[16] How to speak out in such an environment? Non-recognition as victims and the extension of harassment made silence the most recommendable course, concealing the humiliation inflicted by the camp system, attempting to go unnoticed. Rosenberg would become a champion of the Romani cause years later, but could be forgiven if for some time, before new circumstances enabled him to raise his voice, he tried to hide his 'Gypsy' origins or worried about its impact on the popularity his daughter was acquiring as a singer.

The inability to communicate and the sensation of isolation were, then, very intense among the Romanies who survived Nazism. It was not until the mid-1980s that they began to be able to speak out. The suppression that prevented them from doing so started to wane thanks to the courage of a German Sintizza, Philomena Franz. Her example was soon followed by another Roma woman, Austrian Ceija Stojka. The former, able to verbalize her memories only after receiving medical attention, published her memoirs in 1985: 'It's understandable, then, that I say I wrote this manuscript on my knees and weeping.'[17] The latter published hers in 1988, after clearing a further emotional hurdle, her family's opposition. She needed to tell her story and discovered that 'Paper is patient'.[18] The example set by these two women enabled other Roma survivors to contribute to felling those barriers.

The following section discusses what prompted them to use memoir as the genre to record their thoughts and sets that urge in the context of their respective biographical pathways. Be it said here simply that writing, the medium, was instrumental to that end. Paper, not coincidentally, was a patient (to use Ceija Stojka's term) listener in whom to confide everything others could not or preferred not to hear. But writing was also the tool that served to finally widen the circle of potential listeners and readers of memoirs that narrate the history of Romani suffering. Then and now.

The Roma and the Holocaust

On behalf of Roma people

For that reason, the focus of Chapter 5 of this book is primarily on the memoirs written by Roma survivors. A small, but significantly diverse, group was chosen: three women and three men who lived through the Nazi camp system as teenagers or young adults and decades later confronted the task of organizing their remembrances as memoirs, deliberately structured around the Holocaust. Here, by way of background or corroboration, their voices are sporadically supplemented with oral testimony from others gathered under a variety of circumstances. Toby Sonneman's book based on interviews with many members of the Mettbach-Höllenreiner family contains invaluable material in that regard. Nonetheless, the voices of the aforementioned six survivors, whose intentionally chosen memoirs are discussed below in the context of their respective biographies, form the documentary core of this study.

That approach to the subject was adopted because memoirs constitute a particularly articulate literary genre for recording the testimony of witness-intermediaries while leaving ample room for reflecting on identity and politics, on both the individual and collective scales. In the books they managed to publish, these authors narrate their personal suffering while also assuming the role of the Roma people's voice. In a literate cultural medium, written memoirs vest the writer with licence to act as spokesperson. The historical interest of that effect and the analytical potential afforded by the formula, as discussed in the following chapter, offset the documentary bias that must nonetheless not be overlooked. The impact of the presence of other actors who may have mediated in these accounts must also be borne in mind. To contextualize these stories in these and other respects, this section synopsizes the lives of the survivor-authors.

It is only fair, not to mention obvious, to begin with Philomena Franz, author of the first Romani survivor memoirs and one of the loveliest accounts of the Holocaust, to use a deliberate, but descriptive, oxymoron. Franz found in her life prior to the rise of Nazism (particularly her contact with nature) a reservoir of beauty that was to help her emotionally during captivity and that she used later as a writer to create a literary style of her own. Part of a Sinti family settled in Germany for centuries, Philomena was born in 1922. Since childhood, she performed in the family's successful musical and theatrical productions featured at both the Lido in Paris and Berlin's Wintergarten. Together with her many siblings, she was raised in a semi-itinerant lifestyle, for the family alternated its seasonal tours with permanence in their own home. Hers is representative of other German Sinti families who, engaging for centuries in occupations such as music or horse trading, travelled for professional reasons but also had a permanent residence and financial resources, ultimately confiscated by the Nazis. Like other teenagers, in 1938 she was forced to leave school and work in an arms factory. Romani mobility had also been prohibited by Nazi legislation. Caught by police persecution in a steadily narrowing trap, the family was successively subjected to waves of arrests and deportations. Philomena was sent to Auschwitz in 1943 a few months before her twenty-first birthday.

Several of her attempts to flee the camps where she was imprisoned were unsuccessful. Her punishment was torture: on one occasion her sister was hanged publicly. Philomena

Franz survived, was found by Russian troops at the end of the war and returned 'home'. There she discovered that most of her family had been devoured by the camp system. To earn a living, she joined a musical troupe that performed for the Allied forces. She and a Sinto musician who had lost his wife and children at Auschwitz formed a new family, together facing daily post-war hardship with no resources. When they were allowed to live in a borrowed laundry at Cologne 'it was then we felt like genuine human beings'.[19]

Nonetheless, the worst persisted, for the experience at Auschwitz and other camps was always present, in her nightmares when asleep and as indescribable anguish when awake. Clinical treatment of what was diagnosed as depression helped her begin to face her memories head-on in the 1970s. The conclusive impetus to talk about them came, however, when she decided she had to respond to the episode mentioned earlier, when one of her children was called a 'dirty Gypsy' by a classmate. That experience, which left her with the sensation that she could do something about societal perception of her culture, paved the way to a public career. Philomena Franz began to speak at fora and was often interviewed by journalists. In 1980 she published her first book, a fairy tale. Her memoirs were released in 1985. She has been awarded any number of distinctions as a tribute to her struggle against anti-Gypsyism and all racial prejudice. Today Philomena Franz lives near Cologne. Her oeuvre has been re-edited in German several times (the version used here is the 2001 self-publication in which the author included additional texts) and has been translated into both French and Spanish.

The author who wrote the second book of memoirs on the Romani Holocaust (the first in Austria), Ceija Stojka, led a post-war life with many parallels to that of Philomena Franz, notably as regards her decision to raise her voice and fell the walls that isolated victims. But her narrative is the story of someone who was still a child when Nazi persecution was unleashed. Ceija was born in 1933 to an Austrian itinerant family engaging in horse trading. When Austria was annexed to Nazi Germany in 1938, institutional harassment quickly intensified, as discussed in Chapter 2. Ceija's parents lost their freedom to move about and were required to settle their caravan on a lot in Vienna under police surveillance. Ceija recalls her relationship to the neighbourhood and some non-Roma friends, despite Nazi racial legislation that prohibited friendship such as between her older sister and a young man deemed Aryan. Her father and older brothers were subsequently hired as mandatory factory hands while the younger siblings were allowed to continue to go to school for a few years.

A definitive blow came when Ceija's father was arrested, sent to Dachau in 1941 and murdered in 1942 as part of the Nazi's deployment of Aktion T4, a euthanistic operation implemented at Hartheim Castle. Ceija's mother Sidonie, a key figure in the memoirs, was left to care for six children until they were all also arrested and, further to the Himmler Decree, deported to Auschwitz in 1943. Ceija was not yet ten when the number Z6399 was tattooed on her arm. Her younger brother Ossi lost his battle against the typhus endemic at the Auschwitz-Birkenau Camp, while the other members of her family experienced different fates depending on system officials' capricious classifications. In 1944 her two brothers were sent to Buchenwald, while Ceija, her mother and a sister were relocated in the women's camp at Ravensbrück. Their pathways continued to diverge as the Nazi regime decomposed. Ceija and her mother were ultimately imprisoned at Bergen-Belsen until the end of the war, when they were able to return to Vienna. There the family (including in this exceptional case, nearly all her siblings) reunited.

Ceija Stojka was twelve at the time and many years had to pass before she felt able to express her experience of a childhood forfeited to Nazism. With the social and legal harassment perpetrated against Romanies persisting after Hitler's defeat, the suffering and humiliation borne could not be mentioned or recognition as victims demanded. Ceija grew up, had her own children, engaged in street trading and only began to write her story in 1986, under the urging of film-maker Karin Berger. Her first book, a brief account of her family's suffering under Nazi persecution, was published in 1988. It was written in a political environment rarefied by the debate around a Nazi past that stained the reputation of then Austrian president and former United Nations secretary general Kurt Waldheim.[20]

Beginning in those years and through her death in 2013 Ceija Stojka took to jotting down notes and writing notebooks, often illustrated with drawings. Other artistic expressions saw the light in the interim, for in writing and painting she found media in which to both express her experience as a child in the midst of the Holocaust and seek effective healing. Her works attracted interest, her paintings were exhibited, she was distinguished with prizes and a number of documentaries were filmed on her person in the 1990s and the first decade of the new century. Her accounts, aired in the context of a resolute struggle for the recognition of Roma people, both their suffering and their culture, earned her renown in Romani activism. Her successful plastic art exhibitions, in turn, worthily complemented by the documentaries filmed by Karin Berger in interviews with her, have been a very effective means of heightening societal awareness of the historic reality of the Romani genocide at the hands of the Nazis.[21] In addition to the original German edition, the French version of her first book of memoirs is used here because it includes a broader selection of texts published by the author from 1988 to 1992, along with several interviews with Berger.[22]

Two women were the first to raise their voices in writings intended for publication, attesting to a certain relationship between gender and testimonial writing. Ceija Stojka did so despite the opposition of some male members of her family, who approved neither of her opening the Pandora's box of humiliating memories nor of allowing writing to interfere with domestic tasks.[23] From this standpoint, women preceded men in confronting traumatic memory and the need to turn personal experience into a collective right, the right to express sorrow and demand recognition for victims. And they did so defying very strict cultural taboos, a risk also taken by Lily van Angeren when she published her memoirs in 1997.[24] Women may have been able to revisit their experience more effectively than men, raised along the lines of virility that the camp system fully annihilated, thanks to having had to care for their families in a context of silent resistance to the camp system. That idea is explored further in the following chapter.

Be that as it may, the gate opened by the publication of these pioneering Roma women's memoirs eventually encouraged other survivors to follow suit. In 1994 Karl Stojka released his own account through Picus, the Viennese publishers who had

Neither Heard nor Believed: Survivors' Accounts

brought one of his sister Ceija's books to market. Karl, who had lived in the United States and begun to paint in the mid-1980s, also held a solo exhibition organized by the Holocaust Memorial Museum in Washington in conjunction with the Austrian Embassy in the United States. That showing indisputably enhanced the visibility of the Romani genocide and corroborated the Stojka family's role as narrators (a third sibling, Mongo, published his own account in 2000). The catalogue to the exhibition, with brief texts in English explaining the paintings, contributed to that end.[25]

But before the English-speaking book market made a space for Romani survivor remembrance, another woman published her memoirs in a language with a shorter number of readers, Dutch. Born in Germany, Lily van Angeren (maiden name Adele Franz) recomposed her post-war life in the Netherlands and there rose to the challenge of narrating her experience of persecution, captivity and the murder of her family under Nazism. Lily van Angeren was born in 1924 to a family engaging in the itinerant occupations most commonly found among some Sinti communities: music, horse trading and street sales. She was born in a Polish town near the East Prussian border, although her family ultimately settled at Hildesheim (Lower Saxony) when Romanies were deprived of the freedom of movement. Further to the usual pattern, her father was the family's first victim of the criminal police responsible for executing Nazi racial policy. In 1938 he was arrested and sent to the Sachsenhaussen concentration camp. Lily was forced to work in a number of factories until she and other members of her family were deported to Auschwitz-Birkenau in 1943, when she was nineteen years old. There her literacy helped her survive, for she was assigned an office job which also afforded her first-hand access to information on the crimes committed at the camp.

When the *Zigeunerlager* was liquidated in 1944, Lily was transferred to Ravensbrück. Other members of her family did not survive, but she managed to elude one of the so-called 'death marches', the Nazis' attempt to erase the traces of the camp system as it collapsed. She was aided by Dutch troops and in that environment met the man who would later be her husband. In the post-war period Lily attempted to rebuild her life in the Netherlands while seeking the whereabouts of some relatives who had managed to return to Hildesheim. She bore the aching sorrow of her memories and the mortal fear of doctors left by her contact with the Auschwitz infirmary: until her children were born she harboured doubts about whether she'd been sterilized at the camp.

Converting her experience into memoirs served both a healing and a testimonial purpose. Structuring her remembrances in the form of a narrative helped her not only to face the traumas of her Nazi experience, but also to strengthen her intention to demand societal and judicial recognition of Romani genocide victims. Having worked in the Auschwitz office, Lily possessed insider knowledge of how it operated. She was consequently called as a key witness when former SS König was brought to trial in 1987. The court proceedings lasted until 1991 when the Nazi official, who had eluded any responsibility until then, was imprisoned. Lily's memoirs were published in the Netherlands in 1997, but only translated and published in German in 2004.[26] That latter edition is the one used in these pages. She was aided in writing her survivor's account in book form by editors committed to her cause such as Henry Clemens and Hans Dieter

Schmid. From then on and until her death in 2011 Lily brought her testimony to a number of public events organized to seek recognition for and conserve the memory of Romani Holocaust victims.

Just as Lily van Angeren's memoirs were the outcome of collaboration between the witness and empathetic listeners who helped draft them and ready them for publication, Walter Winter's are sourced from a series of four interviews with historians Michael Zimmermann and Thomas W. Neumann conducted from 1991 to 1998. The latter two writers transcribed and organized Winter's account with great respect for the narrator's voice and credited him with the authorship of the resulting book, published in 1999 in German.[27] In it Walter tells his story beginning with his birth in 1919 at the German city of Wittmund, Saxony. He was one of a Sinti couple's nine children. His parents, who engaged in itinerant trading and ran amusement park rides, owned property, including a permanent family home. He remembers his schooling at Wittmund fondly, in particular his participation in sports on the teams of the cities where he grew up. Both Walter and his older brother Erich stood out for their physical prowess. Anticipating trouble with the Nazis' rise to power, his father unsuccessfully tried to keep the family's Romani origins under cover.

As Nazi strike forces or police bullies tightened the circle around them, the Winters found that their teammates and professional association colleagues (their father was highly esteemed in amusement park circles) expelled them from their social circles. When war broke out, the family's automobiles were requisitioned and the men recruited. Erich was called first, followed by Walter, who served in the navy from January 1940 to March 1942. Although highly esteemed by his superiors, Walter left the navy when it became obvious to him that for racial reasons they would never trust him. At the time one of them, while admitting to understanding his decision, could not help from exclaiming, 'But good heavens, what will happen to our sports club?'[28] That was followed by a period of forced labour in local companies until 1943 when Walter, Erich and María Winter were arrested and deported to Auschwitz. All three were young and strong. The two men had military training. They survived largely because they stuck together. When the *Zigeunerlager* at Auschwitz-Birkenau was liquidated they were relocated at Ravensbrück, where María escaped. The two brothers were transferred to yet other camps (Sachsenhaussen) and, as the ultimate irony of military paradox, recruited to fight on the Eastern front, where the German army was in speedy retreat, having suffered one defeat after another. In April 1945 Walter, Erich and other prisoners were dressed in uniform, fed and sent to combat the Soviet troops. Once at their final destination, the problem was to dodge not only the bullets fired by the alleged enemy, but also by the German rank and file, who had been ordered to keep soldier-prisoners from switching to Soviet lines under the promise of liberation.

Although bearing a war wound that had not yet scarred, Walter was able to return home with his brother when fighting in Europe came to an end. The third chapter of this book begins, as the reader will recall, with the discouraging experience of these two survivors who returned only to find anti-Gypsyism persistent and some Nazi officials in their former positions, despite the country's presumed de-Nazification. In the 1990s, when Romani associationism was gathering impetus in Germany after the Dachau hunger strike, Winter began to speak in public and respond to researchers' requests to describe the events he experienced during the Holocaust. 'This book is my statement of opposition,' Winter declared, fearing that the racial discrimination and suffering inflicted by Nazism might be revived with the new ultra-right nationalist movements rearing their head at the time.[29]

As proven by Winter's case, Romani testimonial literature has been driven by the need to adopt a public position on the Holocaust inflicted on these people and at times closely related to the movement and associations demanding this minority's rights. That was true as well for the last two memoirs forming part of the documentary corpus addressed in greater detail in Chapter 5, authored by German Sinti Otto Rosenberg and Ewald Hanstein.

The former was born in 1927 and raised in Berlin by his grandmother. In 1936, when the city was preparing for the Olympic Games to be held there, Otto Rosenberg and his family were incarcerated at the Marzahn Camp for Roma. As he described it, Marzahn was an unhealthy slum where many Berliner Romanies were forced to live under police surveillance as part of a 'cleansing' operation in the Reich's capital. Otto was nine years old when he arrived at Marzahn. While living there he had to work in a local factory and became one of Eva Justin's subjects. When that camp at Berlin was closed down in 1943 he, his grandmother and other family members were deported to Auschwitz. Later when the *Zigeunerlager* was liquidated he was removed to Buchenwald and finally to Mittelbau-Dora, where many of his relatives were murdered in the gas chambers. Otto, seventeen at the time, was forced to work in the underground V2 and V1 missile factory. Among other memories of exhaustion in the final months of the war, Rosenberg recalls the specific torture of having to carry those weapons to his workplace at 3:00 AM at the lively pace set by the music played by a 'Gypsy' band. Later a 'death march' carried him to Bergen-Belsen, where he arrived with no energy to resist. He left after the SS, anticipating the imminent arrival of the Allied troops, withdrew, but only at an uncle's insistence.

As noted earlier, persistent legal and social anti-Gypsyism in post-war Germany prevented Rosenberg from demanding his rights as a victim of Nazism. It was not until the 1980s that he found an environment more favourable to confronting the sorrow and humiliation induced by his memories of both the war experience and of subsequent abuse. As a participant from then on in the Sinti movement to demand their rights, Otto became a prominent activist, engaging in both the claims for indemnity for those who had been imprisoned at Marzahn and the furtherance of a memorial to acknowledge the collective suffering of German Romanies under Nazism. He finally published his memoirs in 1998 with the collaboration of journalist Ulrich Enzensberger, who helped Rosenberg express his remembrances in writing. Originally entitled *Das Brennglas* (burning glass), they were translated immediately into English.[30] Rosenberg's memoirs are among those best known in this type of Romani literature. Their ample dissemination may be largely attributable to Petra and Marianne, his daughters, and their ongoing engagement with education and activism after Otto's death in 2001.

The Roma and the Holocaust

Ewald Hanstein's story runs parallel to Rosenberg's in several ways, although with some peculiarities. Born in 1924, he was a nineteen-year-old youth when jailed at Auschwitz.[31] During the Weimar Republic (1919–33), his father's active association with the German Communist Party in Breslavia, the city where they lived, gave him a first-hand acquaintance with SA violence. Inasmuch as the family had been singled out for their political activism, after Hitler's rise to power they sought a less exposed life in Berlin, but were imprisoned at Marzahn in 1936. Ewald nonetheless managed to escape and live in Berlin for a time, concealing his family's affiliation. He was ultimately arrested and deported to Auschwitz in 1943. Although he survived, neither his mother nor his siblings lived through imprisonment at Auschwitz-Birkenau after being sent there from Marzahn. His father, who had been arrested previously, perished at Sachsenhaussen. When the Auschwitz *Zigeunerlager* was liquidated in 1944, Ewald, after having been taken from one camp to another (including but not only Buchenwald and Mittelbau-Dora), was ultimately evacuated in one of the brutal 'death marches'. He was finally liberated by American troops in April 1945.

After unsuccessful attempts to rebuild his life in post-war Democratic Republic of Germany, he settled at Bremen. The dismissal of his claims for indemnity as a victim of Nazism in 1957 prompted him to become actively involved in Romani associationism and the defence of recognition for survivors. As speaker in schools and other public spaces, he was eventually appointed to the Heidelberg Central Council of Sinti and Roma's governing board and at the end of his life was distinguished with awards and honours for his dedication to the cause of Romani rights. It was in that context that he decided to publish his memoirs, entitled *Meine hundert Leben. Erinnerungen eines deutschen Sinto* (my one hundred lives: memoirs of a German Sinto), released just four years before his death in 2009. Like Rosenberg's, they are the outcome of transcription and editing by a collaborator, Ralf Lorenzen. In his book Ewald Hanstein recognizes how painful remembering is and understands that many cannot or prefer not to engage in that exercise: 'But I want to tell the story as it was,'[32] a self-imposed obligation driven by his long-term commitment to activism.

As must be obvious by now, a combination of two basic motivations underpinned the memorialist urge that drove these Holocaust survivors: the pursuit of emotional therapy and the need to bear witness. Those two intentions lie behind all such literature, although the balance between the two may vary. The perspective in both is forward-looking, although up to now the focus has been on a timeline running from present to past and back. But memoirs are written because there is a future, because their authors wish to influence that future. By writing and publishing their memoirs they participate in a future they hope will differ from the past–present continuum defined in terms of the Holocaust. They want a future where the weight of memory is tolerable. From that perspective, memoirs have a significant therapeutic purpose: they serve to combat isolation by engaging new audiences, even though initially the paper Ceija Stojka found so 'patient' was little more than the recipient of private notes. Memoirs also serve to vent traumas verbally, which is a key to victims' ability to bear them. Many survivors in fact mention the difficulty involved in turning fragmented images of past terror into coherent, communicable discourse. Many also note that attempts to do the opposite, forget and block painful memories, are not always successful. 'I lie awake nights and pictures from Auschwitz loom up. In the past few years it has got increasingly worse. At first I suppressed these things, now it's no longer possible. What you saw,' Walter Winter noted with regret.[33]

By formulating their memoirs, these survivors managed to work through their recollections to overcome the dramatic and traumatic reiteration so aptly likened to a nightmare. LaCapra, a specialist in the study of how the Holocaust has been depicted, distinguishes (but not to their mutual exclusion) two ways individuals may remember traumatic events. One he terms 'acting-out', the tendency to compulsively repeat the past event without taking a distance from the experience, therefore reliving the distress time and again in the present. The other, 'working-through', is what he defines as the ability to establish a mental and emotional distance between a past experience and its present expression. And whilst reformulated memory may not eliminate suffering altogether, some healing may spring from it. The latter strategy also serves a significant testimonial purpose because, according to LaCapra, it enables survivors to become political and ethical actors in their environment, voices with the authority to require listeners to adopt a position on events that call for reparation and should never occur again.[34] When Philomena Franz decided to go to her son's and then other schools to describe her suffering, she was adopting that second attitude. The subsequent formulation and publication of her memoirs consolidated that approach, not only vis-à-vis others, but inwardly: she could turn her own nightmarish remembrances into a message with social and civic intentions and content.

The process is far from simple. To begin with, it can be deeply painful, as many authors of such memoirs have pointed out. Making sense of memories in a global account entails facing up to them, digging up partially forgotten events, delving into blocked remembrance. In other words, it means reliving them. Many Holocaust victims needed outside assistance from privileged listeners who encouraged the authors to undertake the task from the perspective of its utility for society. The significant role played by these mediators between Romani survivors and potential memoir readership must be stressed, because they may have influenced how the account is presented. In that case, the orientation and scope of their modulation are items that must not be overlooked in analysis.

The several books of memoirs discussed here vary widely in that regard. In the 1985 edition of Philomena Franz's book, for instance, her own narrative ends with the war. Reinhold Lehmann, however, who authored the afterword, added a series of brief chapters on post-1945 events, drawn from conversations with Franz. Yet they are unsigned and are written in the same style as the rest of the book. According to the PhD thesis mentioned earlier, in later editions Philomena included more texts of her own and began to earn prestige as a writer above and beyond the value of the remarks added by specialists,[35] Walter Winter's and Otto Rosenberg's memoirs acquired book form with outside collaboration: Zimmermann and Neumann in the former case and Ulrich Enzensberger in the latter. In both books these mediators helped order the text by establishing a chronological structure that enhances their readability. But whereas the historians participating in Winter's book confined their remarks to a clearly defined space, an afterword bearing their signatures, in Rosenberg's memoirs the editors' notes and foreword, along with the drafter's stylistic intentions, may constitute significant interference. As Eve Rosenhaft noted, the editors (particularly in the English version) opted to present the author's voice as a scantly literate youth. However, when dictating his book Otto Rosenberg was already an experienced and highly reputed Romani activist with cultural and verbal resources differing widely from those of a spontaneous teenager whose flat prose prevails in the published account.[36] Perhaps the success of Ceija Stojka's book, in which the voice of the camp child she was appears alongside the recollections of the 55-year-old author, weighed heavily on the decision to highlight Rosenberg's youth and his age at the time of the events narrated. But that undermines the narrator's authority, for his voice in this case is minimized by literary baggage. That style, duly clarified in academically oriented notes, may likewise be attributed to Rosenberg's own desire, informed by his activism, for his memoirs to carry full testimonial and historical value. Such bias and its effect on the text vary widely from one book to another. Hanstein's and von Angeren's are also mediators who played a role in the account. Other highly respectful listeners can be identified, such as Karin Berger, who treated Ceija Stojka's voice with utmost respect in the stories they tell together.

Being aware of such mediation is part of the critical task that makes it possible to turn a document into historical material, for extra-authorial interventions that are not necessarily obvious are involved in any document in one way or another. Whilst all such materials need to be contextualized, particular precaution is called for when drawing from survivors' memoirs, as mentioned in the first few paragraphs of this chapter. That notwithstanding, memoirs are essential to understanding how and why survivors left the camps bodily and emotionally ill, as noted by Ceija Stojka herself, fearful that she might infect her children with that systemic disease.

CHAPTER 5
WHAT LANGUAGE ARE MEMORIES WRITTEN IN?

In the initial pages of the second book in his trilogy on the Holocaust, Primo Levi wondered 'in what language, in what alphabet' memories are written. He used that metaphor as a key to understanding the tricks memory plays, the events repressed that paradoxically affect both the victim of a humiliation and the perpetrator, albeit in different ways.[1] The title of this (as, obviously, of the preceding) chapter was inspired by Levi's query in anticipation of a partial answer: emotions are an element essential to the linguistics of memory in general and more specifically of the wounded memories of Holocaust survivors. That does not mean to say that emotions are the most direct or 'natural' expression of the scars victims carried as a result of their experience in concentration camps and other places where Nazi violence was inflicted. Quite the contrary: the idea is to understand emotions as a response, mediated by experience, to those events as an expressive and cognitive tool that enables survivors to come to grips with, formulate and narrate their recollection of the suffering endured.

This study subscribes to the analyses proposed by the historiographic trend known as the 'history of emotions' (for an introductory guide, see Rosenwein).[2] Further to that line of research, emotions are much more than human beings' direct, biological reaction to a series of stimuli from the outside world that induce fear, hatred, love or desire, depending on the case. Emotions, which in the past were sometimes called 'feelings' or 'passions', are also the result of how a social group lends cultural structure to the relationship between stimulus and emotive reaction and are therefore governed by historic context. Emotions believed natural and universal are actually much more narrowly bounded in space and time. What was deemed terrifying in the Middle Ages is not exactly what caused fear in the nineteenth century (Joanna Bourke, for instance, studied the peculiar fear of being buried alive that arose in the era of scientific and industrial development).[3] What was believed to be humiliating in Spain's Golden Age does not concur with what appears to be the antithesis of honour in Hitler's *Mein Kampf*. Even what people call love differs greatly, depending on the society and historic period: pure homosexual love in classical Greece, for instance, as opposed to romantic love in Victorian England.

The variety of moral codes prevailing in different countries and ages is not the only element that logically influences all manner of cultural references, among them what is deemed characteristically human feeling. Rather, each group formulates a different and changing consensus around how to express and shape emotional content: the most appropriate words, the complementary body language, the expressive limits imposed by social norms and so on. We all learn to feel in society and the expression of our emotions is instrumental to such learning. Historians such as William Reddy accord language an essential role in structuring emotion. Without words people would barely know how to feel, for they help formulate feelings, mentally and socially.[4]

Those ideas are used here to broach the memorialist literature generated by the Romani Holocaust survivors and read their accounts from a fresh vantage point. The intention is to come to understand how the survivors experienced the Holocaust on the grounds of the language of emotion present in all these texts, not only at the time of the events, but also and especially during the subsequent confrontation with their scars, their enduring memories. This book heeds the precautionary advice set out in the preceding chapter about viewing the authorship of these memoirs in the historic context prevailing when they were written. The emotions described are not the 'pure' feelings experienced in the camps, but their subsequent arduous (re)formulation to bear witness to the Holocaust. Rather than conditioning, that circumstance reinforces their validity as historic sources.

Today's words to enlighten yesterday's inaccessibility

From that perspective, emotions are a ray of light beaming through the several layers of time inherent in survivors' memories. They are, first, a way to record and report what happened in the camps and other persecution sites. Many describe fear as an ever-present fellow traveller. Recognizing the indelible mark that emotion left on victims helps acknowledge more clearly a fact that has been documented from other perspectives, namely camp guards' recourse to terror as part of a scheme designed to dominate prisoners in their everyday routine. On that first level, significant parallels can be identified between the Romani survivor memoirs reviewed here and those of other survivors who were able to write and publish their testimony in the early post–Second World War period. For instance, the bewilderment mentioned by many Romani witnesses is described in detail by Jewish psychiatrist Viktor Frankl in his memoirs written in 1945, where he analyses the paralysis stemming from that emotion as characteristic of arrival at the *Lager*, a topic discussed later in this chapter.[5]

Second, the language of emotion in which these accounts are written may serve as a map of the complex world of memory, further to Primo Levi's metaphor. In that regard, some emotions can be seen to prevail over others when reading memoirs such as analysed here. The scars left by moral injury are much more pronounced than those reminiscent of physical pain. Although physical torture in prisons and camps should not be ignored as a determinant of the emotive potential of human beings largely reduced to suffering bodies, other forms of abuse are remembered more distressfully. In the long run other forms of humiliation weighed more heavily on victims' recollections when confronting their experience. That issue is dealt with more fully below.

Third, emotions are also an expressive resource in the hands of those who attributed their isolation and exclusion precisely to their inability to find words with which to make their experience intelligible to others. Mention has been made earlier in this book of that frustration, widely shared by Holocaust survivors. Primo Levi noted that the words used prior (and subsequent) to camp incarceration are vastly insufficient to describe that context: that hunger and cold, fatigue and pain cannot express the hunger, cold, fatigue and pain experienced at Auschwitz. The Romanies who survived Auschwitz concur. According to Josef Reinhardt, 'Auschwitz – it cannot be described'. For Elisabeth Guttenberger, a survivor referred to in Chapter 2, 'Auschwitz cannot be compared to anything else'.[6] The language of emotion can serve to make up for that lack of words, affording the authors of these memoirs a dually powerful resource. On the one hand emotions help them reach an understanding of the disaster that shattered their lives, for the questions they pose are geared to deciphering what happened. They wonder, for instance, how so much hatred could have existed, how the true nature of pre-Nazi relationships with non-Roma could be defined or whether patriotic sentiment was of any value. On the other, emotion also enables victims to verbalize their memories and describe their experience in a language that invokes deep understanding. It places readers in a position requiring a reaction to first-person narratives of such pain, terror or compassion.

Lastly and very closely related to all the foregoing, emotions are Holocaust survivors' vindication, their claim for rights, voiced in their memoirs. In a parallel vein, the dehumanization on which the camp system was based entailed, among others, the 'death of feeling', as noted in Chapter 2. That phrase, cited from Steinberg, is very similar to the expression used by other survivors such as Frankl, who devoted part of his chronicle to a 'lack of feelings', reflecting on prisoners' 'emotional death' as imposed by the Nazi system.[7] Camp inmates' emotions were deliberately suppressed, obviously, and intensified by camp guards as an effective tool for nullifying any possible urge to resist spawned by rebellion or solidarity. Seen from the victims' perspective, the general recollection is that in many circumstances emotional anaesthesia prevented them from reacting with human dignity. Such brutalization weighed on their memory, creating traumas and various shades of guilt.

One of the remembrances most frequently cited in survivors' memoirs is indifference to corpses. Descriptions of the horrific scenario encountered by the Allied forces when liberating Bergen-Belsen Camp are disturbing even today when read from the comfortable distance of our homes. The common grave brimming with corpses was experienced by camp prisoners as daily, hour after hour reality. They were obliged not only to look at their co-victims' dead bodies, but to work among them, live with the ever-present stench of death and cremated human remains, searching and sometimes finding loved ones among the piles of cadavers. The assimilation of horror as routine instituted by camp officials, 'familiarization' to cite the term used by a Jewish survivor, created emotional anaesthesia that later weighed on survivors. Otto Rosenberg remembers it in his memoirs when chronicling the routine way corpses were treated at Auschwitz-Birkenau: 'Piled up. Stored. Stacked. Dumped. Always up, always up. All naked. Every evening the pile was over two meters high. And every evening a lorry with a trailer came to collect this pile and drive it to the crematorium. You don't feel anything any more. The people become, how should I say, unfeeling. They feel nothing any more.'[8] Such is the state of emotional deprivation, attendant upon physical exhaustion, that even camp liberation could be experienced with indifference. While recollecting the destruction of his sentimental fabric at Auschwitz, Primo Levi admits: 'Already for many months I had no longer felt any pain, joy or fear, except in that detached and distant manner characteristic of the *Lager*, which might be described as conditional: if I still had my former sensitivity, I thought, this would be an extremely moving moment.'[9]

Claiming the right to feel was instrumental to rebuilding individual and collective identity, an endeavour the authors of the memoirs analysed here attempted to encourage. These autobiographical accounts explore the authors' own emotions, past and present, and defend the right to recovery after the anaesthesia prompted by the constant pain inflicted by persecution. By formulating these testimonial accounts the narrators also claim their right to feelings that dignify human existence. As discussed later, recognizing the hatred generated by such persecution constitutes a way for survivors to wrest themselves from Nazi shackles by asserting their right to feel emotions without which 'we deny the divinity in us' in the words of Philomena Franz. The title of her memoirs, 'between love and hate', could hardly express that aspiration more eloquently.[10]

Bewilderment: The beginning and the end

In the memoirs analysed here and other survivors' testimonies occasionally cited as supplementary material, the words used to attempt to describe their arrival at concentration camps, Auschwitz in particular, often revolve around feelings of dismay, incredulity and confusion, with underlying bewilderment. Romani narratives mirror Jewish survivors' chronicles when recalling the sights and sounds associated with that initial numbing. Many evoke the chaos heard from inside the railway cars where they had spent days, with orders howled out over the rhythmic noise of the sealed doors being suddenly flung open. Cries of '*Alle raus*' (everybody out) were shouted over a background of barking dogs and the moaning of the newcomers. Antonin Absolon recalled the din, echoing in his oral testimony a metaphor repeatedly used by other survivors: 'I felt like I was in a bad dream.'[11]

Lights, wire fences, watch towers and barracks were the most prominent visual elements in the landscape recalled by Ewald Hanstein, as he struggled with the unsettling separation from his family: 'Where were my sisters? Where my mother and grandmother? All I could see was barbed wire on end, roofs on end, a sea of makeshift barracks.'[12] And yet what was most dismaying for those who, completely confused, were hurled onto the Auschwitz Camp in-ramp, was the human element there. On the one hand they were confronted with the guards' and their collaborators' aggression, gratuitous blows and arbitrary behaviour. On the other they were even more powerfully overcome by the state of the prisoners who had been deported to the camp earlier, described by Ceija Stojka as 'people who looked like animals, emaciated, ghostly'.[13] The sensation that none of that was or could be real was also described by Walter Winter when recalling his arrival at Auschwitz: 'You aren't seeing right,' he told himself when passing by a group of prisoners returning from work, carrying two corpses covered in blood, hands and feet tied to poles ('like deer', he thought). 'Is this going to happen to us?' he then wondered. His bewilderment grew when he reached the barracks only to find that the block elders were other prisoners who collaborated in camp surveillance: 'We stood there unable to comprehend what was happening. It was beyond description. We were completely mesmerized,' he concluded.[14]

Just as prisoner involvement in enforcing in-camp discipline was characteristic of the camp system, new prisoners' bewilderment was intentionally stoked by camp officials to dissuade any attempted disobedience. Such treatment actually began before arrival at the *Lager*. Many of the accounts of the arrest of whole Romani families abruptly deported to Auschwitz in 1943 consistently record glaring facts that reveal intentional police practice: operations were often conducted in the wee hours, pulling adults and children out of bed barely before they knew what was happening, stacking them in lorries that carried them to jail or a camp. When Ceija Stojka narrates her family's arrest (police banging on the door at night, her mother's pleas and the children's fears), she remarks how difficult it was to manage the flow of memories pouring onto the page to avoid what otherwise would be 'an endless book of suffering'. She felt her thoughts rushed much faster than her hand when recalling the details of that episode which, along with her father's arrest, marked the before and after of her family's persecution.[15]

The ritual of dispossession, head shaving and tattooing attendant upon arrival at the camp enhanced the sensation of unreality. Their own bodies were no longer recognizable, and even less those of acquaintances who had been deported earlier. Hence Ceija Stojka's inability to identify her older sister or Philomena Franz's to recognize her godmother. The astonishment induced by what appeared to be incomprehensible generated reactions that endangered prisoners. In some cases they were so numbed they were unable to protect themselves. In others, their response was irrational, as when Philomena Franz provoked the ire of the SS responsible for her deportation when she asked if she could notify her mother to bring her an overcoat. According to Viktor Frankl, such reactions (that at times preceded deportation) were one outcome of the extreme psychological shock experienced by camp newcomers. Although normally short-lived, this sensation spanned a very long emotional distance. Survivors had necessarily begun to function within what Jewish Holocaust survivor Simon Laks referred to as 'habituation', which entailed the emotional mutilation mentioned earlier.[16]

Before reaching a state in which the *Lager* became a new reality, deep suicidal temptations were not infrequent, as Viktor Frankl observed, even deeper than later when prisoners' strength had waned. Lily van Angeren described it in her memoirs, depicting herself in that extreme situation in a dialogue with the electrified fence around Auschwitz-Birkenau: 'If I fall onto you now, I could put an end to all this misery. Your electricity would alleviate hunger, cold, all the pain I'm suffering here. If I have to stay in this hell until I die, I'd prefer to go right now.'[17] On her way back she ran into another prisoner who, discovering she could read and write, landed her a job in the *Zigeunerlager* offices thanks to which she survived Auschwitz.

Even after surmounting the delirious astonishment characteristic of the initial shock and assimilating the camps' crushing daily routine (forced labour, torture, lack of privacy, hunger, disease and discretional murder) prisoners tended to seek refuge in an isolated and largely unreal world, which also severely affected their ability to feel and think. Although the camps did not even vaguely resemble closed universes, for workers and suppliers from nearby villages came and went, prisoners found it very difficult, if not impossible, to connect with the outside world. Ceija Stojka remembers one of those unusual occasions, recalling herself as a child astonished at her fleeting vision when peering from the train that carried her from Auschwitz to Ravensbrück in 1944: 'real people who worked in the fields …, pretty brown cows, … real farms with their livestock and people'.[18]

That reference to a momentary connection to life outside imprisonment, a reality with sensorial quality that for Ceija alluded, as in Plato's cave, to something perhaps once known, conveys how the bewilderment and associated emotions characteristically experienced upon arrival at the camp could be reactivated upon liberation with the arrival of the Allied troops or other events. The combination of physical exhaustion and habituation to camp life (its phantom-like image, practices that inverted any moral code, its daily Russian roulette between life and death) nourished new feelings of confusion. Initial disconcertment paradoxically came full circle because just when survivors should have felt relief, they were suddenly carried to another dimension where they were incapable of any emotional reaction. Simon Lacks assures in his memoirs that whereas the 'state of psychological stupor […] alienated from our regained freedom' declined over the years, it never disappeared altogether.[19]

One prominent component of that bewilderment was the wonder felt over just being alive. In his memoirs, Walter Winter asks how the devil he managed not to be caught in the cross-fire between Germans and Russians on the warfront where he was sent at the last moment: 'Awake at […] nights I often thought "Man, how have you managed to survive all this?"'[20] While clinging to the reply that he was young and strong, he continued to pose the question in his sleepless nights. That reaction is closely related to survivor guilt, discussed in a later section. According to Viktor Frankl, in turn, the feeling invading him in the few minutes immediately after recovering freedom was shame for not experiencing what he theoretically should have upon liberation: joy. As psychiatrist as well as survivor, Frankl tries to explain that this effect was the outcome of having lost the capacity to feel any cheer, the 'depersonalization' associated with the incredulity of recovering what had been constantly yearned for but just as constantly denied.[21]

A number of Romani survivors' testimonies provide an understanding of the cruelty of the paradox inferred by this return to the point of departure. At the end of his memoirs Ewald Hanstein narrates his liberation in a tone that mixes joy and despair. Despite the strong will that had enabled him to go on living (he acknowledges having determined to survive to be able to confront his family's murderers), Hanstein admits that the immense joy invading him with the arrival of the US troops was followed by a 'bottomless void. I looked around in envy of the cheerful American soldiers. When their "work" was over they would go home to their families. I, in contrast, had lost everything, because for a Gypsy home is where the family is'.[22] That same connection between family and return to normality as a desirable, but impossible, aspiration appears in Philomena Franz's memoirs, as she recalls the emotion felt when escaping from Ravensbrück and the parallel desire to return home to her mother. Her next immediate reaction was nonetheless endless anguish: her mother more than likely no longer lived. And besides, 'My head was shaved and I was wearing a prisoner's uniform … did I want to go home looking like that?'[23] Losing her hair was laden with cultural and social significance for Franz as a woman: it was the way her body reminded her it was not going to be easy to move from life in a concentration camp to one in freedom.

The shades of fear

Fear was indisputably one of the emotions most commonly experienced by the victims of racial persecution and deportation to the camps. Indeed, in their memoirs survivors evoke and relive the fears that emerged under those circumstances and remained instilled in them throughout their lives. Those accounts and the supplementary testimonials used here confront the reader with different degrees of an emotion that can come to be physical, like the terror described by Paul Steinberg: 'Terror differs from ordinary fear the way agony differs from simply pain. It's an explosion, a plunge into a pit of blinding light, an epileptic blackout, an orgasm without pleasure. Unlike fear, terror leaves no residue of shame.'[24] As an upper-middle-class Jew, Steinberg had never in his life before deportation felt any other fear than the agitation prompted by lavish gambling. His arrest and subsequent imprisonment at Auschwitz afforded him moments of genuine terror, as he himself admits.

Being regarded a 'Gypsy' in the interwar years familiarized those concerned with fear of persecution and police harassment, a veritable European tradition, as discussed in Chapter 1. Even so, in their memoirs Romani survivors normally identify Hitler's rise to power in 1933 with a qualitative leap in the suffering inflicted, the onset of abuse that differed from earlier persecution. Some scholars studying these narratives have pointed out that the view of pre-Nazi times might be idealized by comparison with what followed. While memory unquestionably restructures remembrance in that and other ways, objectively speaking the progressively narrower limits on Roma peoples decreed by Nazi racial legislation subjected many families to substantially greater and more frightening vulnerability. Otto Rosenberg's memoirs afford a thorough understanding of how fear grew steadily denser among the Romanies imprisoned at the Marzahn-Berlin Camp beginning in 1936. A child's awe inspired by police raids ('the police out on a gigantic spotlight and ran into the blinding light with drawn sabres – just like you sometimes see in the movies') was followed by the sensation that 'more and more people were taken away' 'never to be seen again'. When his mother failed to return from police headquarters in Berlin, from where she was taken to Ravensbrück, he waited for her until nightfall at the bus stop: 'I hardly dared to go home, because it was so dark, so lonely, but I had to go home after all.'[25]

Illustration 40 Hildegard Stein ('Lulu') holding a baby in a Hans Weltzel photo taken at Dessau-Rosslau, Germany. The portrait of this member of the Laubinger family, later deported, evokes the fate of mothers with children at Auschwitz [courtesy of the University of Liverpool Library - Special Collections].

Illustration 41 Sonderkommando works at the Auschwitz crematory, 1944. One of a series of photos taken by members of the Crematorium V command as part of an attempt at resistance and contact with the outside world [Sonderkommando photographs, material in the public domain].

What Language Are Memories Written in?

Subsequent raids that heightened the flow of deportees to the camps and ghettos were other occasions when fear dominated the Romani families arrested and carted off under chaotic circumstances. Walter Winter remembers people being crowded into Bremen jail ('the children were crying') before being sent to Auschwitz: 'It was frightful.'[26] Winter at the time was a strong young man with two similarly strong siblings; the mothers of the children in Bremen were likely to have felt more acute fear than he during deportation [Illustration 41]. Margrette Höllenreiner, for instance, who was shut with her children into one of the cattle cars used to carry prisoners from Munich to Auschwitz, recalling that experience many years later, refers to the dismay she felt for her children: 'We were terrified. No bread, no water, nothing, nothing. Nothing for the children.'[27]

Once in the camps, fear was intrinsic in the atmosphere, for there was no lack of occasions when prisoners perceived the risk of exposure to all manner of suffering. Survivors' memories afford an inkling of the layers and nuances of the fear characteristic of the *Lager*. Otto Rosenberg recalls how 'people trembled' in response to the threats hurled at them by barrack or block elders, arbitrarily designated conveyor belts of SS violence.[28] But there were moments of greater terror, when danger bore a prisoner's name (or more exactly, number), leaving them with the sensation of having been especially and irremediably threatened. Walter Winter describes the time he was about to be executed by one of the guards, who had just shot a Jewish prisoner trying to escape. 'So, now it's your turn' he told Winter while he forced him to approach the electrified fence. 'At that moment my mind went blank. I had a blackout, a complete blackout.'[29] A sudden change of heart on the part of the SS, when he asked whether Winter had been a soldier and received an affirmative answer, saved the prisoner from death just in the nick of time. On occasion those moments of terror are remembered collectively as well as personally, as exemplified by Ceija Stojka when narrating her feelings when her mother, sister and she herself were sent to the Ravensbrück infirmary to be sterilized. Earlier, they had witnessed the suffering and death of other women as a result of that operation. Along with fear, Ceija highlights another sentiment: the enormous relief, expressed with tears, when the doctor's workday finished immediately before it was their turn.[30]

As noted earlier, camp officials routinely used fear as a tool to instil domination, consciously inflicting punishment in public. Referring to such gruesome rituals, Walter Winter notes that the horror inspired by having to witness them had the desired effect of making prisoners wonder every morning whether they would make it to the end of the day. The regime of terror was implemented in many other less formal environments than hangings in the camp square. At Ravensbrück, for instance, the SS threatened the women in Ceija Stojka's group with returning them to Auschwitz and literally to the gas chambers.[31] On other occasions prisoners were suddenly and unexpectedly called out of bed for inspection in the middle of the night, subjected to simulated selection for gassing or similar threats, sometimes carried through and others not.

As Paul Steinberg recalls in his memoirs, an SS 'beat an old Gypsy and then drowned him un a puddle of water eight inches deep, pinning the man's head down with his boot. [...] "Alas, poor Gypsy"', the SS cried out without letting the man raise his head.

147

Steinberg remembers such theatrics as an expression of the pleasure some guards derived from abusing of and then killing prisoners.[32] Another survivor, Julius Hodosi, who was deported to the *Zigeunerlager* with his entire family, also relates such violence and torture to the amusement some guards drew from their own cruelty.[33] But beyond SS enjoyment and flaunting of the violence of which they were unaccountable lords as remembered by Steinberg, the primary aim was to force prisoners to internalize terror-based discipline. Such tactics, Hodosi concludes, kept prisoners in a state of permanent anguish: they never felt safe for even a single moment.

That state of low morale, heart always in throat, always expecting a beating, was fertile soil where another type of fear characteristic of the camps grew: the fear to act. Acting could draw attention and one of the unwritten rules in the *Lager* was to avoid being noticed. There were very few other rules, as there was no logic in the fortune of surviving: actions that would presumably help, such as volunteering for hard labour to avoid the gas chamber, could end in a different manner of death: the gassing order could be repealed at the last moment whilst the prisoner choosing forced labour could fall victim to its worst effects. As Otto Rosenberg puts it, he felt the urge to stay in Bergen-Belsen when the German guards vacated the camp in 1945 not only because he was too exhausted to walk but also because 'I was still afraid that I would make a mistake'. Such lessons must have instilled habits not readily shed after liberation, which was nonetheless a crucial moment that more than likely added consistency to the suite of fears that reigned in the camps. The collapse of the Nazi regime is known to have worsened the ferocity of the camp universe, triggering a mad killing spree, either in the camps themselves or subsequently in the fearful 'death marches' that devoured many of the prisoners who had endured until 1945. The arrival of the Allied troops could add to those fears. 'I did not know: did they intend us ill, or did they intend us good?' Rosenberg writes, admitting that the Allied soldiers inspired as much fear in him as the Germans. A clear expression of that can be found in the account of his brutal encounter with English troops after leaving Bergen-Belsen: lined up with a number of other prisoners, Rosenberg closed his eyes, certain that his last moment had arrived. 'Dear god, now I have survived all this time, the tortures and all the deprivations, and you have got over all the hurdles – and now they come and shoot you!' When he opened them, he discovered that the shot he heard was a photographer's flash. 'Today I would give almost anything for that photograph.'[34]

Fear, logically, becomes a habit very hard to break, particularly given that, as discussed in Chapter 3, during the post-war period Romani Holocaust victims were not acknowledged as such. Rather, they were persecuted, for mainstream society continued to suspect the entire (racial) community of delinquency. It comes as no surprise that Ceija Stojka felt 'enormous fear' when she was jailed in 1948, even though it was only for one night. When she was only fifteen, the Soviet soldiers who occupied the area of Austria where she was travelling with her mother separated her from her family and took her with other youths to the Oberwart headquarters because she had no valid ID.[35] Other episodes in her post-liberation life were similarly tinted by the fear inherited from her childhood in the camps, despite her determination to master it.

Death camp survivors, who had witnessed such extreme horror, were burdened with images very difficult to dismiss. Walter Winter, for instance, describes the sole occasion when he had to work in a gassing facility and his first-hand view of the work performed by the *Sonderkommanden*, the teams of prisoners forced to operate the gas chambers [Illustration 40]. It was one thing to 'know' that the chambers were a mass murder venue (Karl Stojka calls the pathway to the chambers as a 'highway to hell' in his memoirs) and quite something else to see them up close. Winter describes the scene and recalls having to come to an understanding with himself as observer, wondering how he could bear what he was seeing and whether he shouldn't rebel. The description of the deformed and twisted corpses, their removal with cranes and hooks and his own horrified presence, affords readers a glimpse of the images that years later continued to torture him at night. As narrated by another *Zigeunerlager* survivor mentioned in Chapter 2, Maria Peter, so much and such varied fear burrows into and permanently nests in the body. Hence the frequent nightmares that revived the pain inflicted in the camps and similar places: 'I wake up in the middle of the night and my whole body is shaking. These fear-dreams come again and again, they have become a part of me that I can never be rid of.'[36]

Hunger has its priorities

Something so closely related to fear as pain, hunger, as sensation and reality, merits attention, as another experience systematically remembered in association with suffering in camp survivors' memories. Hunger also has a powerful impact on the capacity to feel, imposing on those affected the limits of a tortured and dehumanized body. A hungry body makes finding food an imperious need, the perspective from which prisoners' reactions and ability (or inability) to generate emotional refuge must be understood. Thousands of people underwent that experience who, as Ewald Hanstein notes, 'with no name, face or history', were reduced to a starving mass.[37]

Hanstein provides readers with objective details of the diets imposed in the camps where he was imprisoned. At Auschwitz he recalls that 'the daily rations were insufficient to prevent many from dying of starvation'. At Mittelbau-Dora, where he was assigned to a forced labour detail, 'in the morning we were given a slice of bread, 20 grammes of margarine and half a spoonful of jam … That ration had to last all day'. The outcome was 'we were pure skin and bones'.[38] Circumstances worsened near the end of the war especially at places such as Bergen-Belsen, remembered by many survivors as the last step on the stairway to hell. There, Otto Rosenberg remembers being 'only skin and bones', practically unable to stand up, who like his fellows ate potato peelings, 'even though they were blue with rot. That was no longer of any importance. When you found a bone, who knows from whom, from a dog or some other animal, you broke it open and sucked it clean, just so that you had a little bit of taste'.[39] Similarly, Philomena Franz recalls internment at a smaller camp while Auschwitz-Birkenau was being torn down as: 'Hunger and nothing more than hunger. I was caught by a guardess as I tried to find a few potato peels in the kitchen trash.'[40]

That combination of undernourishment and the obligation to perform intense physical labour led to an overall state of exhaustion that killed prisoners silently, as anticipated by camp system officials and graphically described as the 'work to death' strategy discussed earlier. Those who survived saw their self-consuming bodies change in odd ways ('skeletons disguised with skin and rags'). As Viktor Frankl put it, 'Each of us could calculate with fair accuracy whose turn would be next.'[41] Such estrangement could be especially painful when prisoners were confronted with their loved ones. Upon arrival at Ravensbrück, for instance, Philomena Franz discovered that her sister was there: 'One day I ran into her face-to-face, but I failed to recognize her.'[42]

Hunger also determines priorities, a fact of life about which much has been said and written. Those able to subsist deployed all their resources to finding something to eat besides the standard watery soup. The most daring took huge risks, which proved to be a key to survival. In a concentration camp 'a piece of bread is worth more than a thousand-mark note', according to Otto Rosenberg:

> If you see that you have a chance to get something, then you have to muster all your courage to do it. I was beaten several times. I had to take this into account when I went to the kitchen to get something or other, for example potato peels or later on in Ellrich food the army threw away. I grabbed it, put it in my cup and ran. If they caught me, my number was written down. Either I was beaten immediately or I was called up later, by number. But I did not care, the main thing was that I had something to eat.[43]

In that same vein, Walter Winter gives an account of a great feat: distracting a whole bag of potatoes under the guards' very noses while unloading a lorry. Deprived of such opportunities, other prisoners, including Ceija Stojka and her mother, had no qualms about eating the weeds sprouting around the edges of the barracks or sucking on the nourishing sap of a tree they called, in reference to the value attributed it, 'the tree of life'.[44]

Hunger not only devours the body, inspiring a series of primitive reactions and repressing feelings, but may also be experienced as the source of long-lasting emotional wounds. Sophie Höllenreiner, who was deported with her children first to Auschwitz and then to Ravensbrück and Mauthausen and lastly to Bergen-Belsen ('the worst'), obtained in the fourth a piece of bread she tucked away for her children to share. As she hid it, she fondled it physically and mentally, magnifying the nourishment it would afford them. She intended to dole it out gradually, keeping some for the next day, but when one of the younger ones found it and wept, she had no choice but to hand it out immediately. The bread disappeared instantaneously and barely calmed her children's hunger. Asked years later what her worst memory was, she chose that among many other episodes: 'To this day, I still think of this piece of bread in my pocket.'[45]

In a way hunger became a symbol of a wider spectrum of suffering, a condensed summary of the camp system that did not limit its symbolic existence to memory as expressed in words, but extended menacingly into any other moment in post-camp life.

Describing with enhanced joy the view of the countryside and farm labour she observed when travelling through Austrian fields in 1948, Ceija Stojka writes that a scene of simple harvesting could suffice for an abrupt change of mood, as she relived her stay at the *Lager*: 'when I see turnips, I always feel ill: the memory of Bergen-Belsen is called up instantaneously.'[46]

Enduring wounds

Concentration camp survivors' accounts would logically be expected to narrate painful episodes. Surprisingly, however, physical pain can be found in only a few short passages. The corporal punishment inflicted by the guards is certainly portrayed in detail on occasion, including context, the thrashing, the effect on resistance. But such scenes do not abound. More than that, the bodily pain with which survivors were tortured is not uncommonly referred to in these memoirs generically, without going into detail, with admirable contention. For instance, both Walter Winter and Philomena Franz were subjected to solitary confinement in a *Stehbunker*, a very small cell with standing room only. Winter only describes the hatchway entrance. Franz claims not to know how she survived and notes that after the ordeal she had to be brought to the infirmary to cure the wounds on her arms. Both put greater expressive effort into describing their siblings' physical pain when they were punished in their respective presence: either succinctly but dramatically, as Franz does by saying she still remembers her sister's screams when hanged in public, or more descriptively, as when Winter depicts his brother's condition after being whipped by one of the camp SSs.

In any event, physical pain is not a major theme in survivors' memoirs, but more often present only between lines. That is especially obvious in comparison to the persistent mention of other types of pain that would seem to have wounded more deeply. Particularly striking in this regard is the unanimity in the memoirs reviewed here around the moral damage caused by the offence to a series of principles deemed instrumental to gender, family and social relations in Romani culture. A number of violations against such fundamentals were felt as profoundly humiliating, wounding in ways survivors felt obliged to address in their memoirs, despite the effort that required in some cases. They also reflect on the taboos they had to surmount to be able to explain how cultural precepts on which pre-Holocaust Romani identity was based were nullified in the camps. Such damage called for even more complex memory reformulation than the recollection of physical pain.

As the passages below show, such remembrances revolve around body cover, family organization, inter-sex relations and rites commemorating life events such as birth and death. The destruction of behavioural pillars in those areas severely affected personal dignity and social honour. Whilst many of such types of humiliation would be as painful for other communities of prisoners, account must be taken of the peculiarity of the *Zigeunerlager* as family camps, a scenario that intensified the suffering inflicted by the violation of ethical and aesthetic codes underpinning social relations in Romani culture. That is not to say, however, that all these prisoners were characterized by cultural uniformity. Nor should they be viewed in an anthropologically reductionist light that would very likely tend to indiscriminately attribute to them traditions more specifically characteristic of nomad groups (such as some Sinti and Lovara). In the latter, the separation between men and women and some codes of hygiene are so essential that Lily van Angeren, for instance, recalls as torment the fact that 'men were obliged to sleep in the lower bunks and women in the upper'. She goes on to explain to readers that 'among Gypsies for men to sleep underneath women is a taboo that the Germans would naturally not heed'.[47]

More generally, Romani survivors associate two specific camp venues with their recollection of humiliations difficult to forget: one was the latrines and the other the 'sauna', the building where prisoners were occasionally disinfected and deloused. When addressing what happened there they are confronted with what they themselves call a violation of essential taboos. Otto Rosenberg remembers the latrines with horror: 'That was so terrible. Women pulled a cloth over their face, but it was terrible. Here one of the greatest taboos was broken. It was a normal way of relieving yourself but a torture and insult to our people'.[48] Ewald Hanstein expressed the same feelings and in his memoirs explains what that insult meant to him:

> They took not only our lives but also our dignity. That happened especially when we answered Nature's call: the latrines were in an oblong hut with a long beam running over a ditch. There, men, women and children had to sit together, whether or not we even knew one another. For Sinti and Roma peoples, men's respect for women is particularly important.[49]

The 'sauna' was the second place associated with collective humiliation, where guards systematically showed their contempt for the need for intimacy relative to body exposure described in these memoirs. Exposure of the naked body to the rest of the community, especially by women and most painfully by older women, was experienced and remembered as an aggression that caused an impact of a magnitude difficult to express. Rosenberg recalls with particular sorrow the experience of coming face to face with his grandmother, who tried to hide behind the small child she was with: 'Then I turned away. I knew how embarrassing it was for her, in front of her grandson. Women with their grown-up sons and men, naked in front of their daughters – there can be no greater torment'.[50]

Both men and women narrate such events, although humiliation was felt differently by the two sexes. Walter Winter needs more connotative adjectives for these than for other occasions to describe his feelings when women found themselves in such a situation: 'The women stood there naked, old women too, with whom I had been acquainted prior to Auschwitz. It was shameful, humiliating, you cannot imagine'.[51] The shame of being seen naked in public perceived from a woman's perspective is present in Lily van Angeren's, Philomena Franz's and Ceija Stojka's memoirs, intensified in all three cases by the SS guards' lecherous smirks. They also often mention the deep humiliation elderly women felt when their need to cover their bodies was disdained. In their memoirs, younger women described such aggressions as a blow to all women's self-esteem, thereby raising their voices in defence of older women unable to raise theirs.

In the latter context, head shaving played a dually symbolic role, as for women it meant more than the loss of an attribute of what they deemed their femininity and an element of their beauty. It served as well as a major insult to women's honour. The issue is recalled with regret in many episodes, even before arrival at the camps. Rosenberg gives an account of an old woman in Marzahn who tried to slip by Ritter and Justin unnoticed: 'Then they cut off her hair. Just imagine, such an old woman! Then all she had on her head were these bristles!'[52] In addition, in the camps disinfection entailed shaving all bodily hair, pubic hair included. 'Especially for elder women it was a particularly unbearable humiliation,' in Lily van Angeren's words.[53] As she contends, the fact that women who had never even talked about their sex had to bear being shaved by just anyone and in the presence of the German guards contributed to her own loss of faith in a God who allowed such things. Ceija Stojka also mentioned the torture inflicted by putting the razors in the hands of prisoners, whereby a son might be forced to shave his own mother.

On occasion such accounts of the violation of cultural codes around gender and sex were underpinned by the infliction of sexual assault or abuse that scarred survivors' memories. Lily van Angeren courageously describes the time she was willing to trade her body for a potato, to be able to grant her dying brother's last wish.[54] Although it was Lily herself who consented to the cook's terms, other women came to her aid, paying the price as she 'organized' a little more food for them all. Personal suffering, in itself difficult to bear, was intensified by the sorrow of witnessing the suffering borne by others. Hermine Horvath, a survivor whose testimony is on display at the Auschwitz-Birkenau State Museum, introduces an important element to be considered in this latter regard. Remembering the predatory voracity of one of the SSs 'who took women any time and wherever he wanted', she adds: 'husbands or any other family members simply had to look away.'[55] In addition to the direct harm done to victims, then, sex violence against women could also be experienced as a blow to masculine honour, a humiliating situation that caused severe damage to the virility of those concerned and unable to react [Illustration 42].

The implications weighed on families after the war, when their relations, and male-female relations in particular, were strained by the impositions and concessions that necessarily had to be made by the family at the Auschwitz *Zigeunerlager*.[56] Other effects of life in the camps would deepen the sensation of unmitigated shame that did so much damage to the mainstays of Roma people's gender and social identity. One example was the fracture of the basic patterns of family coherence and obedience resulting from the practice of choosing young males as block elders, obviating the greater respect traditionally accorded their seniors, who were relegated to irrelevance. Another was sterilization, conducted up to the very last minute (Winter recalls his own brother's and that of other prisoners at Ravensbrück shortly before the end of the war), remembered as the irreparable deprivation of the right to have children in future.

Illustration 42 Georg Laubinger in the 1930s. Imprisoned at Buchenwald Camp in 1938, Georg was finally released from Bergen-Belsen in 1945. Neither his wife nor his children survived Nazi persecution [Courtesy of the University of Liverpool Library - Special Collections].

The denial of another essential right, to bury their dead, is likewise described as an open wound in all the survivors' memoirs. Such deprival generated especially raw pain, so ably expressed by Ceija Stojka in her account of her brother Ossi's death at Auschwitz: 'How could I forget it?' she writes, as she narrates the scene of the child dying in the infirmary, whose hand she attempts to hold. 'A guard came rushing toward me and hit me on the head, but that was nothing because my sorrow was much greater. We were not allowed to even weep over the loss of our loved one.'[57] The memoirs also form part of an effort, made long afterward, to enact the rituals owed to the dead, while claiming the acknowledgement due them as victims. Ewald Hanstein relates the two needs clearly in his memoirs when he notes that a post-war visit to the camp at Auschwitz inspired in him the courage to use the remembrance of his experience there to speak out: 'It may be the dead who give me strength.'[58]

Dignity, in the end, is a luxury reserved to the free. The camp system was designed to nullify that sensation and leave a trail of shame in its place. Walter Winter touches the raw nerve of suffering when in his memoirs he replies to an argument he very likely heard quite often in the post-war period, to the effect that people outside the camps also suffered during the war. Of course, he concedes, 'other people suffered in the war.

Soldiers too, but they had weapons and were free. When there was an air raid, they could take shelter. They could fight against the enemy they faced. We in the camps were forced to accept everything; we were completely powerless.'⁵⁹

Anger and sympathy

Although the physical and mental state in which people imprisoned in Nazi camps for racial reasons conditioned their ability to call up emotions that would nourish reactions such as resilience, survivors' memoirs devote some space to just that. Their assertions in that respect can be inferred from their accounts of two opposing feelings, anger and sympathy, as experienced both during incarceration and after liberation. Any such comparison must nonetheless be drawn against the backdrop of the osmotic relationship between the two periods established by emotive memory.

The narrators themselves tend to establish differences, aware of the crucial distance between how they may have reacted at Auschwitz and how later. That may explain why their descriptions of camp events seldom include any reference to a feeling as closely related to resistance as anger. Philomena Franz, whose determination to risk escape time and again may be attributed to the rebellious streak in her personality, gifts her readers with the depiction of a few moments of hatred representative of her resistance. As punishment for running away from Ravensbrück she was sent to Oranienburg to be interrogated and from there sent back to Auschwitz. While waiting in line for the return trip, she was singled out by the commander: 'You can be sure those wings of yours are going to be clipped,' he jeered. 'You won't fly off so quickly next time.' Philomena Franz describes her inner reaction categorically but pithily: 'I felt an irresistible temptation to gouge his eyes out.'⁶⁰

On that occasion, however, she knew she had to control her impulse. In contrast, Walter Winter describes an episode in which he and other prisoners instinctively vented their anger by beating an SS. They acted in the dark, and although the guard chosen was the least cruel of any in the camp, Winter admits they felt immediately terrified when realizing the possible consequences of their behaviour. Fury was a luxury in the camps. And yet the system filled survivors with hatred. Otto Rosenberg speaks openly about that feeling in his account of his return to Berlin on foot after liberation, a treacherous route even at that late date given the presence of sharpshooters and other hazards. The group he was in therefore decided to stop for a while at a farm where a woman lived alone with her children. He admits they did not beg for, but demanded food: 'I was full of hate and had the intention to kill. To kill all the people, not only those who had tortured us in the camp. You did not accept us as Germans, and now that we are getting out, we are going to put you Germans to death too.' But he also describes the healing power of humanitarian behaviour and his recovery when the involuntary hostess sat the group at her table: 'We stayed there for several days, or maybe one or two weeks. We slept in the house, we ate together with the children, and the woman cooked for us. In other words quite fantastic.'⁶¹

The Roma and the Holocaust

With the collapse of the Nazis, feelings of hatred and vengeance marked survivors' post-war lives. Although he left that farm as a person less haunted by primary hatred, Rosenberg describes his disturbed mental state. Ewald Hanstein, in turn, claims that his desire for revenge against those who murdered his loved ones nourished his will to survive the *Lager*. Acknowledging resentment, as other survivors (such as Jean Améry) did, converting it into part of their right to open the eyes of those who had closed them to the Holocaust, was a complex component of the attempt to process traumatic memory. It is consequently an overarching theme in survivors' testimonies that cannot be broached with inconsistent moralism. In the case of the Roma, as Eve Rosenhaft notes, it should not be seen in the light of stereotypic 'Gypsy vengeance', for the violent expression of demands for apology found in these survivors' testimonies must be understood in the context of the ongoing anti-Gypsyism in post-war Germany.[62] Otto Rosenberg's narrative on how difficult it was to obtain indemnity for the harm caused to his family (bureaucratic insistence on receiving documents that had been requisitioned by the police in the Nazi era or the requirement to exhume his mother's body) illustrates the meanness of the governmental and societal reaction to the absence of any legal or economic protection for Romani survivors in the harsh post-war years. Otto Rosenberg's memory of his anger with one official calling him a 'fat pig' and adding 'You are all Nazis' as he destroyed his desk, must be viewed against that backdrop.[63]

Hatred is a complex reaction, among others in terms of its evolution over time. In confronting his own emotions as part of the determination to deal with his traumatic memories, Walter Winter attests to the rancour he felt towards the perpetrators. In his experience, after the war there was barely any room for anything besides everyday affairs and the attempt to start over in hard times. 'It is only in the last twenty years, when things have become a little more settled, that the memories have returned and I have had to come to terms with what I experienced under the Nazis. The more I think about my suffering the more hate I feel.' That expression must also be set in its historic scenario. The rise of a Romani movement demanding redress in 1980s Germany helped Winter and others assume their (individual and collective) right to memory, a right that entailed (as his case exemplifies) the expression of feelings. The reaction of ex-Wehrmacht or SS corps members in chance encounters with former Auschwitz prisoners during summer holidays (for instance) was particularly troublesome. What to think when, seeing the number tattooed on victims' bare arms, they claimed: 'I had nothing to do with the camps'?[64]

The complexity of the emotional mix of hatred, anger and revenge can be perceived by comparing the expression of those feelings in survivors' memoirs to the space devoted by the authors to the opposite sentiments: love, sympathy and pardon. Philomena Franz embodies the most obvious intersection between the two suites of emotions. The very title of her book ('between love and hate') is an allusion to the tortuous route she had to follow to let go of her urge to wreak 'terrible revenge' alongside feelings of sympathy and pardon, at times even toward those who stood by the perpetrators.[65]

The inclusion of remembrances of scenes of sympathy described in detail symbolizes the lifeline those moments and sentiments may have been in the past and a subsequent present. Just as she acknowledges the harsh reality of other prisoners who collaborated with the system, in her memoirs Franz evokes recollections of inter-prisoner solidarity. In some cases reality is intensified and idealized a posteriori, such as when she refers to the close companionship among the Romanies at Ravensbrück extolled by the guards as an example for other groups of prisoners. In others, situations are perceived indirectly rather than as the explicit object of the episode recalled. Indications of the assistance lent to the weakest links in the chain seep through the slits in the hut where Franz underwent solitary confinement in the form of references to the cigarettes or bread she remembers being given by other prisoners. Children, either individually or collectively, also prompted protective sentiments in adults. Walter Winter felt so concerned about the welfare of the parentless children in his barracks that he asked Mengele himself for more food for them. Philomena Franz took a motherless Polish Romani girl under her wing as long as she could. Ceija Stojka remembers the affection of an elderly likewise Polish woman with no children of her own who cared for all the children in their barracks.

The authors also relive shows of sympathy by those outside the camp universe and even the camp guards, all of which rendered processing the conflicting emotions even more complicated. Franz is particularly magnanimous in her recollections. In one instance she cites a German soldier's generous moral support when he found her weeping in a park in Stuttgart because part of her family had been deported; and in another she describes how a young SS made a sincere effort to lift her spirits when she herself was sent to a camp. In a third, she remembers a woman in a town near Ravensbrück in charge of bringing food to her cell after her re-arrest following an attempted escape: 'The mayor's wife came to see me and cared for me. As she kept cows, every morning she would bring me a bowl of milk saying "drink this down quickly, child".'[66] It was also a glass of milk offered by another woman in an SS's home ('I don't know if she was his wife or a servant') that triggered affectionate memories in Rosenberg: 'That was as if the sky made the great big sun to shine and it was raining May rain – that is what it was like, such joy. Oh yes, there are still good people!'[67]

The power of small deeds that restituted some of the human dignity so intensely eroded by the camp system underlies other remembrances involving the actions of a precious few SSs. Walter Winter describes the case of one who assumed the risk of carrying messages between him and his parents. Although that was because they were acquainted before the war and had shared good times, dancing included, as young men, Winter makes a point of that generosity because 'I want it to be known'.[68] In her testimony another Auschwitz-Birkenau *Zigeunerlager* survivor, Hermine Horvath, recalls a young SS, a camp newcomer, who empathized with the sorry condition of the camp children and brought them bread from the storehouse: 'The next day this SS-man who hadn't lost his good heart wasn't there anymore. I don't know what happened to him.'[69] Acknowledging, albeit with reservations, the acts of empathy on the victimizers' end must have been difficult for victims when confronting the narrative of their memories as survivors. The reward for admitting such kind behaviour, beyond the need to continue to believe in humanity in some way, may have served as support for claiming their right to having and expressing lofty sentiments that the camp system had attempted to nullify.

The Roma and the Holocaust

Nostalgia: Yearning for places lost

In his memoirs Primo Levi evokes a feeling characteristic of concentration camps described with what he found to be a lovely German word, *Heimweh* (homesickness, longing for one's home), translated into Italian by the author as *dolore della casa*.[70] It was 'dolore' that only appeared when he wasn't working, he says, because the harsh physical punishment imposed by forced labour left no room for refuge in memory. Levi also notes, however, that when prisoners could allow themselves a small space of their own, awake or asleep, that feeling prompted surprisingly clear memories. 'Nostalgia' may be a less literal but more precise translation to express a yearning for places lost, those physical and emotional scenarios that serve to define the only thing known for sure: the place of origin.

The Romani memoirs reviewed here frequently describe the grief of remembering pre-Nazi life destroyed by racial persecution, materialized in stories about family, childhood, neighbourhood and other relationships. Studies on this genre of literature comment on their idealization of the past in the wake of camp experience. That third-party reaction is understandable, naturally. Nonetheless, in light of the conspicuous agreement in these memoirs around a series of particulars they must be interpreted as

Illustration 43 **Three Pulika family teenagers smiling for their non-Roma friend Jan Yoors.**
Pre-Nazi life is remembered by memoir authors as a relatively peaceful time [US Holocaust Memorial Museum, Washington, courtesy of Kore Yoors].

something more than romanticized remembrances of pre-1933 life. The focus should not be on the possible resemblance or otherwise to objective 'reality'. Rather, analysis of these narratives should serve to understand how Romani collective memory assessed (suffered) the loss of a series of intangibles on which the community had built a feeling of belonging, wrested from them by Nazism. The authors of these memoirs attempt to repair that pillage through their narratives, which hold the power to restore at least part of those worlds, whether real or imaginary [Illustration 43].

Evocation of home is one of the most characteristic expressions of that loss. It is woven into remembrance drawn from different environments and origins. For Philomena Franz, for instance, home is a radiant caravan fitted out with all the conveniences, a 'wondrous home on wheels', with mahogany cupboards, leaded glass mirrors, drawers for the tableware and so on.[71] It was an essential element of semi-nomadic life, for in winter they resided in their permanent family home. In contrast, for Elisabeth Guttenberger home consisted in a structure built to last in 'a very beautiful part of the city [Stuttgart] with many gardens and parks', where they lived congenially with the rest of the neighbourhood.[72] A number of other things were lost along with the narrators' abodes: whilst Guttenberger stresses the benevolent interpersonal relations with neighbours in what she refers to as the happiest period of her life, Franz underscores the beauty of the natural surroundings encountered on their journeys. Seeing spring leaves sprouting on trees, slowly growing fruit, playful sunbeams, the melodious chirping of birds and so on, she remembers it all in detail and delight, converting her memories into a lifeline during hard times.

Otto Rosenberg, in turn, remarks with pride on the dignity of the material sparsity in which they were raised by his grandmother, who 'took great care of us to make sure we were well off. We were not rich (…) she often sat there and mended stockings, or sewed a patch on a pair of trousers, or turned a shirt and a collar – we were always clean and decent'.[73] Alongside the hygiene, which contrasted with the filth reigning in the camps they were taken to, several survivors include references to family reunions, especially to the most extensive and festive, in their recollections of a home lost. Walter Winter, for instance, remembers the importance for them of meeting with family in the context of their semi-nomadic life, either in their travels from one fair to the next when their father would change their route to be able to spend the night at Walter's grandparents' home ('there we'll all be together') or sought to meet up at some stop along the way with other family members ('they simply had to see one another again').[74] Such events were necessarily celebrated with a party where music always played a prominent role [Illustration 44].

Memories of home include recollections of a series of places associated with pre-Nazi life. While the authors acknowledge the presence of anti-Gypsyism, they equate those times with amiable relations with non-Roma. Guttenberger's mention of open sociability is echoed by Lily van Angeren's recollections of neighbours whose home she visited to read with their children or Ceija Stojka's about friends in Vienna. Ewald Hanstein recalls that interpersonal relations with mainstream society were not necessarily contentious, and 'although we *Zigeuner* were always subject to prejudice and discrimination', they also enjoyed some friendly relations. Hanstein contends that in those times he had 'a happy

Illustration 44 Gustav and Rudolf Thormann at Dessau-Rosslau, Germany, 1936. Violinists in the family tradition, the two cousins fell victim to Romani genocide [Courtesy of the University of Liverpool Library - Special Collections].

childhood until the Nazis arrived'.[75] Childhood, and in that context school, were other places on the map of a lost past longed for at the camps.

Those places are associated in the narratives with feelings of safety, pleasure and joy. Philomena Franz recalls how much she learned from her grandfather, who explained the marvels of nature as they travelled. Walter Winter relates how time flew as he helped his father work their fields in winter. Lily van Angeren writes that 'life was good to us … As a child, I could play with other children as I pleased'. For her, freedom was the word that best described that childhood universe lost: 'Freedom was a luxury we pleasured in every day. We barely mentioned it then, but looking back I now realize how free we were'.[76] All these memories comprise a sentimental universe that serves as a counterpoint to feelings of a stolen childhood discussed in Part I of this book: the justifiable sensation lurking behind the complaint of those who experienced the camps as children for having been deprived of the benefits typical of early life and for barely having known what being safe or protected meant [Illustration 45].

School is also associated with nostalgia for childhood. Philomena Franz remarks on her enrolment in the schools in the towns visited, where she learned and played with other children while surprising teachers with all she knew about biology and geography. Walter Winter devotes a full chapter to school in his memoirs, first remembering a teacher who told his father he would take care of Walter if he allowed him to stay at the teacher's home to go on to secondary school, rather than conditioning his education to the opportunities open in their travels. 'I was particularly good at drawing with pencil or quill and Mr. Cordes thought I could become an architect.'[77] Although he also mentions the occasional hostility of some students (cries of 'Gypsy, Gypsy'), his overall assessment of his times as a child is benevolent. Teachers are also affectionately recalled by other survivors. Elisabeth Guttenberger, for instance, credits her survival at Auschwitz to a teacher in Stuttgart who enabled her to finish elementary school and acquire the literacy that proved to be so useful in the camp offices: 'My teacher had quite a personality and was an opponent of the Hitler regime,' she recalls.[78]

Childhood is fertile soil for feelings of belonging that spread socially into other terrains. 'How much home (*Heimat* in the original) does a person need?' asks an Austrian Jew, Jean Améry. Born as Hans Chaim Mayer, he survived Auschwitz and later went into exile in Belgium (in whose anti-fascist resistance he had participated during the war), adopting a new name and language as an outcome of the need to dissociate from German culture, where Nazism had thrived.[79] Améry committed suicide in 1978 after having published several books imperative to understanding the effects of the camp system on its victims. His oeuvre consequently contains some of the most painful and courageous reflections on all the word *Heimat* means and paradoxically cannot be fully translated to other languages (home, house, shelter, country, fatherland and so on, depending on the context). It was nonetheless the basis for the sense of origin referred to everything that ties people to places that have meaning for them, childhood being one such place, closely linked to the safety

Illustration 45 Romani family alongside their caravan photographed by Jan Yoors between 1934 and 1939. Childhood is one of the essential losses in the context of the forfeiture of happier times for those remembering the Holocaust [US Holocaust Memorial Museum, Washington, courtesy of Kore Yoors].

afforded by the family. Another, the country-nation where one believes to belong, evokes filial pride, the cultural elements of which are shared and for which some people are even prepared to give their lives.

This book views sorrow for the loss of country on the same plane as the aching for loss of home. Such yearning was felt by Romani prisoners in both the concentration camps and later after release, their lives conditioned by ongoing legal and social harassment. Any discourse on national identity included in these memoirs and other Romani testimonies must therefore not be overlooked but considered in terms of a feeling of national belonging betrayed by the brutal comparison of what was believed ('we're Germans') and the treatment received ('you're trash'). The tension between feelings of belonging and exclusion runs throughout these narratives. The former are often present in episodes where the authors explicitly perceive themselves to be German (or Austrian). Such is the case of the feelings of pride in their families' participation in the German army during the First and Second World Wars. And Walter Winter, as noted, was likewise proud of his brother's and his own prowess in sports that earned them popularity on local teams: everyone knew they were Romanies, says Winter, but they were liked and sought out. In his words, for that and other reasons during their youth they believed being legally and culturally German was compatible with being Sinti and they spoke both languages, each as appropriate.

Even at the time of their first arrest, some survivors claimed their rights from the perspective of citizens who perceived themselves as such. Lily van Angeren remembers her aunt reacting with indignation when the police denied her a service (social assistance) under the pretext that it was exclusive to Germans: 'Only Germans? What are we? Aren't we Germans? We hold German citizenship. Or did our people fight in the Great War for a country that wasn't ours?' Lily herself thought for some time that she had nothing to fear because they were Germans.[80] The Nuremberg laws and many subsequent legal and law enforcement measures made them realize that institutionally and socially, under the Nazi regime they were not in fact Germans.

But like many Jews, many Romanies refused to believe that harsh truth until they saw the concentration camps, for their lifestyles and cultural references made them feel indisputably German. Be it said that the Roma people living in areas under Third Reich rule were not a uniform community, as explained in Part I. Alongside groups who engaged in a nomadic life, more accustomed to traditional police harassment, other families had homes, jobs and relations woven into mainstream society, to the extent that they saw no contradiction in combining their two identities. There were even people of Romani descent who, far from feeling wholly outcast, participated in organizations akin to the Nazi party, in keeping with trends shared in 1930s Germany.

Self-perception as German citizens was a trap that ensnared some Romani families, delaying their reaction to the growing ferocity of legal and police aggression. Lily van Angeren recalls sharing their cell after arrest with a man dressed in tails who refused to consent to such treatment. Faced with the possibility of deportation to Poland as someone deemed to be foreign or racially inferior, the man so elegantly dressed reacted: 'They have absolutely no right ... I'm German, I carry a German passport and I work

What Language Are Memories Written in?

in this country.'[81] It is therefore not surprising that the need for attachment to country and the acrimonious destruction of those anchors during the Third Reich gave rise to glaring paradoxes. Jewish survivors described such mixed feelings as substantial to their experience, as illustrated by Imré Kertész's reflections on her Hungarian homeland in her merciless narrative, *Fateless*.[82] We also see them in Romani witnesses' memoirs, likewise expressive of the tragedy of a violently betrayed feeling of belonging. Otto Rosenberg's acknowledged childhood admiration for uniformed police and soldiers constitutes a good example [Illustration 46]. He recalls an old Prussian helmet with its classical spike, a gift from his brother Max when the family was imprisoned at Marzahn.

> I polished it until the scales shone. In those days I played a lot with the son of a Roma family who was my age. He had a little dog. And one day this little boy appeared in a military uniform, with a helmet and Swastika and combat belt and a sable, the whole works. I thought that it was lovely, I would have liked to have that too.[83]

Illustration 46 Uniformed police in charge of watching over the Marzahn-Berlin Camp.
'I must admit, I admired those soldiers, those big, blond, blue-eyed men in their pretty uniforms,' Rosenberg recalls in his memoirs as an example of how impressed he was with military poise [German Federal Archive – Digital image Archive].

The Roma and the Holocaust

Imprisonment, forced labour, deportation and above all life in the camps left the survivors with the justifiable conviction that their feelings of patriotic belonging were worth nothing, for they had been completely betrayed. Hugo Höllenreiner, interviewed by Toby Sonneman, summarized very neatly the effect of the camps on national identity, which also helps determine the relevance of Améry's question on how much fatherland people need. 'We were, and we are, German citizens. I have a family tree that shows we've lived for 500 years in Germany. We always had decent homes and jobs and we lived like any other citizens'. Nonetheless, he added, although 'I was a Munich boy, it didn't count. I was a Gypsy'.[84] Hugo and his whole family were deported to Auschwitz: he was one of the six children a desperately thrilled Sophie Höllenreiner had saved a slice of bread for at Bergen-Belsen. His cousin Ludwig, Shukar in Romanes, also allowed Sonneman to record his memories in their interview. His parents were very proud to be Germans: his father Eduard Höllenreiner had been awarded a medal in the Great War and, due to the inconsistencies of Nazi racial policy toward the Roma, was enrolled in the German army until nearly the end of the Second World War. Although that saved his wife and son from going to Auschwitz, one after another of their relatives was deported. Their home at Munich became a centre of information and refuge for those attempting to escape that fate. Eduard consequently returned from the front with his patriotic and military pride completely shattered. According to his son, he never forgave the Germans, whom he deemed murderers until the end of his days.

Guilt

As discussed in earlier sections of this book, the feelings of guilt instilled in victims by the camp system, one of the longest lasting scars of incarceration, were based on a particularly perverse mechanism. Prisoners were obliged to live in demeaning circumstances and deliberately humiliated in an attempt to sap their will and ability to resist. That left in the survivors the anguish of not having behaved with sufficient human dignity during the *Lager* ordeal. In the camps in general and Auschwitz in particular the system attacked the moral and cultural references prisoners had been raised in. As Laks summarizes in his memoirs,

> Auschwitz was a certain kind of 'negative' world to which we were abducted. White became black and black, white; values were turned around 180 degrees. To put it more emphatically, every one of us had one of two possibilities before him: either to beat and torture his neighbors or to be beaten and tortured by them. Feelings of dignity and humanity were regarded as an offense; logical reasoning, as a sign of madness; compassion, as a sign of pathology, psychic and moral.[85]

But survivors, ultimately returning to the world from which they had been abducted, demanded accountability of themselves and publicly described their experience to recover the cultural references that afforded them the dignity of which they had been deprived. Guilt therefore became a classical theme in Holocaust memorialist literature. Many survivors were tortured by the thought that they were among a precious few saved whilst vast numbers were drowned, to resort again to Primo Levi's expression. Or as Viktor Frankl said in words that likewise attest to the grief-laden relief of having escaped alive, for those who live, 'we know: the best of us did not return.'[86]

Such contradictory feelings around surviving the camp experience materialize in the Roma memoirs reviewed here in a series of introspective questions also found in other Romani as well as in Jewish accounts. One of the core themes broached is solidarity or more precisely, feeling ashamed of not having been sufficiently solidary. Under the conditions prevailing in the camps human decency was a luxury that ran counter to self survival. Nonetheless, some of these narrators recall being guilt-ridden even at the time, for deceitful camp strategy made them feel partly responsible for deaths for which only the system was to blame. In that vein Nico Rost, a famous anti-fascist, felt grief over partially causing the death of a prisoner at Dachau for not having 'organized' a piece of bread for him ('I feel abominable, as if I hadn't done my duty'), he writes in his diary on 17 April 1945.[87] Otto Rosenberg faults himself for another prisoner's suicide after having denied him a potato from his ration. 'If I had known that, I would have given him a potato. But now it's too late,' he says, summarizing in just a few words the memory of his feelings then and the anguish of reliving them.[88]

The unease over having been somehow 'privileged' by the system is another variation on this guilt complex. Clearly, those not subjected to forced labour who spent their working hours performing jobs in offices, the 'sauna', the canteen or other indoor facilities were more likely to survive. Food was also somewhat less scarce in those places. Lily van Angeren remembers the advantage she and her sister Waltraud were afforded by landing jobs in the Auschwitz-Birkenau office and infirmary, respectively, thanks to being literate. 'The sole drawback of the new job,' Lily remarks, 'was that they took me to a different barracks, away from my family', but she also notes that 'the office staff had more privileges than the other camp inmates', especially larger rations.[89] Rosenberg also notes that benefit, deeming the time spent working in the sauna as a way to recover. 'I was again able to stabilize myself.'[90] But such past benefits became a moral burden later when reflecting on their fortune as survivors, for they knew (and many acknowledged) that salvation came at the cost of others' annihilation, at times direct and open. That was how Hermine Horvath felt when remembering that the infirmary doctor saved her from the gas chamber on several occasions, favouring her over others: 'In front of the people who were selected for death I always feel ashamed, because once more I had been lucky.'[91]

At other times guilt weighed on remembrance of the rest of the family, imagined or known to be suffering more during imprisonment. When Lily van Angeren was removed to Ravensbrück she felt 'depressed and even guilty' when wondering about the fate of her sister and her family who remained at Auschwitz, whilst she in contrast received larger rations working in the new camp's infirmary. She comes back to that issue in her description of the relief she felt when she later found refuge among the Dutch liberation troops. 'We felt guilty over how well-off we were while our families continued to live that horrible nightmare.'[92] Such emotions could be even more acute after liberation and the return to life in society. In this new stage, the question posed by many survivors around why they were among the lucky few who lived through the camp experience acquired a particularly painful dimension where family members were concerned. Ewald Hanstein recalls: 'Sometimes when I go to bed I see their faces clearly around me: my mother Maria's, my father Peter's, my sisters Gertrud, Elisabeth, Lydia and Ramona's, my brother Gregor's, my grandmother's and all the others'. None of them survived Auschwitz ... why me?'[93]

Unsurprisingly, at times survivors reflect on the advantage or disadvantage of family ties in the camp context, against the backdrop of the dilemma of having to choose between solidarity and the conditions for survival. Walter Winter, who spent most of his incarceration with two young siblings, Erich and Maria, both endowed with significant resilience, wonders whether to survive it was 'more difficult being together with brothers, with family, than being alone', without coming to any clear-cut conclusion: 'It was sometimes advantageous and sometimes not.'[94] A sibling's support and protection, such as in the case recollected, could obviously be an advantage, but having to protect could be a drawback, for that self-demand put a further stain on prisoners' strength, already stretched to the limit. Otto Rosenberg believes it was better to be alone, for that way behaviours and decisions affected no one else: 'What I wanted to do, that I decided for myself and did it too. That was one reason why I survived.'[95] His grandmother, with several family children under her wing at Auschwitz, was taken to the gas chamber when the camp was evacuated.

Several survivors recall liquidation of the Auschwitz *Zigeunerlager* in terms of intra-family tension intertwined with feelings of guilt. Such an event could hardly be remembered any other way, given how camp officials handled evacuation in August 1944. Before all the surviving Romanies at Auschwitz were sent to the gas chamber, those still able to work were relocated at Ravensbrück and other camps. Many survivors remember the anguish of separation from their families as rumours flew about the fate awaiting one and the other group. Amelie Schaich, for instance, a teenager sent to the *Zigeunerlager* from Mulfingen orphanage, remembers the last words she heard from her younger siblings: 'You're leaving and we will be burned.'[96] That the scene may have been partially rewritten a posteriori by a tortured memory (Amelie may not have in fact known her siblings' fate and recomposed that tragic moment later, after being told of the mass murder of all the Roma prisoners who remained at Auschwitz) is of scant relevance here. What Amelie felt when recalling that moment was that her own salvation was a debt owed to her dead siblings.

Walter Winter's more structured narrative provides details about those events and unravels the knot of tensions and feelings of guilt that afflicted survivors. His account describes the tragic regrouping of prisoners to be relocated immediately before camp liquidation from the perspective of someone chosen to leave. Those few were told that if they had served in the German army they could take close family members with them.

What Language Are Memories Written in?

According to Winter, of the 500 Wehrmacht soldiers who had been deported, only around 150 were still living. Despite his lack of authorial skill, his description of the conditions in which the operation took place is gripping. When the ex-soldier prisoners were called up by their number, they were to step forward and point to the family members who would board the lorries to be taken from Auschwitz. Walter Winter writes that when his turn came, his sister, two cousins and a few other relatives were lined up behind him, but he had to run to find his wife (a prisoner whom he had said he married solely to be able to substantiate the family relationship). Prepared finally to answer when his number was called, he felt someone pull on his shirt and beg in Romanes: 'Walter, take us with you.' He turned to see an old acquaintance standing behind him with her husband and six-month old baby. On hearing his number called for the third time, at the last minute just as the door was closing, he managed to get his entire group into the lorries leaving Auschwitz. He says he felt a wave of relief at the time, but adds: 'I wanted to take the entire block – the entire camp – but it wasn't possible.'[97]

Just as Winter remembers all those he was unable to take with him, when Hanstein describes his own survival at the end of his memoirs he explicitly mentions memories of his mother and six siblings who did not leave Auschwitz, whilst he was sent to another camp as a useful worker. Casting blame on those not responsible was a form of torture the *Lager* inflicted even after closure, a post mortem achievement forming part of its basic mechanism consisting in requiring prisoners to participate in many ways in upholding the camp system. In that respect liberation offered little respite, as Hanstein notes. He contends that whilst the arrival of the allied soldiers saved the victims from dying of hunger, cold or disease, no one could free them of the remembrance of their experience, tattooed on their minds as indelibly as the prisoner's number on their arms.[98]

From disappointment to distress to mistrust

According to Viktor Frankl, the two sentiments that prevailed among survivors trying to recompose their lives after liberation from the Nazi camps were bitterness and disillusionment. The former arose in response to coming home to find all or some loved ones missing or to repeatedly hearing from friends or relatives that 'we suffered too'. The latter came after realizing that the happiness so long yearned for during imprisonment could not be restored because suffering persisted in the form of memory, as Hanstein noted. Going home, or what was left of it, was particularly difficult for Romani Holocaust survivors, both for the type of existential suffering so familiar to anyone who had left the *Lager* alive and for the specific circumstances that characterized Romani families' lives in post-Nazi Germany (and Europe).

As discussed in Chapter 3, until quite a few years after the war German society and hence international public opinion failed to collectively come to terms with the fact that the population as a whole stood largely behind the Nazi regime. In the interim many survivors of Nazi racial persecution lived cloaked in a silence only broken by organizations able to demand acknowledgement of responsibility. A number of Jewish agencies helped thousands of people institute proceedings for redress with the appropriate authorities or leave the countries where they had been persecuted, en route to a new life in Israel. Even so, the severity of the Holocaust was not addressed by the societies that had been involved in the Second World War until the 1960s, when a number of high-profile cases and historic research positioned the issue on their moral and cultural agendas.

As noted earlier, however, the Jewish Holocaust became an essential public issue for European social conscience considerably sooner than when the general public began to acknowledge the existence of Romani genocide (in research, legal proceedings or memory). Therefore the devastation of returning to a home where no one was waiting for them persisted among Roma survivors for a very long time. The 'none of us should have come back' uttered by French Resistance participant Charlotte Delbo, who survived Auschwitz, may have acquired even deeper meaning for Romani survivors in Germany due to the incredibly long time social silence lasted.[99] Even as recently as the early 1990s, Ludwig-Shukar Höllenreiner, who had lived in a number of Nazi camps as a child, contended that nothing had changed since the end of the war. As he explained in an interview, Germans had not assimilated the genocide of the Roma people, eluding all responsibility by simply laying the blame on Hitler. Particularly galling was the persistence of that immediate post-war attitude fifty years later. He told interviewer Toby Sonneman that he would answer her questions because she was from the United States and he hoped his words would be heeded in that country, whereas in his own they were taken as lies or overstatements. 'I wouldn't tell this to a German. It goes in one ear and out the other. Half of them don't believe you. They think it is a made-up story.'[100]

That impression could be perceived very early on, even upon liberation itself, as can be gathered from Lily van Angeren's account of her encounter with the Allied troops:

> No matter who did the interrogating, they mistrusted us. Why had we been arrested? What had we done? Where had we been jailed? ... The same as an SS inquiry, but by police wearing a different uniform. Almost no-one believed our story. It was very hard to convince them that being Gypsy sufficed to be sent to a concentration camp. We were tremendously frustrated by that disbelief, but it didn't matter to anyone.[101]

As can be inferred from that account, the anguish felt by other groups of survivors was intensified among the Roma due to the peculiarity of their racial exclusion and the disbelief around their description of what had happened in the camps. The sceptical attitude of the allied troops who questioned van Angeren was no more than the tip of the iceberg of the underlying suspicion of delinquency to which all Romani survivors were subject, prolonging Nazi anti-Gypsy discourse.

Lily van Angeren ultimately found a new life in the Netherlands, although not before managing to solve the bureaucratic problems stemming from having no official papers. Most of the Romani survivors whose testimony is discussed here, however, had to remain in Germany (or Austria), living in racially hostile societies while contending with the very harsh circumstances characterizing the post-war economy. With no governmental assistance and little or nothing to start from after Nazi seizure of their assets, Romanies were hard put to reorganize family life, typically riddled with new suffering. Philomena Franz and her husband engaged first in musical performances and then in selling antiques in Cologne, initially enduring much hardship to be able to support their children. The Winters, in turn, managed to found a small company that provided amenities (e.g. jugglers, acrobats) in fairs, despite all the bureaucratic hurdles. The work involved was so intense at first that, as mentioned earlier, Walter was scantly able to find the time to devote to remembering the past. Rosenberg and Hanstein went from job to job and from one place of abode to another (the latter moving from the German Democratic to the Federal Republic) before forming their own families. The Stojkas first occupied a flat left vacant by the Nazi collaborator owners, but returned to their itinerant lifestyle when the latter recovered it. On reaching adulthood Karl decided to leave Austria. After enrolling in the French Foreign Legion he emigrated to the United States, whereas Ceija had children very early on and stayed in Vienna, where she worked with her mother selling rugs. In all these cases, the initial paucity of resources made the return to life in freedom very difficult. Otto Rosenberg, for instance, remembers that the caravan where they first lived was so cold in winter that their small daughter had to wear gloves in bed.

The sentiment prevailing under such conditions was distress, due in Rosenberg's case, for instance, to the recurrence of the troubling question of why he had survived and his siblings and other relatives hadn't.

> The whole family (…) not one person was able to survive. Even though my brothers were much stronger and tougher than I. I was the smallest! I cannot understand that. They say: you have your freedom now, be happy. There was no way I could be all that joyful, because I missed my brothers and sisters, always, to this very day. When the holidays came and people celebrated, or the families sat together, that was when this inner thing, this nervous strain came. That was very hard.[102]

Hanstein's memoirs relate similar feelings. With their narratives, both introduce the reader to their grim post-war state of mind, beset by chagrin over the loss of their respective families, several generations of which were practically annihilated [Illustration 47]. Despair over the loss of the possibility of fatherhood intensified the grief in some cases, projecting the harm done in the camps into the future. 'A great sorrow' is what Sophie Höllenreiner felt for her son Mano even fifty years after he was sterilized at Ravensbrück as a young boy.[103]

Disappointment and distress go hand-in-hand with a third feature characteristic of the emotional attitude prevailing among Romani survivors: mistrust. Walter Winter explains the reasons by comparing social relations in his father's day to his own work environment, identifying a huge difference before and after the war. His very sociable father, he says, was on friendly terms with his amusement park ride colleagues. He was very popular, always inviting the others to a round of drinks. 'But today I am a different person. What I have been through has made me distrustful. Totally distrusting. In the past I was not so.'[104] As Rosenhaft notes, that wariness, widely shared by Romani survivors in post-war Germany, was the logical outcome of a series of experiences where the trust placed in others had been betrayed in one way or another under Nazi rule.[105] That was often because the scientists and engineers who worked for the Ritter racial unit not only pressured those they wanted to study and classify with ethnographic methods, but also often approached them with empathy or a friendly attitude. Eva Justin, who spoke Romanes well, earned such trust among her interviewees that they gave her a name in their language, Lolitschai [Illustration 48]. Like her, other professionals who had focused attention on the Roma were often seen, if not as friends, at least as potential

Illustration 47 Laubinger family men posing for a group photo, Dessau-Rosslau, Germany, 1935. Photo dated only a few years prior to a series of arrests and deportations that took the lives of several generations of this family [Courtesy of the University of Liverpool Library – Special Collections].

intermediaries with the authorities, a possible aid as police harassment intensified. Photographer Hans Weltzel and the Laubinger family provide an example of the close relationship at times established between observer and observed [Illustration 49].[106]

Although the intentions differed greatly from case to case, from Justin's open manipulation to Weltzel's dubious responsibility, the hopes of any possible support or collaboration were ultimately dashed. Moreover, feelings of trust betrayed were deepened by the knowledge that such relationships enabled non-Romanies to gather information on Roma genealogies and lifestyles. And whilst the reasons that led some Romani patriarchs to furnish Nazi authorities with data (in the context of Himmler's plans for a racial reserve), transferring that information had obviously pernicious effects that contributed further to post-war suspicion and scepticism. Those sentiments were reinforced by the survivors' awareness that informers in the Romani community had collaborated with the Nazi racial police, as Walter Winter recalls about a relative known to have participated in such betrayals who arrived at Auschwitz so branded.

There was very good reason for mistrust to spread quickly after the war, complicating even more the already difficult determination to start over. On the one hand the camp-imposed severance of traditional hierarchies and gender codes induced tension in post-war family life. On the other, whole sets of rules governing social behaviour were invalidated by the realization that Romani efforts to live on congenial terms with non-Roma society had been completely ignored. Walter Winter's memoirs include an account of his disappointment over the futility of his strenuous endeavour to behave

Illustration 48 Eva Justin interviewing Romani women and children in Racial Hygiene Unit, photograph taken between 1936 and 1940. 'Participatory observation' was a technique in which subjects were tricked into trusting the interviewer [German Federal Archive – Digital image archive].

Illustration 49 Hedwig Laubinger-Steinbach posing for Hans Weltzel at Dessau-Roßlau in 1939. The friendly relations between photographer and family proved to be of no assistance to the Laubingers when deported, although Hedwig managed to survive in hiding during the war [Courtesy of the University of Liverpool Library - Special Collections].

further to the instructions received on integrating his Romani legacy into mainstream social life. He notes that his stay in the army revealed the uselessness of his determination to progress, even though his attempts to meet all his obligations could hardly have gone unnoticed by his superiors. 'We Sinti were motivated. "Be inconspicuous! Always be, when possible, better than the others!" So that they could not call us "asocial" or "lazy". This ambition was second nature, "You must be better than the others, so as not to stand out".'[107]

Given how little it helped to waste emotional intelligence on that determination, Romani genocide survivors and their families were more often than not faced in the post-war period with the complex challenge of reinventing a cultural space that could serve as guides to social behaviour. Some assumed the need to reflect on their individual and collective identity: writing memoirs was a way to tackle the elusive redefinition of identity, retaining ties to the past while pursuing future commitments.

Pride, courage, values, power

The autobiographies of Romani survivors meditate on their identity, introducing their readers to all the features they deem characteristic of their sense of being as individuals as well as members of the community. In some cases, such meditation is explicit, as in the case of pioneers Philomena Franz and Ceija Stojka, whereas in others it can only be perceived by reading between the lines. Whether one or the other, that exercise attests to the effort involved in facing the difficult task of structuring survivors' traumatic memories of the Holocaust while also attempting to build bridges between past and future by writing about them.

Their stories consequently include considerations around Romani identity, cultural fundamentals and connections to mainstream culture. Such considerations embody power, clearly political power in the fullest meaning of the term: they appeal to potential readers with an attitude that demands societal change. Adopting such a position in the political and collective domain is on occasion attendant also upon making decisions about individual identity and how it plays out within community bounds. In both regards, the endeavour seeks not only to conserve elements characteristic of Romani cultural but to ensure their future relevance.

When they refer to their own and their families' lives before the Holocaust in their memoirs, survivors assume the responsibility of informing readers about their culture. They master the mistrust referred to in the preceding section and attempt with an abridged description to demand respect for what they deem to be Romani customs and values and thereby portray their culture in a favourable light [Illustration 50]. Where Philomena Franz describes how the Sinti lived in harmony with nature and honoured their elders, Walter Winter stresses the importance of work and exertion in his family. Otto Rosenberg highlights the affection with which children were raised and Ceija Stojka the meaning of music as a social and family cultural heritage, an element also emphasized as essential to Romani identity by other authors. At times the minor details remembered acquire exemplary value, such as in Franz's description of family meals around the hearth: 'We fried bacon and put potatoes in the fire. We had roasted apples for dessert. We drank sour milk my grandmother served in clay bowls with a thick layer of cream on top.'[108] It is up to readers to compare that domestic abundance to camp system starvation rations and wonder about such meaningless loss (drawing similar conclusions by contrasting the cleanliness of narrators' homes to camp squalor).

One especially interesting feature of these accounts is that nearly all stress the narrator's ability to read and write. Whilst Roma culture is commonly believed by mainstream society to be essentially illiterate, these memoirs include specific claims to the contrary: 'We all knew how to read and write. How could we have learnt our lines otherwise?' asks Philomena Franz, referring to her family's theatrical performances.[109] Ewald Hanstein explicitly remembers being taught to read and write by his mother, setting that legacy on an equal footing with the musical and political training received from his father.[110] In her account, Lily van Angeren refers to how much she loved learning to read and fondly relates her parents' insistence that she go to school and do her homework.[111] Otto Rosenberg, in turn, while regretting that a childhood spent in concentration camps deprived him of the opportunity to attend school, proudly recalls that some members of his family owned books and drafted and elegantly penned texts for others.[112]

The Roma and the Holocaust

Using memoirs as the primary substantiation of the discussion in this chapter indisputably magnifies the prevalence of literacy, a bias addressed in the introduction, although it is no less indisputable that orality was a core feature of Romani culture for centuries. Nonetheless, the 'illiterate Gypsy' stereotype not only undervalues non-written forms of culture but is a prejudice of unjustifiable breadth that attributes a lack of cultural heritage to an entire people. The authors of these memoirs make an effort to refute that as well as other stereotypes. To that end, they refer in their accounts to reading and writing as forms of expression not foreign to traditional Romani culture, while acknowledging their immediate importance to them personally as a key to fulfilling the self-imposed obligation to bear witness to and demand responsibility for the Holocaust. Whereas Walter Winter regrets not having written down the names of the Auschwitz Camp guards, Ceija Stojka is keenly aware that she must rely on the written record of her remembrances to claim a place in her country's memory of Romani victims of the Nazi regime.

Here the question is not to simply acknowledge the power of print as mainstream society's most prominent cultural vehicle, but rather to reinterpret writing as a narrative format compatible with Romani culture and usable by Romani authors. These memoirs therefore constitute powerful tools: the power to refute stereotypes, to demand a place in official memory, to describe shared history in their own telling, to open eyes and ears and so on. This crossroads of cultural, biographical and political coordinates generated a specifically Romani literature characterized by culture-specific themes and original narrative styles, as discussed by Marianne Zwicker.[113] The claim that their culture can also be expressed in writing does not, however, entail forsaking oral tradition, but rather invokes its reformulation in a number of directions. The value of traditional oral storytelling, its role as an element in conveying collective memory and the role of the elderly in that task are all present in these memoirs of the Holocaust. References can be found when they call up life prior to persecution or when they describe episodes under Nazi rule that attest to the effort to keep a record of acts of cohesion and emotional consolation.

Otto Rosenberg, for instance, relives the image of his grandmother telling stories for their group during reclusion at Marzahn and Ceija Stojka remembers her mother in that same role in the camps where they were imprisoned. But aware that the camp system had annihilated most of the community storytellers, this new generation of narrators seeks formulas to prevent the loss of such a vast cultural capital. Some pay tribute to storytelling in their recollections, including it in their summary of the features comprising the core of a culture that needed to be conserved in the face of the extinction threatened by the Nazi regime. Such oral narration and memory stand alongside music, care for the weak, communion with nature and love of freedom as the building blocks of a collective Romani identity that rests on this and similar discourse. In that context, writing memoirs must be viewed against the backdrop of the Romani associational movement that was emerging not only in Germany but in other regions, as discussed earlier. In 1961 Ionel Rotaru, pioneer of the French movement, summarized the features he deemed to form Romani cultural identity for an Israeli journalist interested in an international organization presided by his interviewee. The list included elderly storytellers, understood as guardians of community tradition.[114]

The authors of the memoirs reviewed here contribute to the attempt to propel Romani oral tradition toward the future, given its malleability, comparable to that of written sources, and its susceptibility to restructuring in new surrounds. First, the short stories, poems or short-short stories included by Philomena Franz and Ceija Stojka in later editions or whole new versions of their autobiographies quite obviously drew for inspiration from community oral tradition, as respects style and plots both.[115] Second, the decision to raise their voice publicly induced these authors and the other narrators discussed here to speak at schools for Roma and non-Roma audiences, as well as in other settings, thereby broadening oral narrative and vesting it with new civic meaning. That reformulation of orality, alongside literary activity, gave narrators such as Franz and Stojka power as women whose ability to communicate and represent was ultimately acknowledged both in- and outside the Romani community.

The interpretation of women's role in Romani culture is where these authors build another bridge connecting past and future [Illustration 51]. The gender-related peculiarity of the earliest survivor literature on the Romani Holocaust was mentioned in a previous section: the first authors to use this narrative format to fell the walls of silence were women. And by adopting written and published testimony as their vehicle of expression, they changed the rules of gender behaviour in the family and social environments in which they had been raised, understood as cultural references lying at the root of family and social architecture in any human community. The everyday routine imposed by the camp system had obliterated the shared cultural patterns that make harmonious interpersonal relations possible and generate social cohesion. Elders' authority had been undermined, men's honour destroyed, respect for women annihilated and so on. During the post-war period, some Romani survivors defied the still (albeit precariously) persistent limits defined for the two sexes' behaviour and the expression of their respective roles to fulfil their self-imposed duty to bear witness to the Holocaust.

From that perspective, in her memoirs Lily van Angeren discusses her very personal dilemma in a manner potentially beneficial to others. On the one hand, she informs the reader how certain taboos weighed on her as a member of the Romani community, such as any mention of her woman's body which should never be a subject of public conversation but at most dealt with discreetly with other women in the family. Public mention of operations, pregnancies and childbearing, including Nazi physicians' conduct in those regards, is 'taboo for us'. And yet when she poses the question of whether those community rules should perpetuate the silence around what the Roma suffered under the Nazi regime, all that was done to them against their will, she decides: 'I can ignore my taboos, even if only to ensure the half-million "Zigeuner" gassed under Hitler's rule are not forgotten, but I cannot ignore those upheld by others. That would be immoral.'[116] Hers is consequently an account referred solely to her own experience in shattering taboos that respectfully avoids any reference to other cases. It is an option chosen to bravely clear the path for other women.

Romani women's ability to work around gender identities to comply with what they deemed their duty to bear witness to the Holocaust and its consequences can also be found in Ceija Stojka's accounts. As she told Karin Berger in a conversation subsequently published by the latter, her partner could not understand why she would take up a pen for anything else than to write a postcard to their children, to be read by them only. Women were bound by the limits of discretion and the private dimension. For that reason, Ceija began to write her memoirs only when she was alone, seeking times of brief respite from her household chores. As she cooked and cleaned, she says, she continued to write mentally, returning to the open universe of the written page.[117] Without shirking from her inherited role, whereby home and kitchen were her assigned territory (Berger remembers her busy cooking meals during their interviews), Stojka began to occupy formerly unprecedented public spaces: publishing companies, exhibition halls and other venues.

The private realm was compatibilized with the public dimension in a number of ways. Taking a stand in an area so apparently private (albeit socially determined) as gender roles has roots in as well as effects on presence in the public arena. Ceija Stojka needed to widen the circle of potentially feminine tasks within the Romani community because she wanted to claim a place for Nazi genocide victims in her country's social conscience and memory. As Zwicker notes, the intention to leave a record of their testimony as survivors in connection with the demand to be able to call Austria or Germany their 'country' is present in both Stojka's and Philomena Franz's oeuvre.[118] That demand for fatherland is formulated in both their memoirs in the form of a story that remembers and emotionally reformulates pre-Nazi life landscapes, primarily rural in Franz's book and urban in Stojka's.

To nullify the pernicious effect of Nazism on that feeling of belonging, in their memoirs these authors call upon German and Austrian society to assume the Romani Holocaust as a component of the national past and consequently of its present official memory. They afford the fatherland a new opportunity in an attempt to include Roma in its history, integrated not only in the official accounts of the tragic events of the Holocaust but also in the heritage inherent in Romani communities' historic presence on national soil. The use of German as the language of Franz's and Stojka's memoirs carries a message to the effect that 'we form part of a culture that expresses itself in that language'. In a similar vein, Ceija Stojka's use of phrases in Romanes in some paragraphs of her book denotes the assertion of her right to deem the roots of her two cultural identities to be compatible.

At a time when an autonomous associational movement was consolidating, it comes as no surprise that such positions both made an impact on and were influenced by the discourse conveyed by Romani platforms and representatives. Nor should the differences in the meaning attributed to the term fatherland in these autobiographies be deemed unusual. Ceija's brother Karl Stojka, writing his after she had published hers, opts for interpreting Romani identity as something not rooted in any given country, but as a suite of cultural features shared by his people internationally.[119] Other memoirs are very closely linked to their authors' activism, as noted in connection with Hanstein and Rosenberg. At the same time, the new political-cultural atmosphere that, beginning in the 1980s, encouraged Romani survivors to raise their voices, rendered testimonies of people not directly involved with the organized Sinti and Roma movement likewise very timely. Nonetheless, in one way or another and by way of conclusion, this set of documents identifies a series of political values. The pithy opening sentences in Philomena Franz's introduction to her memoirs illustrate that point very clearly: 'We are all entitled, even today, to talk about our suffering. To find ourselves anew, to honour the victims and to tell the young: that was the way it was and it should never happen again.'[120]

As Franz notes, these narrators are exercising a right. The decision itself to do so calls for courage, an attitude generally acknowledged by their editors and collaborators. To cite only a couple of examples, it is highlighted by Ralf Lorenzen and Henning Scherf, authors, respectively, of the foreword and afterword to Ewald Hanstein's memoirs; and Wim Willems who titled his introductory comments to Lily van Angeren's account 'The courage to testify'.[121] That right and that courage, beyond any personal therapeutic value for the narrators themselves, are understood by the survivors to be the outcome of a dual commitment to their community. On the one hand, they acknowledge a debt to the fallen, with their 'message from the murder victims', as Ewald Hanstein belligerently contends. 'We need no memory that evades the confrontation between victims and executioners to relieve consciences. We need memory present in the railway cars, on the [selection] ramp, that sees faces, that hears cries of despair.'[122]

At the same time, they hope with their written testimony to contribute to the project of building a different future for later generations. They aim both to make youngsters socialized in the mainstream culture aware of what happened and understand where racial cleansing policies can lead (summarized in the refrain that it should never happen again) and to enable further generations of Romanies to value and preserve their cultural legacy and history. These narrators' focus on portraying the Roma people in a positive light in contrast to the prevailing stereotypes is consequently attendant at times upon an appeal to an ideal interethnic Roma and non-Roma readership. The challenge they pose themselves is huge and not only for obvious reasons, such as the persistence of cultural racism, the self-interested political use of demands, the emergence of new and different educational priorities, the tendency of any society to engage in collective amnesia around disturbing episodes of its past and so on. It also involved grounding future Romani identity on more than their people's status as Holocaust victims, as pointed out by some of these authors.

The objective of the second part of this book is to depict the emotional architecture that structures these memoirs. In that respect, it endeavours to highlight the valour underpinning these attempts to open a door to the future by those who dared to confront a past characterized by racial persecution under the Nazis. In their role as victims maimed by camp experience, they themselves determine what language memories are written in: 'That is [all] correct, that is all true,' says Walter Winter about the accounts of the camp system found in many history books, adding: 'but you don't read about feelings.' There are things, he maintains, such as constant fear, that 'people cannot begin to comprehend. Yet I remember everything.'[123]

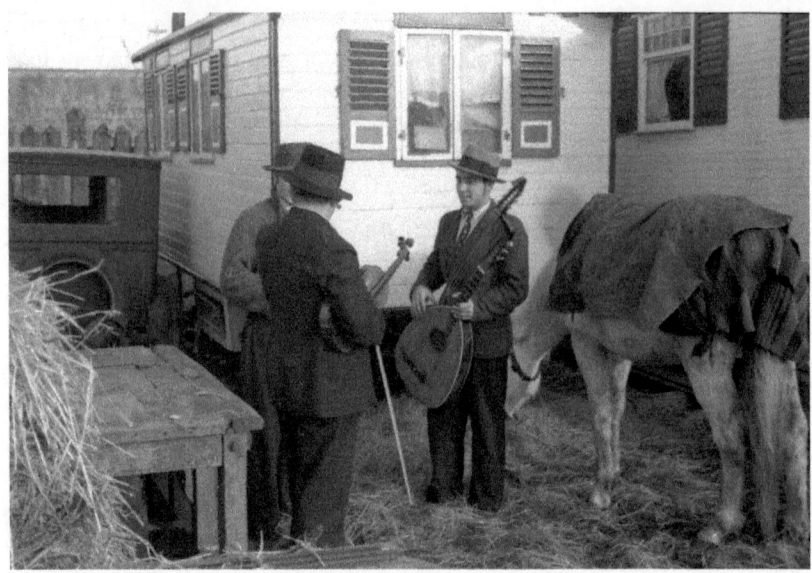

Illustration 50 Musicians Lolo Adell (violin), Frans Basili (laud) and Josef Basili (rear) at Haarlem, the Netherlands, 1940. These three Auschwitz survivors represent the value of music in Romani culture, a bridge spanning the Holocaust experience [NIOD, Institute for War, Holocaust and Genocide Studies, Amsterdam].

Illustration 51 Pauline Thormann (Lotte), left. Practically her whole family died at Auschwitz. She was sent to Ravensbrück as apt for work immediately before the *Zigeunerlager* was liquidated [Courtesy of the University of Liverpool Library - Special Collections].

ANNOTATED BIBLIOGRAPHY

This bibliography is intended to provide readers with supplementary information of particular interest. Its annotated listing of the bibliographic and documentary sources cited only briefly in the body of the study or in footnotes to enhance readability can be used both for comparison and to explore the matters addressed in greater depth. It is consequently arranged not by author in alphabetical order but by chapter, broken down by sections. The ultimate aim is to make it easier for readers to locate the references they deem of interest. This section of the book, rather than a more or less lengthy list of resources, is meant as a guide to smooth navigation. Nonetheless, the list is nowhere near exhaustive. It refers solely to the publications cited in the book, along with occasional mentions of others which, while not explicitly cited, may help readers find their bearings in the vast field of Holocaust literature.[1]

The **Introduction** summarizes debates on the singularity or otherwise of the Holocaust and the intentions pursued, along with terms used in the field and similar issues. Such issues are discussed in the following studies, some of which are cited in full in the text: *The Holocaust in History* by Marrus, Michael R. [Hannover, NH, London: University Press of New England, 1987]; *The Holocaust in Historical Context* by Kratz, Steven T. [Oxford: Oxford University Press, 1994]; *Hitler's Willing Executioners. Ordinary Germans and the Holocaust* by Goldhagen, Daniel [New York: Alfred Knopf, 1996]; *Hitler and the Jews. The Genesis of the Holocaust* by Burrin, Philipe [London: Edward Arnold, 1994]; *Ethics and Extermination: Reflections on Nazi Genocide* by Burleigh, Michael [Cambridge: Cambridge University Press, 1997]; and *Telling Lies about Hitler. The Holocaust, History and the David Irving Trial* by Evans, Richard J. [London: Verso Books, 2002]. To set the violence specific to the Holocaust against the backdrop of the general culture of violence prevailing in Europe at the time, the Introduction drew from: *Fire and Blood. The European Civil War, 1914–1945* by Traverso, Enzo [Translated by David Fernbach. London: Verso Books, 2017], originally published in French as Traverso, Enzo, *A feu et à sang. De la guerre civile européenne (1914–1945)* [Paris: Stock, 2007].

In connection with the Romani genocide in particular, Anton Weiss-Wendt reviews names and interpretations in the introductory pages to the most recommendable book on the subject: *The Nazi Genocide of the Roma. Reassessment and Commemoration* by Weiss-Wendt, Anton [New York, Oxford: Berghahn Books, 2013]. For a discussion of the Romani experience in relation to the interpretation of the Holocaust as an exclusively Jewish issue, see Milton, Sybil, 'The Context of Holocaust' [*German Studies Review* 13, no. 2 (1990): 269–83] and 'Gypsies and the Holocaust' [*The History Teacher* 24, no. 4 (1991): 375–87]; and two studies by Friedlander, Henry, 'Step by Step: The Expansion of

Murder, 1939–1941' [*German Studies Review* 17, no. 3 (1994): 495–507] and *The Origins of Nazi Genocide: From Euthanasia to the Final Solution* [Chapel Hill, NC: University of North Carolina Press, 1995].

The following provide valuable insight into terminology from the standpoint of Romani intellectuals: 'Romanies and the Holocaust: A Re-evaluation and Overview' by Hancock, Ian F. [In *The Historiography of Holocaust*, edited by Dan Stone, 383–96. New York: Palgrave Macmillan, 2005]; by the same author 'On the Interpretation of a Word: Porrajmos as Holocaust' [*The Holocaust in History and Memory* 3 (2010): 19–23]; and by Courthiade, Marcel, 'How to call the genocide perpetrated against the Roma in Nazi times?' [Rromani INALCO. Accessed 20 May 2021. https://rrominalco.hypotheses.org/le-genocide-des-rroms/how-to-call-the-genocide-perpetrated-against-the-rroms-in-nazi-times].

The caveat on photographs also mentioned in the Introduction is based on the essential essay by Sontag, Susan, *Regarding the Pain of Others* [New York: Farrar, Straus and Giroux, 2003].

Contributions by historians, anthropologists and cultural scholars were consulted for **Chapter 1**. One of the classic treatises on the pre-Nazi history of Roma people in Europe, by Fraser, Angus M., *The Gypsies* [Oxford: Blackwell, 1992], draws from traditional approaches in a number of ways, affording a very useful overview. For a more up-to-date interpretation see *Gypsies and Other Itinerant Groups. A Socio-historical Approach* by Lucassen, Leo, Wim Willems, and Annemarie Cottar [Basingstoke: Macmillan, 1998]. That study views the arrival of Romanies in Europe in the context of host country governmental practice, as well as the stereotypes generated accordingly. British anti-Gypsy legislation is addressed, in Appendix I in particular, in the book by Mayall, David, *Gypsy-Travellers in the Nineteenth Century Society* [Cambridge: Cambridge University Press, 1988] and in greater detail by Morgan, John E. in '"Counterfeit Egyptians": The construction and implementation of a criminal identity in early modern England' [*Romani Studies* 26, no. 2 (2016): 105–28]. For a more extensive discussion of British governmental logic and English society attitudes see Cressy, David, *Gypsies. An English History* [Oxford: Oxford University Press, 2018]. The situation in Spain is summarized by Sánchez Ortega, María Helena in 'Evolución y contexto histórico de los gitanos españoles' [In *Entre la marginación y el racismo. Reflexiones sobre la vida de los gitanos*, edited by Teresa San Román, 13–61. Madrid: Alianza Editorial]. The scene describing their arrival in France is drawn from: '*Journal d'un bourgeois de Paris, 1405–1449, publié d'après les manuscrits de Rome et de Paris par Alexandre Tuetey inédit* [Paris: H. Champion, 1881].

The effects of artistic, scientific and political endeavour on the emergence of stereotypes, a cultural development decisive for the historic process broached in this book, have been studied in a particularly valuable series of publications. The portrayal of 'Gypsies' as 'others' profoundly different from mainstream society is addressed in an indispensable book by Willems, Wim, *In Search of the True Gypsy. From Enlightenment to Final Solution* [London: Frank Cass, 1997]. Equally essential is a book by Mayall, David, *Gypsy Identities 1500–2000: From Egipcyans and Moon-Men to the Ethnic Romany*

[London: Routledge, 2004]. Leonardo Piasere authored two imperative studies on physical anthropology and its contribution to scientific stereotypes: Piasere, Leonardo, 'Crania Cingarica. La construcción antropológica del cuerpo gitano' [*Historia Social* 93 (2019): 103–22]; and Piasere, Leonardo, and Gianluca Solla, ed. *I filosofi e gli zingari* [Rome: Aracne, 2018]. The role of children's and teenage literature in the creation of such adverse stereotypes with long-term political implications is analysed in depth by Kommers, Jean in *Kinderroof of Zigeunerroof? Zigeuners in Kinderboeken* [Utrecht: Van Arkel, 1993] and *Gypsies in Nineteenth-Century Children's Books. A Comparative Study of Four National Literary Traditions* [Leiden: Brill, 2022]. The portrayal of Spanish 'Gitanos' and its spill-over into all European Romani communities is brilliantly studied by Charnon-Deutsch, Lou in *The Spanish Gypsy. The History of a European Obsession* [University Park: Pennsylvania State University Press, 2004]. Another possible source on the subject is: Sierra, María, 'Cannibals Devoured: Gypsies in Romantic Discourse on the Spanish Nation' [In *Enemies within: Cultural Hierarchies and Liberal Political Models in the Hispanic World*, edited by María Sierra, 167–221. Newcastle upon Tyne: Cambridge Scholars Publishing, 2015]. For a comparison between Orientalism and Gypsyism, see Lee, Ken, 'Orientalism and Gypsylorism' [*Social Analysis* 44, no. 2 (2000): 129–65].

This section on stereotype-building also refers to documents used as historic sources: Romer, Isabella F., *The Rhone, the Darro and the Guadalquivir, A Summer Ramble in 1842* [London: Richard Bentley, 1843]; Mérimée, Prosper, *Carmen* [Paris: Michel Lévy Frères, 1846]. The literal quotes cited in English were copied from Mérimée, Prosper, *Carmen* [Translated by Lady Mary Lloyd. New York: Limited Editions Club, 1941]; Borrow, George, *The Zincali. An Account of the Gypsies of Spain* [London: John Murray, 1841]; Liszt, Franz, *Des Bohémiens et leur musique en Hongrie* [Paris: Librairie Nouvelle, 1859]; and Knox, Robert, *The Races of Man: A Fragment* [Philadelphia: Lea and Blanchard, 1850]. Similarly, the discussion draws from the memoirs authored by Höss, Rudolf, *Commandant of Auschwitz, The Autobiography of Rudolf Hoess* [Cleveland, New York: The World Publishing Company, 1959] and from Leni Riefenstahl's motion picture *Tiefland* [1954. Riefenstahl Film, GmbH, Germany], filmed during the Second World War but not released until 1954.

The final section in Chapter 1 references studies published in English to afford the reader a closer look at the circumstances prevailing in Romani communities in a number of European countries from the early twentieth century until Hitler's rise to power and to establish a connection between prior harassment and subsequent Romani genocide. These include: *The Crisis of Genocide. Annihilation: The European Rimlands 1939-1953*, Vol. 2 by Levene, Mark [Oxford: Oxford University Press, 2013]; 'The National Socialist "Solution of the Gypsy Question": Central Decisions, Local Initiatives, and Their Interrelation' by Zimmermann, Michael [*Holocaust and Genocide Studies* 5, no. 3 (2001): 412–27]; 'Development and Institutionalization of Romani Representation and Administration. Part 2: Beginnings of Modern Institutionalization [Nineteenth Century-World War II]' by Klímová-Alexander, Ilona [*Nationalities Papers* 33, no. 2 (2005): 155–210]; 'Underclass Gypsies. An Historical Approach on Categorisation and Exclusion in France, in the Nineteenth and the Twentieth Centuries' by About, Ilsen

[In *The Gypsy 'Menace'. Populism and the New Anti-Gypsy Politics*, edited by Michael Stewart, 95–114. London: Hurst, 2012]; and *The Rights of the Roma. The Struggle for Citizenship in Postwar Czechoslovakia* by Donert, Celia [Cambridge: Cambridge University Press, 2017].

Further to the effort made to synopsize the literature, **Chapter 2** contains occasional references to certain original sources. The list of publications on the Romani genocide in general is headed by the book by Zimmermann, Michael, *Rassenutopie und Genozid. Die nationalsozialistische 'Lösung der Zigeunerfrage'* [Hamburg: Christians, 1996]. The aforementioned article in English by the same author ('The National Socialist "Solution"') summarizing that book provides a highly recommendable guide to the subject. Although more recent research reveals the need to update Zimmermann's overview, his publications continue to be essential to the study of Romani genocide under Nazi rule. A similar comment is applicable to a concise and clear-sighted summary of the most essential data published as a supplement to the memoirs penned by Philomena Franz: Benz, Wolfgang, 'Vom Vorurteil zum Massenmord: Die nationalsozialistische Verfolgung der Zigeuner' [In *Zwischen Liebe und Hass: Ein Zigeunerleben*, authored by Philomena Franz, 109–25. Freiburg: Herder, 1992]. Tribute is due in this context to Susan Tebbutt for her compilation and publication in English of a series of other early studies in Tebbutt, Susan, ed. *Sinti and Roma. Gypsies in German Speaking Society and Literature* [New York, Oxford: Berghahn Books, 1998]. Tebbutt herself authored some of the most significant chapters and included contributions by other researchers who had been working on the subject. One pertinent chapter was authored by Eiber, Ludwig, 'The Persecution of the Sinti and Roma in Munich 1933–1945' [In *Sinti and Roma. Gypsies in German Speaking Society and Literature*, edited by Susan Tebbutt, 17–33. New York, Oxford: Berghahn Books, 1998]. The chapter summarizes his book *Ich wußte es wird schlimm. Die Verfolgung der Sinti und Roma in München 1933–1945* [Munich: Buchendorfer Verlag, 1993].

The initial estimates of the number of victims, which have been growing as research progresses, can be found in Huttenbach, Henry R., 'The Romani *Porajmos*: The Nazi Genocide of Europe's Gypsies' [*Nationalities Papers* 19, no. 3 (1991): 373–94]. For percentages, see also Browning, Christophe, 'The Nazi Empire' [In *The Oxford Handbook of Genocide Studies*, edited by Donald Bloxham and A. Dirk Moses, 407–25. Oxford: Oxford University Press, 2010]; and Kapralski, Slawomir, 'The consequences of the genocide for Roma memories and identities' [In *The Legacies of the Roma Genocide in Europe since 1945*, edited by Celia Donert and Eve Rosenhaft, 284–303. London, New York: Routledge, 2022]. The studies consulted to contextualize the literature on the Romani experience in the wealth of studies on the Holocaust included one by Hilberg, Raul, *The Destruction of the European Jews* [New York, Holmes and Meier, 1985]; and two by Friedländer, Saul: *Nazi Germany and the Jews, 1933–1939* [New York: Harper Collins, 1997] and *The Years of Extermination: Nazi Germany and the Jews, 1939–1945* [New York: HarperCollins, 2007].

The most recent overview of the Romani Holocaust is the aforementioned collection of papers, edited by Weiss-Wendt, Anton, *The Nazi Genocide of the Roma. Reassessment and Commemoration* [New York, Oxford: Berghahn, 2013]. It constitutes an apt counterpoint to Lewy, Gunther, *The Nazi Persecution of the Gypsies* [Oxford: Oxford University Press, 2000]. While well documented, the latter treatise nonetheless fails to correctly appraise the scope of the Romani genocide, which is minimized relative to Jewish suffering. A book recently published by Kay, Alex J., *Empire of Destruction. A History of Nazi Mass Killing* [New Haven: Yale University Press, 2021] contains a review of the present state of the art in Chapter 10, entitled 'Genocide of the European Roma' [239–53], whilst in Chapter 4, 'Murder of Psychiatric Patients and Roma in the Soviet Union' [99–115], it identifies Roma peoples as victims of persecution.

Overall, research on the persecution and annihilation of European Romanies has been territorially fragmented, a wholly logical outcome of the geographic scope and diversity of the local circumstances involved. Information on Austria, so closely related to the German experience, can be found in Freund, Florian, 'Genocidal Trajectory: Persecution of Gypsies in Austria, 1938–1945' [In *The Nazi Genocide of the Roma*, edited by Anton Weiss-Wendt, 44–71. New York, Oxford: Berghahn, 2013] and Baumgartner, Gerhard, 'Identifying the Roma and Sinti victims forcefully deported in autumn 1941 to the "Zigeunerlager" Litzmannstadt' [In *Beyond the Roma Holocaust: From Resistance to Mobilisation*, edited by Thomas M. Buchsbaum and Slawomir Kapralski, 41–58. Krakow: Österreichische Botschaft Warschau/Taiwpn Universitas, 2017]. Events in Czechoslovakia are addressed by Jirí Lípa in a book by several authors whose general premise is that the Holocaust cannot be understood without interpreting the various groups of victims as something more than merely ancillary to the Jewish experience: Lípa, Jirí, 'The Fate of Gypsies in Czechoslovakia under Nazi Domination' [In *A Mosaic of Victims: Non-Jews Persecuted and Murdered by the Nazis*, edited by Michael Berembaum, 207–15. New York: New York University Press, 1990].

Research in western European countries such as Italy and France has been later in coming under the false presumption that the Roma were not intensely persecuted there on racial grounds. On Italy, see Boursier, Giovanna, 'La persecuzione degli zingari nell'Italia fascista' [*Studi Storici* 37, no. 4 (1996): 1065–82]; Boursier, Giovanna, 'Gypsies in Italy during the Fascist dictatorship and the Second World War' [In *The Gypsies during the Second World War. In the Shadow of the Swastika*, edited by Donald Kenrick, 13–35. Paris: Hatfield, Centre de Recherches Tsiganes/University of Hertfordshire, 1999]; and Trevisan, Paola, '"Gypsies" in Fascist Italy: from expelled foreigners to dangerous Italians' [*Social History* 42, no. 3 (2017): 342–64]. The following studies were consulted in connection with France: Filhol, Emmanuel, and Marie-Christine Hubert, *Les Tsiganes en France. Un sort à part 1939–1946* [Paris: Perrin, 2009]; Foisneau, Lise, and Valentin Merlin, 'French Nomads' Resistance, 1939–1946' [In *Roma Resistance during the Holocaust and Its Aftermath. Collection of Working Papers*, edited by Evelin Verhás et al., 57–101. Budapest: Tom Lantos Institute, 2018]; Foisneau, Lise, 'Mass arrests and persecutions of "Nomads" in France, 1944–1946. Post-liberation purges or evidence of anti-Gypsysim?' [In *The Legacies of the Roma Genocide in Europe since 1945*, edited by Celia Donert and Eve Rosenhaft, 21–37. London, New York: Routledge, 2022]; and

Heddebaut, Monica, *Des Tsiganes vers Auschwitz. Le convoi Z du 15 janvier 1944* [Paris: Éditions Tirésias/Michel Reynaud, 2018].

Essential to research on Romania and the deportation to Transnistria are the studies by Viorel Achim, in particular *The Roma in Romanian History* [Budapest: Central European University Press, 1998]. Achim also helped document the interesting novel set in those environments by Morar, Ioan T., *Negru și Roșu* [Bucharest: Editura Polirom, 2013]. New sources and interpretations are identified in a more recent article by Solonari, Vladimir, 'Ethnic Cleansing or "Crime Prevention"? Deportation of Romanian Roma' [In *The Nazi Genocide of the Roma*, edited by Anton Weiss-Wendt, 96–119. New York, Oxford: Berghahn, 2013]. The Balkans are also the object of new research on the political, ethnic and religious persecution of Romanies. One, for instance, is Trubeta, Sevasti, 'Gypsiness, racial discourse and persecution: Balkan Roma during the Second World War' [*Nationalities Papers* 31, no. 4 (2003): 495–514]. The general context is viewed in terms of the intersection with the religious issue in Motadel, David, *Islam and Nazi Germany's War* [Cambridge, MA: The Belknap Press of Harvard University Press, 2014]. The Ustacha's practices are specifically analysed in a chapter by Korb, Alexander, 'Ustacha Mass Violence Against Gypsies in Croatia, 1941–1942' [In *The Nazi Genocide of the Roma*, edited by Anton Weiss-Wendt, 72–95. New York, Oxford: Berghahn, 2013]. On Bulgaria see Crowe, David M., *A History of the Gypsies of Eastern Europe and Russia* [New York: St. Martin's Griffin, 1994]. Information on Jasenovac can be found in Mojzes, Paul, *Balkan Genocides. Holocaust and Ethnic Cleansing in the Twentieth Century* [Lanham: Rowman and Littlefield Publishers, 2011]. The measures adopted against Romanies in Southeastern Europe are summarized in the open access report *The Roma Holocaust/Roma Genocide in Southeastern Europe* [coordinated by the Auschwitz Institute for the Prevention of Genocide and Mass Atrocities and the Roma Program at the François-Xavier Bagnoud Center for Health and Human Rights-Harvard University. 2022. Last accessed 8 September 2022. https://www.auschwitzinstitute.org/news/launch-for-the-roma-holocaustroma-genocide-in-southeastern-europe-research-report/].

New studies on the former Soviet Union based on unpublished sources reconstruct the murder of Romanies in mass killing unit executions and other types of actions. Included in that group are two reports by Holler, Martin, 'The Nazi Persecution of Roma in Northwestern Russia: The Operational Area of the Army Group North, 1941–1944' [In *The Nazi Genocide of the Roma*, edited by Anton Weiss-Wendt, 153–80. New York, Oxford: Berghahn, 2013]; and 'The National Socialist Genocide of the Roma in the German-occupied Soviet Union' [Council of Europe *Report for the Documentary and Cultural Centre of German Sinti and Roma*. 2009. Last accessed 8 September 2022. https://www.coe.int/en/web/roma-genocide/russian-federation#Scientific_publications]; and one by Mikhail Tyaglyy, 'Nazi Occupation Policies and the Mass Murder of the Roma in Ukraine' [In *The Nazi Genocide of the Roma*, edited by Anton Weiss-Wendt, 120–52. New York, Oxford: Berghahn, 2013]. Roma peoples' circumstances in the Soviet Union before and after Nazism are studied in Lemon, Alaina, 'Roma (*Gypsies*) in the Soviet Union and the Moscow Teatr Romen' [*Nationalities Papers* 19, no. 3 (1991): 359–72].

Territorial studies provide insight into common traits and local peculiarities, similarities and differences that can be used to depict a more nuanced portrait of Nazi persecution of European Romanies. Other studies address issues such as repression and specific features of complex camp structures. Himmler's fantasies on a racial reserve, for instance, are the subject of an article by Lewy, Guenter, 'Himmler and the 'Racially Pure Gypsies" [*Journal of Contemporary History* 34, no. 2 (1999): 201-14]. With an entirely different purpose associated with the intersection between gender and race, Sybil Milton aims her sights on women as the target of domination during persecution and imprisonment in 'Hidden Lives: Sinti and Roma Women' [In *Experience and Expression. Women, the Nazis, and the Holocaust*, edited by Elizabeth R. Baer and Myrna Goldenberg, 53-75. Detroit: Wayne State University Press, 2003]. The pathway that led to exclusion and deportation has also been broached from a biographical perspective. The Romani boxer Rukeli is studied by Nirenberg, Jud in *Johann Trollmann and Romani Resistance to Nazis* [Iowa City: Win by KO, 2016]. His story also inspired the novel by Fo, Dario, *Razza di Zingaro* [Milan: chiarelettere editore, 2016]. Sintizza Erna Lauenberger's (Unku's) life is used similarly in Lauenberger, Janko, and Juliane von Wedemeyer, *Ede und Unku - die wahre Geschichte. Das Schicksal einer Sinti-Familie von der Weimarer Republik bis heute* [Gütersloh: Gütersloher Verlagshaus, 2018]. The pillaging of Romani cultural property is mentioned in Petropoulos, Jonathan, 'The Polycratic Nature of Art Looting: The Dynamic Balance of the Third Reich' [In *Networks of Nazi Persecution. Bureaucracy, Business and the Organization of the Holocaust*, edited by Gerard D. Feldman and Wolfgang Seibel, 103-17. New York, Oxford: Berghahn, 2004].

Two subjects of particular relevance to the Romani experience are discussed in these studies of specific features of the Holocaust. One is the adulterated scientific apparatus designed as a vast laboratory whose findings were applied to perpetrate the massacre. The other is the light shed on all that is known about the Auschwitz-Birkenau Camp (and hence life and death in other camps as well). The collaboration of highly reputed contemporary scientists such as Dr Robert Ritter in establishing the criteria used by the Nazi police to racially classify Roma peoples is amply documented in Zimmermann's aforementioned study ('The National Socialist "Solution"'). Beyond Dr Ritter and team's specific circle, that practice spread to many other countries, as noted in a chapter of a book edited by Zimmermann the year he died: Achim, Viorel, 'Gypsy Research and Gypsy Policy in Romania' [In *Zwischen Erziehung und Vernichtung. Zigeunerpolitik und Zigeunerforschung im Europa des 20. Jahrhunderts*, edited by Michel Zimmermann, 156-74. Stuttgart: Franz Steiner Verlag, 2007]. Certain paradoxes arise in this connection, particularly when attempting to interpret professionals' intentions. The paradigmatic example, photographer Hans Weltzel, is analysed by Rosenhaft, Eve in 'A photographer and his "victims": Reconstructing a shared experience of the Romani Holocaust, 1934-1964' [In *The Role of the Romanies. Images and Counter Images of 'Gypsies/Romanies' in European Cultures*, edited by Nicholas Saul and Susan Tebbutt, 178-207. Liverpool: Liverpool University Press, 2005]. More general studies, such as Lifton, Robert Jay, *The Nazi Doctors. Medical Killing and the Psychology of Genocide* [New York: Basic Books, 2000] that include Romanies with other groups of prisoners, were consulted as sources to document scientific horror at its most base, medicine as practised in Nazi camps. Further information on Roma people and a general interpretation of their fate can also be found in Müller-Hill, Benno, *Murderous Science: Elimination by Scientific Selection of Jews, Gypsies, and Others. Germany: 1933–1945* [New York: Oxford University Press, 1988]; Friedlander, Henry, *The origins of Nazi Genocide. From Euthanasia to the Final Solution* [Chapel Hill: University of North Carolina Press, 1995]; and Weindling, Paul, *Victims and Survivors of Nazi Human Experiments. Science and Suffering* [London: Bloomsbury, 2014]. The third contains a section specifically on the abuse of Romanies in scientific experiments.

The creation of the *Zigeunerlager* in the Auschwitz-Birkenau extermination camp, a pivotal theme in Romani genocide, is described in Zimmermann's aforementioned studies ('The National Socialist "Solution"'; *Rassenutopie und Genozid*). More information on the subject can be found in a book that combines chapters written by specialists with extracts from survivors' memoirs and records on file at the Auschwitz-Birkenau State Museum archive, and specifically in Volume 7 of the museum's series: Kapralski, Slawomir, Maria Martyniak, and Joanna Talewicz-Kwiatkowska, *Roma in Auschwitz, Voices of Memory Series* [Auschwitz: International Center for Education about Auschwitz and the Holocaust, 2011]. This is an updated and more accessible version of the *Memorial Book: The Gypsies at Auschwitz-Birkenau* [Munich, New York: State Museum of Auschwitz-Birkenau - Documentary and Cultural Centre of German Sinti and Roma, 1993], also occasionally cited in the body of the text.

The Auschwitz *Zigeunerlager* should of course be set in the general context of the Nazi camp system, as attempted here with the support of studies such as written by D'Almeida, Fabrice, *Ressources inhumaines. Les gardiens de camps de concentration et leurs loisirs* [Paris: Librairie Arthème Fayard, 2011], and other sources of pioneering research on 'Gypsy' camps as a whole. That would include the early internment camps for Roma in Germany as well as the Buchenwald and Ravensbrück concentration camps, addressed respectively by Fings, Karola in 'Romani and Sinti in the concentration camps' and Sparing, Frank in 'The Gypsy camps' [both in *From 'Race Science' to the Camps. The Gypsies during the Second World War*, edited by Karola Fings, Herbert Heuss and Frank Sparing, 39–70 and 71–109. Hatfield: University of Hertfordshire Press, 1999]. The *Zigeunerlager* nonetheless featured a series of peculiarities that are better perceived in testimonies such as studied by Turda, Marius, 'The ambiguous victim: Miklós Nyiszli's narrative of medical experimentation in Auschwitz-Birkenau' [*Historien* 14, no. 1 (2014): 43–58]. In it the author analyses the memoirs of a former doctor and prisoner forced to assist Mengele at Auschwitz. The present book also relates the Auschwitz *Zigeunerlager* in some cases to events at other camps, such as the *Zigeunerkapelle* reported on by Pike, David W., *Spaniards in the Holocaust: Mauthausen, the Horror on the Danube* [London: Routledge, 2000]. Analysis of how the family as an essential structure in Romani communities affected Roma life in the camp system draws from the thoughts expressed in that regard by Rosenhaft, Eve, 'The Gypsy's Revenge. Betrayal and personal retribution as themes in the post-Holocaust experience and memory of German Sinti' [In *Beyond Camps and*

Forced Labour II. Proceedings of the Second Conference on Post-Holocaust Experience and Memory, edited by J.D. Steinert and Inge Weber-Newth, 406–13. Osnabrück: Secolo, 2008].

Chapter 2 also cites documentary sources. More specifically, these include the eight volumes and annexes composing the unpublished series of papers collected and translated into English by the allies as preliminaries to the Nuremberg trials: *Nazi Conspiracy and Aggression* [Office of United States Chief of Council For Persecution of Axis Criminality, 1946]; Höss, Rudolf, *Commandant of Auschwitz. The Autobiography of Rudolf Hoess* [Cleveland, New York: The World Publishing Company, 1959]; Kermish, Joseph, ed. 'Emmanuel Ringelblum's Notes, Hitherto Unpublished' [*Yad Vashem Studies* VII (1968), 117–18]; Arendt, Hannah, *Eichmann in Jerusalem. A Report on the Banality of Evil* [New York, 1963. Internet Archive. Last accessed 3 September 2022. https://archive.org/details/eichmann-in-jerusalem-a-report-on-the-banality-of-evil-by-hannah-arendt]; and the memoirs of a Resistance fighter who involved his Romani friends in the struggle against Nazism: Yoors, Jan, *Crossing. A Journal of Survival and Resistance in World War II* [London: Weidenfeld & Nicholson, 1972].

In a similar vein, *La Bible des Roms. La tradition Tsigane dévoilée par Zanko et recueillie par le Révérend Père Chatard*, 1959 [Reprint, Marseille: Gaussen - Association Tchatchipen, 2017], in turn, is a book that echoes the voice of Zanko, a French internment camp survivor. Ceija Stojka's memories of being a child in the camps are captured in the documentary film directed by Karin Berger, *Unter den Brettern hellgrünes Gras* [2005. Austria: Navigator Film Produktion].

The discussion in **Chapter 3** on post-war German and European denial of the Romani Holocaust and the persistence of institutional and social persecution, in addition to Wolfgang Benz's aforementioned study ('Vom Vorurteil zum Massenmord'), draws from: Milton, Sybil, 'Persecuting the Survivors: The Continuity of "Anti-Gypsyism" in Postwar Germany and Austria' [In *Gypsies in German-Speaking Society and Literature*, edited by Susan Tebbutt, 35–48. New York, Oxford: Berghahn Books, 1998]; Margalit, Gilad, 'The Justice System of the Federal Republic of Germany and the Nazi Persecution of the Gypsies' [In *The Nazi Genocide of the Roma*, edited by Anton Weiss-Wendt, 181–204. New York, Oxford: Berghahn Books, 2013]; Foisneau, Lise, 'Mass Arrests and Persecutions of "Nomads" in France from 1944 and 1946: Post-Liberation Purges or Evidence of Antigypsyism?' [In *The Legacies of the Roma Genocide in Europe since 1945*, edited by Celia Donert and Eve Rosenhaft, 21–37. London, New York, Routledge, 2022]; two publications by Matei, Petre, 'Compensation Claims from Romania in the ITS Collections. Between the Victims and the State' [*Jahrbuch des International Tracing Service* 5 (2016): 160–86] and 'Roma in 1980s Communist Romania and Roma Discourse on Holocaust. Between Compensation and Identity' [In *The Legacies of the Roma Genocide in Europe since 1945*, edited by Celia Donert and Eve Rosenhaft, 214–41. London, New York: Routledge, 2022]; and studies by Marushiakova, Elena, and Vesselin Popov, 'State Policies under Communism' [2013. Last accessed 15 September 2022. https://www.researchgate.net/publication/235700092_State_Policies_towards_Roma_Gypsies_under_Communism] and Reuss, Anja, '"Returning to Normality?": The

Struggle of Sinti and Roma Survivors to Rebuild a Life in Postwar Germany' [In *Jewish and Romani Families in the Holocaust and Its Aftermath*, edited by Eliyana R. Adler and Kateřina Čapková, 141–55. New Brunswick: Rutgers University Press, 2021].

On victims' claims, from individual initiatives to the action taken by Romani associationism, including defence of the right to memory, see: Maximoff, Mateo, 'Germany and the Gypsies: From the Gypsy's Point of View' [*Journal of the Gypsy Lore Society* XXV (1946): 104–8]; Baumann, Ulrich, 'From the Gypsy's Point of View - Politique et Mémoire au travers de la vie et l'ouvre de Matéo Maximoff' [*Etudes Tsiganes* 60 (2017): 115–33]; the aforementioned article by CIlona Klímová-Alexander ('Development and Institutionalization'); Liégeois, Jean-Pierre, 'Naissance du pouvoir tsigane' [*Revue française de sociologie* 16, no. 3 (1975): 295–316]; Margalit, Gilad, and Yaron Matras, 'Gypsies in Germany - German Gypsies? Identity and Politics of Sinti and Roma in Germany' [In *The Roma: A minority in Europe. Historical, Social and Cultural Perspectives*, edited by Roni Stauber and Raphael Vago, 203–216. Oxford: Berghahn Books, 2007]; in *The Nazi Genocide of the Roma* [Edited by Anton Weiss-Wendt, 229–59. New York, Oxford. Berghahn Books, 2013], the chapters by Blumer, Nadine, 'Commemorating Sinti and Roma and Jews in Germany's National Narrative' and Kapralski, Slawomir, 'The Memory of Genocide and Contemporary Roma Identities'; and lastly, an article by Sierra, María, 'Creating *Romanestan*: A Place to Be a Gypsy in Post-Nazi Europe' [*European History Quarterly* 49, no. I.2 (2019): 272–92].

The discussion in Chapter 3 on research progress, in addition to the publications cited in Chapter 2 on the subject, drew from some earlier studies: Novitch, Miriam, *Le génocide des Tziganes sous le régime nazi* [Paris: Comité pour l'érection du Monument en mémoire des Tziganes assassinés à Auschwitz, 1968]; and the decisive book by Puxon, Grattan and Donald Kenrick, *The Destiny of Europe's Gypsies* [London: Sussex University Press, 1972]. Progress in research can also be systematically traced thanks to an article on the state-of-the-art by About, Ilsen, and Anna Abakunova, 'The Genocide and Persecution of Roma and Sinti. Bibliography and Historiographical Review' [International Holocaust Remembrance Alliance. 2016. Last accessed 8 September 2022. https://www.holocaustremembrance.com/resources/publications/genocide-and-persecution-roma-and-sinti-bibliography-and-historiographical]. Particularly suggestive in this regard is Rosenhaft, Eve, 'At Large in the "Grey Zone": Narrating the Romani Holocaust' [In *Unsettling History. Archiving and Narrating in Historiography*, edited by Sebastian Jobs and Alf Lüdtke, 149–79. Frankfurt: Campus, 2010].

This chapter also alludes to analyses of museum discourse, as in van Baar, Huub, 'From "Time-Banditry" to the Challenge of Established Historiographies: Romany Contributions to Old and New Images of the Holocaust' [In *Multidisciplinary Approaches to Romany Studies*, edited by Michael Stewart and Máton Rövid, 153–71. Budapest: Central European University, 2010]; as well as two by Radonic, Ljiljana: 'People of Freedom and Unlimited Movement: Representations of Roma in Post-Communist Memorial Museums' [*Social Inclusion* 3, no. I.5 (2015): 64–77]; and '"Unadaptable people" - Roma and "our" Victims in Post-Communist Memorial Museums' [In *The Legacies of the Roma Genocide in Europe since 1945*, edited by Celia Donert and Eve

Rosenhaft, 261–83. London, New York: Routledge, 2022]. On cinema, see: Lewis, Ingrid, *Women in European Holocaust Films, Perpetrators, Victims, and Resisters* [London: Palgrave/Macmillan, 2017]. Settela Steinbach's experience was researched by Wagenaar, Aad, *Settela* [Translated by Janna Eliot. Nottingham: Five Leaves, 2005, with an afterword by Ian Hancock]. It was originally published in Dutch as Wagenaar, Aad, *Settela. Het meisje heeft haar naam terug* [Amsterdam: De Arbeiderspers, 1995].

Baumgartner et al. authored what is arguably the most recommendable online resource aspiring to enhance dissemination of these issues: Baumgartner, Gerhard, Irmgard Bibermann, Maria Ecker, and Robert Sigel, *The Fate of European Roma and Sinti during the Holocaust. Teacher's Manual* [Translated by Chris March. Austrian Bundesministerium für Bildung und Frauen, Fondation pour la Mémoire de le Shoah, Paris, and International Holocaust Remembrance Alliance. (n.d.). Last accessed 3 September 2022. https://www.romasintigenocide.eu/en/home]. Other online sources deployed include the websites *Digital Exhibition about Genocide of Sinti and the Roma* (n.d.). Last accessed 5 September 2022 [https://romasinti.eu/]; *Forgotten Victims: The Nazi Genocide of the Roma and Sinti* [(n.d.). Last accessed 10 September 2022 [https://www.un.org/en/exhibits/forgotten-victims]; the blog 'Beyond Stereotypes: Cultural Exchanges and the Romani Contribution to European Public Spaces' [BESTROM Project. (n.d.). Last accessed 3 September 2022. https://bestrom.org/]; the website 'Giving Memory a Future. The Sinti and Roma in Italy and around the World' [Università Cattolica del Sacro Cuore and USC Shoah Foundation. (n.d.). Last accessed 8 September 2022. https://sfi.usc.edu/education/roma-sinti/en/conosciamo-i-roma-e-i-sinti/chi-sono/nel-mondo-e-in-italia.php]; the series of articles on the National WWII Museum site, including one authored by Rosenhaft, Eve, 'Strangers in Their Own Land: Romani Survivors in Europe 1945' [National WWII Museum, 20 September 2021. Last accessed 9 September 2022. https://www.nationalww2museum.org/war/articles/romani-holocaust-survivors-1945]; the slideshow of the exhibition 'Don't Forget the Photos' [(n.d.). Last accessed 8 September 2022. https://dontforgetthephotos.wordpress.com]; and the documentary film directed by Müller, Jana, *What Happened to Unku?* [Alternatives Jugendzentrum Dessau, 2008. https://www.nationalww2museum.org]. Another documentary well worth viewing is Navarro, David, *Mi Holocausto - My Holocaust. Philomena Franz*, edited in Spain in 2022 from recordings of interviews with Franz [BESTROM Project. (n.d.). Last accessed 4 September 2022. https://miholocausto.com/]. The text also cites a play included in the book edited by Rau, Simon, Eve Rosenhaft and Eva Shock-Quinteros, *Und Wohin Jetzt? Die 'Zigeunerpolitik' im Deutschen Kaiserreich und United Kingdom* [Bremen: Universität Bremen, 2022].

Only two documentary sources are cited in Chapter 3. The first is: *Basic Handbook. ABC of German Administration and Public Services* (1944), compiled by the National Archives of America (NARA), originally classified and now accessible [(n.d.). Last accessed 29 September 2022. https://www.fold3.com/image/270203948]. Thanks are owed to Miguel Martorell for alerting the present author to the section titled 'Gypsies' on pages 97 and 98 of that document. The second, featuring an appearance by Settela Steinbach, is a film made by van der Burg, Michael, a Jewish prisoner at Westerbork Camp. It forms part of the Open Beelden repository on the page Westerbork

Films by Rudolf Breslauer [Westerbork Films Collection, UNESCO Album. 20 January 2020. Last accessed 3 November 2022. www.openbeelden.nl/media/1223905/WESTERBORK_FILMS_COLLECTION__UNESCO_ALBUM__20200120]. Shot at Westerbork, Netherlands, in 1945, it features the famous scene with Settela Steinbach (minute 6:21).

In addition to the Romani survivor memoirs that constitute the core of this book, other resources have been deployed in **Part II** to effectively contextualize their accounts. Reference in that regard must be made firstly to scientific literature on the historical meaning and appropriate methods for studying such documents. Of particular relevance are the considerations around the sudden flare of testimonial perspective in contemporary history addressed by Wieviorka, Annette in *The Era of the Witness* [Translated by Jared Stark. Ithaca: Cornell University Press, 2006], initially published as Wieviorka, Annette, *L'ère du témoin* [Paris: Plon, 1998]. Historiography owes some of the most classical contributions to the structuring of Holocaust survivor recollections and testimonies to LaCapra, Dominick, *Representing the Holocaust: History, Theory, Trauma* [Ithaca: Cornell University Press, 1994]. Observations on the impact of gender on Holocaust experience and testimony are also addressed hereunder, as described in Waxman, Zoe V., *Writing the Holocaust: Identity, Testimony, Representation* [Oxford: Oxford University Press, 2006].

In the sparse scientific output specifically dealing with Romani survivor memoirs, the two most comprehensive analyses adopt a cultural and literary approach. The more systematic of the two is Zwicker, Marianne C., 'Journeys into Memory. Romani Identity and the Holocaust in Autobiographical Writing by German and Austrian Romanies' [PhD. diss., University of Edinburgh, Edinburgh, 2009]. With the focus on a series of memoirs, some of which are also discussed hereunder, Zwicker analyses and interprets the narratives from the standpoint of author identity-building, contextualized with rigorously contrasted biographical data. The second study, which uses similar literary material and a more anthropological perspective, French, Lorely, *Roma Voices in the German-Speaking World* [New York, London: Bloomsbury, 2015], nonetheless contains a few biographical inaccuracies. Two further analyses, conducted from historiographic perspectives more in line with the present approach, were consulted for studies on Romani Holocaust memoirs. One is the aforementioned chapter by Rosenhaft, Eve ('The Gypsy's Revenge') and the other a book (the second chapter in particular, 'Victims' Stories') by von dem Knesebeck, Julia, *The Roma Struggle for Compensation in Post-War Germany* [Hatfield: Hertfordshire University Press, 2011].

As noted in Chapter 5, a substantial share of the tools used for a contextualized analysis of the discourse found in these six accounts chosen to represent Roma camp experience has its roots in the history of emotions. A useful entry in that line of historiography can be found in Rosenwein, Barbara H., 'Worrying about Emotions in History' [*American Historical Review* 107, no. 3 (2002): 834–6]. Of the various studies in connection with that intellectual current, this book draws explicitly from: Bourke, Joanna, *Fear: A Cultural History* [Emeryville: Shoemaker Hoard, 2006]; and Reddy, William M., *The Navigation of Feeling. A Framework for the History of Emotions* [Cambridge: Cambridge University Press, 2001].

Annotated Bibliography

In another vein, the effort to interpret and interrelate the narratives in Romani victims' memoirs draws heavily from a comparative reading of the memoirs of other groups of Nazi Holocaust survivors, primarily by Jewish authors but also by prisoners persecuted on political grounds. Even bearing in mind the biographical differences, the uneven opportunity for exchange with others and many other circumstances distinguishing the narrators, such relational reading would appear to afford indisputable advantage when broaching an interpretation of the events narrated.

Of the many published to date, the memoirs and autobiographical writings authored by people of Jewish descent sent to the camps as racially inferior consulted most intensively for Chapters 4 and 5 include two of the three volumes on Auschwitz by the author of an indispensable analysis of the camp system: Levi, Primo, *Se questo è un uomo* [Turin: Einaudi, 1946]; and *I sommersi e i salvati* [Turin: Einaudi, 1986]. The literal quotes cited in English were copied respectively from Levi, Primo, *If This Is a Man/The Truce* [Translated by Stuart Woolf. 1st edn. The Orion Press, 1969. Reprint, London: Abacus, 2003. (Kindle edn) (n.d.)], and Levi, Primo, *The Drowned and the Saved* [Translated by Raymond Rosenthal. 1st edn. Michel Joseph, 1988. New York: Vintage Books, 1989. Reprint London: Abacus, 2013].

Likewise imperative is the account by Steinberg, Paul, *Chroniques d'ailleurs* [Paris: Éditions de la Seine, 1997]. The literal quotes cited in the text were copied from Steinberg, Paul, *Speak You Also: A Survivor's Reckoning* [Translated by Linda Coverdale. New York: Metropolitan Books/Henry Holt and Co., 2000. (Kindle edn) (n.d.)]. In a book of memoirs written immediately after the war, Austrian psychiatrist Viktor Frankl attempted to filter his own memories through professional observation. His insights on prisoners' emotional responses proved very useful for the present discussion. Originally published as Frankl, Viktor, *Ein Psycholog erlebt das Konzentrationslager* [Vienna: Verlag für Jugend und Volk, 1946], it was translated into English more than ten years later as Frankl, Viktor: *Man's Search for Meaning, an Introduction to Logotherapy* [Translated by Ilse Lasch. Boston: Beacon Press, 1959]. A Polish musician who conducted the Auschwitz orchestra published his memoirs in English as Laks, Simon, *Music of Another World* [Translated by Chester A. Kiesel. Evanston: Northwestern University Press, 1989], based on a rework of the book cowritten with Coudy, René, *Musiques d'un autre monde* [Paris: Mercure de France, 1948]. Another book of memoirs relevant to this chapter was authored by Jean Améry and meticulously translated into English as *At the Mind's Limits: Contemplations by a Survivor of Auschwitz and Its Realities* [Translated by Sidney and Stella P. Rosenfeld. Bloomington: Indiana University Press, 1980]. Améry felt able to confront the blank page much later than Frankl, in 1964, in the wake of the Frankfurt proceedings on Auschwitz. His reflection on the prisoner's conundrum was initially published in German as Améry, Jean, *Jenseits von Schuld und Sühne: Bewältigungsversuche eines Überwältigten* [Munich: Szczesny, 1966].

Imre Kertész penned a well-known first-person narrative that straddles fiction and biography in her description of a Hungarian teenager's experience as a victim of Nazism, rendered in print as *Fateless* [Evanston: Northwestern University Press, 1992]. In his diary Viktor Klemperer, another professional, resorted to his acquis to set his personal suffering at arm's length from his insightful dissection of Nazism. The original German language book was published as *LTI. Notizbuch eines Philologen* [Berlin: Aufbau/Verlag Berlin: 1947]; and translated and published in English as *The Language of the Third Reich: LTI, Lingua Tertii Imperii: A Philologist's Notebook* [Translated by Martin Brady. London: Bloomsbury, 2013].

Only two of the many testimonies by camp system survivors persecuted on political grounds are cited hereunder. The first is the diary written by Dutch anti-fascist Nico Rost, begun in the concentration camp itself and reworked in several later editions. As the diary seems never to have been published in English, the literal quotes cited in that language in the text were translated from the Spanish version, *Goethe en Dachau* [Barcelona: Contraescritura, 2016]. The justification for that decision lies in the wisdom informing translator Nuria Molinés's inclusion of the quotes in a number of languages. Her Spanish version also contains a camp vocabulary in German, an editorial option that very effectively conveys the idiomatic chaos that reigned in the camps. The present analysis also resorts to the highly personal literary reworking of camp experience written by a member of the French Resistance: Delbo, Charlotte, *Auschwitz et après: Aucun de nous ne reviendra* [Paris: Gonthier, 1965], published in English as *Auschwitz and After* [New Haven, London: Yale University Press, 1997].

The reasons for choosing certain editions of the Romani memoirs on which the analysis in Chapters 4 and 5 is based (and which are likewise cited in Part I) are discussed in the text. The full editorial details are listed here, arranged by the date of the original edition, given the significance of that information.

The first was Franz, Philomena, *Zwischen Liebe und Hass. Ein Zigeunerleben* [1st edn. Freiburg: Herder, 1985]. The author's 2001 self-publication containing supplementary materials (from which some of the literal quotes cited in the text in English were translated) was used. The Spanish edition includes a study by Sierra, María, 'Philomena Franz, Narrator of the Romani Holocaust' [BESTROM Project. (n.d.). Last accessed 4 September 2022. (https://bestrom.org/blog-2/105-philomena-franz,-narrator-of-the-romani-holocaust)]. Franz's book was followed by Stojka, Ceija, *Wir Leben im Verborgenen: Erinnerungen einer Rom-Zigeunerin* [Vienna: Picus, 1988]. For the reasons set out in Chapter 4, the French version (from which the literal quotes cited in the text in English were translated) was also used here: *Nous vivons cachés. Récits d'une Romani à travers le siècle* [Translated by Sabine Macher. Paris: Isabelle Sauvage, 2018]. A very impactful later account is also referenced hereunder: *Träume ich, dass ich lebe? Befreit aus Bergen-Belsen* [Vienna: Picus, 2005]. Lily van Angeren's memoirs were first published in Dutch as *Lily: het unieke levensverhaal van een zigeunerin* [Amsterdam: Forum, 1997], and translated into German a few years later as '*Polizeilich zwangsentführt'. Das Leben der Sintizza Lily van Angeren-Franz* [Translated by Martina den Hertog-Vogt. Hildesheim: Gebrüder Gerstenberg, 2004]. That second publication, the one consulted for this book, is the original from which the literal quotes cited in the text in English were translated.

Like van Angeren's, Otto Rosenberg's memoirs are the outcome of collaboration with writers entrusted with recording the interviews, conducted in this case by Ulrich

Enzensberger, originally published in German as *Das Brennglas* [Berlin: Eichborn, 1998] and soon after translated into other languages. It was published in English as *A Gypsy in Auschwitz, as told to Ulrich Enzenberger* [Translated by Helmut Bögler. London: London House, 1999], from which the literal quotes cited in the text were copied. One year after the first edition of Rosenberg's memoirs were published, Walter Winter wrote his. Based on a series of interviews recorded by historians Thomas W. Neumann and Michael Zimmermann, who annotated and edited the manuscript, it was initially published in German as *WinterZeit. Erinnerungen eines deutschen Sinto, der Auschwitz überlebt hat* [Hamburg: Ergebnisse, 1999]. The literal quotes cited in the text in English were copied from *Winter Time. Memoirs of a German Sinto Who Survived Auschwitz* [Translated by Struan Robertson. Hatfield: University of Hertfordshire Press, 2004], which carries a foreword by the translator. The sixth and last book of memoirs used as part of the documentary corpus on which the analysis in Part II of this book is based is Hanstein, Ewald, *Meine hundert Leben. Erinnerungen eines deutschen Sinto* [Bremen: Donat, 2005]. The literal quotes cited in the text in English were translated from that version.

Supplementary testimonies from a number of sources are also referenced hereunder. One of the books that proved highly valuable, in addition to the recollections set out in the aforementioned volume on the Auschwitz-Birkenau *Zigeunerlager Memorial Book: The Gypsies at Auschwitz-Birkenau* [Munich, New York: State Museum of Auschwitz-Birkenau - Documentary and Cultural Centre of German Sinti and Roma, 1993] is Sonneman, Toby, *Shared Sorrows. A Gypsy Family Remembers the Holocaust* [Hatfield: University of Hertfordshire Press, 2002]. That choral reconstruction of a Sinti family harshly punished by the Holocaust is based on an extensive series of interviews conducted by Toby Sonneman, herself the daughter of a Jewish refugee in the United States. Ian Hancock helped Sonneman contact Reili Mettbach, another Romani survivor also living in the United States, who became involved in her project. He travelled to Germany with Sonneman where he introduced her to his family, a key to the collaboration involved in a book that interweaves the history of Romani and Jewish persecution, while consistently respecting the specificity of the former genocide.

The two documentary sources used in Chapter 5 are Stojka, Karl, *The Story of Karl Stojka: A Childhood in Birkenau* [Washington DC: United States Holocaust Memorial Museum, 1992]; and Gentily, Anne-Marie. 'Un *Sionisme* gitan: conversation avec Vaida Voevod III' [*La Terre Retrouvée* (15-IX-1961)].

NOTES

Foreword

1. Philomena Franz (b. 1922) was deported to Auschwitz in 1943. She survived it and other camps. She was the first Romani to publish her testimony as a Nazi genocide victim. She has long been involved in defending her people's rights, including the right to a place in History. She presently lives near Cologne, where she continues to bear witness to the events she experienced.

Introduction

1. Toby Sonneman, *Shared Sorrows. A Gypsy Family Remembers the Holocaust* (Hatfield: University of Hertfordshire Press, 2002), 62.
2. Marianne C. Zwicker, 'Journeys into Memory. Romani Identity and the Holocaust in Autobiographical Writing by German and Austrian Romanies' (PhD diss., University of Edinburgh, Edinburgh, 2009).
3. María Sierra, *Holocausto gitano. El genocidio romaní bajo el nazismo* (Madrid: Arzalia Ediciones, 2020).
4. The sole exception to that general principle are the terms 'anti-Gypsy' and 'anti-Gypsyism'. Their extensive use in the social sciences and throughout this book informed the decision not to set them in quotation marks.
5. Dominick LaCapra, *Representing the Holocaust: History, Theory, Trauma* (Ithaca: Cornell University Press, 1994).
6. 'Holocaust', *Encyclopaedia Britannica* (n.d.), https://www.britannica.com/event/Holocaust (accessed 23 April 2022).
7. Enzo Traverso, *A feu et à sang. De la guerre civile européenne (1914–1945)* (Paris: Stock, 2007); published in English as *Fire and Blood. The European Civil War, 1914–1945* (London: Verso Books, 2017).
8. Anton Weiss-Wendt, *The Nazi Genocide of the Roma. Reassessment and Commemoration* (New York, Oxford: Berghahn Books, 2013).
9. Guenter Lewy, *The Nazi Persecution of the Gypsies* (Oxford: Oxford University Press, 2000).
10. Sybil Milton, 'Gypsies and the Holocaust', *The History Teacher* 24, no. 4 (1991): 375–87; and 'The context of Holocaust', *German Studies Review* 13, no. 2 (1990): 269–83; Henry Friedlander, 'Step by Step: The Expansion of Murder, 1939–1941', *German Studies Review* 17, no. 3 (1994): 495–507; and *The Origins of Nazi Genocide: From Euthanasia to the Final Solution* (Chapel Hill, NC: University of North Carolina Press, 1995).
11. David Navarro, *My Holocaust. Philomena Franz* (Beyond Stereotypes: Cultural Exchanges and the Romani Contribution to European Public Spaces (BESTROM, 2022), https://miholocausto.com/ (accessed 4 September 2022).

Notes

Chapter 1

1. *Journal d'un bourgeois de Paris, 1405–1449, publié d'après les manuscrits de Rome et de Paris par Alexandre Tuetey inédit* (Paris: H. Champion, 1881), 219–20.
2. David Cressy, *Gypsies. An English History* (Oxford: Oxford University Press, 2018).
3. John E. Morgan, '"Counterfeit Egyptians": The Construction and Implementation of Criminal Identity in Early Modern England', *Romani Studies* 26, no. 2 (2016): 105–28 (quote on p. 120).
4. Leo Lucassen, Wim Willems and Annemarie Cottar, *Gypsies and Other Itinerant Groups. A Socio-historical Approach* (Basingstoke: Macmillan, 1998).
5. María Sierra, 'Cannibals Devoured: Gypsies in Romantic Discourse on the Spanish Nation', in *Enemies within: Cultural Hierarchies and Liberal Political Models in the Hispanic World*, ed. María Sierra (Cambridge: Cambridge Scholar Publishing, 2015).
6. Isabella F. Romer, *The Rhone, the Darro and the Guadalquivir. A Summer Ramble in 1842*, Vol. 2 (London: Richard Bentley, 1843), 115.
7. Ken Lee, 'Orientalism and Gypsylorism', *Social Analysis* 44, no. 2 (2000): 129–65.
8. George Borrow, *The Zincali. An Account of the Gypsies of Spain* (London: John Murray, 1841), 77.
9. Prosper Mérimée, *Carmen*, trans. Lady Mary Lloyd (New York: Limited Editions Club, 1941; Kindle edn, n.d.), Ch. 2.
10. Franz Liszt, *Des Bohémiens et leur musique en Hongrie* (Paris: Librairie Nouvelle, 1859).
11. Leni Riefenstahl, *Tiefland* (Riefenstahl Film, GmbH, 1954) [filmed in 1940–4 in the midst of the Second World War but not released until ten years after it ended].
12. Robert Knox, *The Races of Man: A Fragment* (Philadelphia: Lea and Blanchard, 1850), 108.
13. Leonardo Piasere and Gianluca Solla, *I filosofi e gli zingari* (Rome: Aracne, 2018); Leonardo Piasere, 'Crania Cingarica. La construcción antropológica del cuerpo gitano', *Historia Social* 93 (2019): 103–22.
14. Borrow, *The Zincali*.
15. Ibid., 264.
16. Ibid., 53–4, 309.
17. David Mayall, *Gypsy Identities 1500–2000: From Egipcyans and Moon-Men to the Ethnic Romany* (London: Routledge, 2004); and David Mayall, *Gypsy-Travellers in the Nineteenth Century Society* (Cambridge: Cambridge University Press, 1988); Wim Willems, *In Search of the True Gypsy. From Enlightenment to Final Solution* (London: Frank Cass, 1997).
18. Piasere, 'Crania Cingarica', 103–22.
19. Jean Kommers, '*Gypsies' in Nineteenth-Century Children's Books* (Leiden: Brill Academic Publishers, Inc., 2022); and *Kinderroof of Zigeunerroof? Zigeuners in Kinderboeken* (Utrecht: Van Arkel, 1993).
20. Ibid., 47, 48; Mérimée, *Carmen*, Ch. 3.
21. Lou Charnon-Deutsch, *The Spanish Gypsy. The History of a European Obsession* (University Park: Pennsylvania State University Press, 2004).
22. Alexandre Zanko, *La Bible des Roms. La tradition Tsigane dévoilée par Zanko et recueillie par le Révérend Père Chatard* (1959; repr. Marseille: Gaussen – Association Tchatchipen, 2017).

Notes

23. Alaina Lemon, 'Roma (*Gypsies*) in the Soviet Union and the Moscow Teatr Romen', *Nationalities Papers* 19, no. 3 (1991): 359–72.
24. Ilona Klímová-Alexander, 'Development and Institutionalization of Romani Representation and Administration. Part 2: Beginnings of Modern Institutionalization [Nineteenth Century-World War II]', *Nationalities Papers* 33, no. 2 (2005): 155–210.
25. Michael Zimmermann, 'The National Socialist "Solution of the Gypsy Question": Central Decisions, Local Initiatives, and Their Interrelation', *Holocaust and Genocide Studies* 5, no. 3 (2001): 412–27; and *Rassenutopie und Genozid. Die nationalsozialistische 'Lösung der Zigeunerfrage'* (Hamburg: Christians, 1996).
26. Zimmermann, 'The National Socialist "Solution"'.
27. Ilsen About, 'Underclass Gypsies. An Historical Approach on Categorization and Exclusion in France in the Nineteenth and the Twentieth Centuries', in *The Gypsy 'Menace'. Populism and the New Anti-Gypsy Politics*, ed. Michael Stewart (London: Hurst, 2012).
28. Celia Donert, *The Rights of the Roma. The Struggle for Citizenship in Postwar Czechoslovakia* (Cambridge: Cambridge University Press, 2017).
29. Zimmermann, 'The National Socialist "Solution of the Gypsy Question"'; *Rassenutopie und Genozid*.
30. Mark Levene, *The Crisis of Genocide. Annihilation: The European Rimlands 1939–1953*, Vol. 2 (Oxford: Oxford University Press, 2013).

Chapter 2

1. Alex J. Kay, *Empire of Destruction. A History of Nazi Mass Killing* (New Haven: Yale University Press, 2021).
2. Slawomir Kapralski, 'The Consequences of the Genocide for Roma Memories and Identities', in *The Legacies of the Roma Genocide in Europe since 1945*, ed. Celia Donert and Eve Rosenhaft (London, New York: Routledge, 2022).
3. Weiss-Wendt, *The Nazi Genocide of the Roma*, 4.
4. Friedlander, *The Origins of Nazi Genocide*.
5. Sevasti Trubeta, 'Gypsiness, Racial Discourse and Persecution: Balkan Roma during the Second World War', *Nationalities Papers* 31, no. 4 (2003): 495–514; Martin Holler, 'The National Socialist Genocide of the Roma in the German-Occupied Soviet Union', in *Report for the Documentary and Cultural Centre of German Sinti and Roma* (Heidelberg: online, 2009), https://dokuzentrum.sintiundroma.de/en/?s=report+for+the+documentary+and+cultural+centre+of+german+sinti (accessed 8 September 2022).
6. David Motadel, *Islam and Nazi Germany's War* (Cambridge, MA: The Belknap Press of Harvard University Press, 2014).
7. Weiss-Wendt, *The Nazi Genocide of the Roma*.
8. Ludwig Eiber, 'The Persecution of the Sinti and Roma in Munich 1933–1945', in *Sinti and Roma. Gypsies in German Speaking Society and Literature*, ed. Susan Tebbutt (New York, Oxford: Berghahn Books, 1998), 23.
9. Raul Hilberg, *The Destruction of the European Jews* (New York: Holmes and Meier, 1985).
10. Saul Friendländer, *Nazi Germany and the Jews, 1933–1939* (New York: Harper Collins, 1997).

11. Walter Winter, *Winter Time. Memoirs of a German Sinto Who Survived Auschwitz* (Hatfield: University of Hertfordshire Press, 2004).
12. Frank Sparing, 'The Gypsy Camps', in *From 'Race Science' to the Camps. The Gypsies during the Second World War*, ed. Karola Fings, Herbert Heuss and Frank Sparing (Hatfield: University of Hertfordshire Press, 1999).
13. Otto Rosenberg, *A Gypsy in Auschwitz, as Told to Ulrich Enzenberger* (London: London House, 1999).
14. Riefenstahl, *Tiefland*.
15. Rosenberg, *A Gypsy in Auschwitz*.
16. Jud Nirenberg, *Johann Trollmann and Romani Resistance to Nazis* (Iowa City: Win by KO, 2016); Dario Fo, *Razza di Zingaro* (Milan: chiarelettere editore, 2016).
17. Gilad Margalit, 'The Justice System of the Federal Republic of Germany and the Nazi Persecution of the Gypsies', in *The Nazi Genocide of the Roma. Reassessment and Commemoration*, ed. Anton Weiss-Wendt (New York, Oxford: Berghahn Books, 2013).
18. Philomena Franz, *Zwischen Liebe und Hass. Ein Zigeunerleben* (Freiburg: Herder, 1985; repr., self, 2001), 41.
19. Zimmermann, 'The National Socialist "Solution of the Gypsy Question"'; and *Rassenutopie und Genozid*.
20. Janko Lauenberger and Juliane von Wedemeyer, *Ede und Unku – die wahre Geschichte. Das Schicksal einer Sinti-Familie von der Weimarer Republik bis Heute* (Gütersloh: Gütersloher Verlagshaus, 2018).
21. Kay, *Empire of Destruction*, 245.
22. Wolfgang Benz, 'Vom Vorurteil zum Massenmord: Die nationalsozialistische Verfolgung der Zigeuner', in *Zwischen Liebe und Hass: Ein Zigeunerleben*, auth. Philomena Franz (Freiburg: Herder, 1985; repr., 1992).
23. Winter, *Winter Time*.
24. *Nazi Conspiracy and Aggression*, Office of United States Chief of Council For Persecution of Axis Criminality, Vol. 3 (1946), 496.
25. Eiber, 'The Persecution of the Sinti and Roma'.
26. Sonneman, *Shared Sorrows*.
27. Slawomir Kapralski, Maria Martyniak and Joanna Talewicz-Kwiatkowska, *Roma in Auschwitz, Voices of Memory Series*, Vol. 7 (Auschwitz: International Center for Education about Auschwitz and the Holocaust, 2011), 66.
28. Jonathan Petropoulos, 'The Polycratic Nature of Art Looting: The Dynamic Balance of the Third Reich,' in *Networks of Nazi Persecution. Bureaucracy, Business and the Organization of the Holocaust*, ed. Gerard D. Feldman and Wolfgang Seibel (New York-Oxford: Berghahn Books, 2004), 103–17.
29. Nirenberg, *Johann Trollmann*.
30. Jirí Lípa, 'The Fate of Gypsies in Czechoslovakia under Nazi Domination', in *A Mosaic of Victims: Non-Jews Persecuted and Murdered by the Nazis*, ed. Michael Berenbaum (New York: New York University Press, 1990).
31. Ibid., 211.
32. Emmanuel Filhol and Marie-Christine Hubert, *Les Tsiganes en France. Un sort à part 1939-1946* (Paris: Perrin, 2009); Lise Foisneau, 'Mass Arrests and Persecutions of "Nomads" in France, 1944–1946. Post-Liberation Purges or Evidence of Anti-Gypsysim?', in

Notes

The Legacies of the Roma Genocide in Europe since 1945, ed. Celia Donert and Eve Rosenhaft (London, New York: Routledge, 2022).

33. 'Un camp pour les Tsiganes – Saliers, 1942–1944', Musée de la Résistance et de la Déportation de l'Isère – Maison des Droits de l'Homme, Grenoble (27 November 2015 to 23 May 2016).

34. Monica Heddebaut, *Des Tsiganes vers Auschwitz. Le convoi Z du 15 janvier 1944* (Paris: Éditions Tirésias-Michel Reynaud, 2018).

35. Adam Czerniakow, *The Warsaw Diary of Adam Czerniakow: Prelude to Doom*, ed. Raul Hilberg (Chicago: Robert R. Dee, 1999).

36. Joseph Kermish, 'Emmanuel Ringelblum's Notes, Hitherto Unpublished', *Yad Vashem Studies* VII (1968): 117–18.

37. Mikhail Tyaglyy, 'Nazi Occupation Policies and the Mass Murder of the Roma in Ukraine', in *The Nazi Genocide of the Roma. Reassessment and Commemoration*, ed. Anton Weiss-Wendt (New York, Oxford: Berghahn Books, 2013).

38. Florian Freund, 'Genocidal Trajectory: Persecution of Gypsies in Austria, 1938–1945', in *The Nazi Genocide of the Roma. Reassessment and Commemoration*, ed. Anton Weiss-Wendt (New York, Oxford: Berghahn Books, 2013).

39. Hannah Arendt, *Eichmann In Jerusalem. A Report on the Banality of Evil*, Internet Archive, May 2020, https://archive.org/details/eichmann-in-jerusalem-a-report-on-the-banality-of-evil-by-hannah-arendt (accessed 3 September 2022).

40. Saul Friedländer, *Nazi Germany and the Jews; and Saul Friedländer, The Years of Extermination: Nazi Germany and the Jews, 1939–1945* (New York: HarperCollins, 2007).

41. Giovanna Boursier, 'Gypsies in Italy during the Fascist Dictatorship and the Second World War', in *The Gypsies during the Second World War. In the Shadow of the Swastika*, ed. Donald Kenrick (Paris: Hatfield, Centre de Recherches Tsiganes/University of Hertfordshire, 1999).

42. Paola Trevisan, '"Gypsies" in Fascist Italy: From Expelled Foreigners to Dangerous Italians', *Social History* 42, no. 3 (2017): 342–64.

43. Viorel Achim, 'Gypsy Research and Gypsy Policy in Romania', in *Zwischen Erziehung und Vernichtung. Zigeunerpolitik und Zigeunerforschung im Europa des 20. Jahrhunderts*, ed. Viorel Achim (Stuttgart: Franz Steiner Verlag, 2007); and *The Roma in Romanian History* (Budapest: Central European University Press, 1998).

44. Paul Mojzes, *Balkan Genocides. Holocaust and Ethnic Cleansing in the Twentieth Century* (Lanham: Rowman and Littlefield Publishers, 2011), 58; and Alexander Korb, 'Ustacha Mass Violence against Gypsies in Croatia, 1941–1942', in *The Nazi Genocide of the Roma. Reassessment and Commemoration*, ed. Anton Weiss-Wendt (New York, Oxford: Berghahn Books, 2013).

45. David M. Crowe, *A History of the Gypsies of Eastern Europe and Russia* (New York: St. Martin's Griffin, 1994).

46. Kay, *Empire of Destruction*, 66.

47. Holler, 'The National Socialist Genocide of the Roma'.

48. Holler, 'The National Socialist Genocide of the Roma'; and 'The Nazi Persecution of Roma in Northwestern Russia: The Operational Area of the Army Group North, 1941–1944', in *The Nazi Genocide of the Roma*, ed. Anton Weiss-Wendt (New York, Oxford: Berghahn Books), 153–80.

49. *Nazi Conspiracy and Aggression*, Office of United States Chief of Council For Persecution of Axis Criminality, Vol. 6 (1946), 496.

50. Holler, 'The National Socialist Genocide of the Roma'.
51. Tyaglyy, 'Nazi Occupation Policies'; Kay, *Empire of Destruction*, 112.
52. Gerhard Baumgartner, 'Identifying the Roma and Sinti Victims Forcefully Deported in Autumn 1941 to the "Zigeunerlager" Litzmannstadt', in *Beyond the Roma Holocaust: From Resistance to Mobilisation*, ed. Thomas M. Buchsbaum and Slawomir Kapralski (Krakow: Österreichische Botschaft Warschau – Taiwpn Universitas, 2017), 41–58.
53. Levene, *The Crisis of Genocide. Annihilation*.
54. Guenter Lewy, 'Himmler and the 'Racially Pure Gypsies'', *Journal of Contemporary History* 34, no. 2 (1999): 201–14.
55. Paul Weindling, *Victims and Survivors of Nazi Human Experiments. Science and Suffering* (London: Bloomsbury, 2014).
56. Zimmermann, *Rassenutopie und Genozid*.
57. Kapralski et al., *Roma in Auschwitz*.
58. Ibid., 81 (Polish prisoner), 80 (Romani soldier).
59. Ibid., 74 (Peter), 86 (German Romani), 73 ('elegant woman'), 68–9 (Baker).
60. Ibid., 98.
61. Levene, *The Crisis of Genocide*.
62. Benz, 'Vom Vorurteil zum Massenmord'.
63. Franz, *Zwischen Liebe und Hass*, 51.
64. *Memorial Book: The Gypsies at Auschwitz-Birkenau* (Munich, New York: State Museum of Auschwitz-Birkenau – Documentary and Cultural Centre of German Sinti and Roma, 1993).
65. Imre Kertész, *Fateless* (Evanston: Northwestern University Press, 1992).
66. Zimmermann, *Rassenutopie und Genozid*.
67. Franz, *Zwischen Liebe und Hass*; Sonneman, *Shared Sorrows*, 65–6 (Mettbach); *Memorial Book*, 1497 (Guttenberger).
68. Kapralski et al., *Roma in Auschwitz*, 75.
69. Ibid.
70. *Memorial Book*, 1520.
71. Rudolf Höss, *Commandant of Auschwitz, The Autobiography of Rudolf Hoess* (Cleveland, New York: The World Publishing Company, 1959), 234.
72. Kapralski et al., *Roma in Auschwitz*, 97.
73. Primo Levi, *If This Is a Man / The Truce*, trans. Sturt Woolf (Miami: The Orion Press 1969; Kindle edn, Abacus, 2003), Ch. 13, 'October 1944'.
74. Zimmermann, *Rassenutopie und Genozid*.
75. Kapralski et al., *Roma in Auschwitz*, 90.
76. Ibid., 91.
77. Zimmermann, *Rassenutopie und Genozid*; Kapralski et al., *Roma in Auschwitz*.
78. Kay, *Empire of Destruction*, 252.
79. *Memorial Book*, 1517.
80. Ibid., 1498.
81. Höss, *Commandant of Auschwitz*, 140–1.

Notes

82. Primo Levi, *The Drowned and the Saved* (London: Abacus, 1989; repr. 2013), 132; *If This Is a Man*, Ch. 1, 'The Journey'.
83. Kapralski et al., *Roma in Auschwitz*.
84. Levi, *The Drowned and the Saved*, 21.
85. Kapralski et al., *Roma in Auschwitz*, 97.
86. Franz, *Zwischen Liebe und Hass*; *Memorial Book*, 1518.
87. Palise Taicon, Auschwitz Prisoners Database (n.d.), https://www.auschwitz.org/en/museum/auschwitz-prisoners/ (accessed 12 September 2022); Kapralski et al., *Roma in Auschwitz*, 60.
88. Eve Rosenhaft, 'The Gypsy's Revenge. Betrayal and Personal Retribution as Themes in the Post-Holocaust Experience and Memory of German Sinti', in *Beyond Camps and Forced Labour II. Proceedings of the Second Conference on Post-Holocaust Experience and Memory*, ed. J.D. Steinert and Inge Weber-Newth (Osnabrück: Secolo, 2008).
89. Kapralski et al., *Roma in Auschwitz*, 76.
90. Levi, *If This Is a Man*, Ch. 9, 'The Drowned and the Saved'.
91. Rosenberg, *A Gypsy in Auschwitz*, 65–6.
92. Simon Laks, *Music of Another World* (Evanston: Northwestern University Press, 1989).
93. Kapralski et al., *Roma in Auschwitz*, 88.
94. Laks, *Music of Another World*, 82.
95. David W. Pike, *Spaniards in the Holocaust: Mauthausen, the Horror on the Danube* (London: Routledge, 2000).
96. Laks, *Music of Another World*.
97. Sonneman, *Shared Sorrows*; Levi, *If This Is a Man*, Chapter 4, 'Ka-Be'.
98. Laks, *Music of Another World*.
99. Pike, *Spaniards in the Holocaust*, 113.
100. Karola Fings, 'Romani and Sinti in the concentration camps', in *From 'Race Science' to the Camps. The Gypsies during the Second World War*, ed. Karola Fings, Herbert Heuss and Frank Sparing (Hatfield: University of Hertfordshire Press, 1999).
101. Kapralski et al., *Roma in Auschwitz*, 10.
102. Ibid., 69.
103. Rosenberg, *A Gypsy in Auschwitz*, 28.
104. Sonneman, *Shared Sorrows*, 94–9.
105. Ceija Stojka, *Wir Leben im Verborgenen: Erinnerungen einer Rom-Zigeunerin* (Vienna: Picus, 1988); Karin Berger, *Unter den Brettern hellgrünes Gras* (Navigator Film Produktion, 2005).
106. Friedlander, *The Origins of Nazi Genocide*.
107. Kapralski et al., *Roma in Auschwitz*, 87.
108. Ibid.
109. Robert Jay Lifton, *The Nazi Doctors. Medical Killing and the Psychology of Genocide* (New York: Basic Books, 2000).
110. Kapralski et al., *Roma in Auschwitz* (Babbit), 95; (Wierzbicka), 92.
111. Marius Turda, 'The ambiguous victim: Miklós Nyiszli's Narrative of Medical Experimentation in Auschwitz-Birkenau', *Historien* 14, no. 1 (2014): 43–58.

Notes

112. Ibid.
113. Kapralski et al., *Roma in Auschwitz*, 101.
114. Winter, *Winter Time*; Rosenberg, *A Gypsy in Auschwitz*.
115. Levi, *The Drowned and the Saved*, 173.
116. Kapralski et al., 22; *Roma in Auschwitz*, 124–5.
117. Lise Foisneau and Valentin Merlin, 'French Nomads' Resistance, 1939–1946', in *Roma Resistance during the Holocaust and Its Aftermath. Collection of Working Papers*, ed. Evelin Verhás et al. (Budapest: Tom Lantos Institute, 2018).
118. Verhás et al. (ed.), *Roma Resistance during the Holocaust and Its Aftermath. Collection of Working Papers* (Budapest: Tom Lantos Institute, 2018).
119. Jan Yoors, *Crossing. A Journal of Survival and Resistance in World War II* (London: Weidenfeld and Nicholson, 1972).
120. Holler, 'The National Socialist Genocide of the Roma'; Alaina Lemon, 'Roma (*Gypsies*) in the Soviet Union and the Moscow Teatr Romen'.
121. C. Stojka, *Wir Leben im Verborgenen*.
122. Ibid.; Rosenberg, *A Gypsy in Auschwitz*, 84.
123. Zoe V. Waxman, *Writing the Holocaust: Identity, Testimony, Representation* (Oxford: Oxford University Press, 2006).
124. Sybil Milton, 'Hidden Lives: Sinti and Roma Women', in *Experience and Expression. Women, the Nazis, and the Holocaust*, ed. Elizabeth R. Baer and Myrna Goldenberg (Detroit: Wayne State University Press, 2003).

Chapter 3

1. Winter, *Winter Time*, 117.
2. Thomas W. Neumann and Michael Zimmermann, 'Postscript: Sinti and Roma in Post-War Germany', in Walter Winter, auth., *Winter Time. Memoirs of a German Sinto Who Survived Auschwitz* (Hatfield: University of Hertfordshire Press, 2004), 153–69.
3. Sybil Milton, 'Persecuting the Survivors: The Continuity of "Anti-Gypsyism" in Postwar Germany and Austria', in *Gypsies in German-Speaking Society and Literature*, ed. Susan Tebbutt (New York, Oxford: Berghahn Books, 1998).
4. Benz, 'Vom Vorurteil zum Massenmord'; ibid., 122.
5. *Basic Handbook. ABC of German Administration and Public Services* (National Archives of America, NARA, 1944), 98.
6. Margalit, 'The Justice System of the Federal Republic of Germany'.
7. Neumann and Zimmermann, 'Postscript: Sinti and Roma in Post-War Germany'; Margalit, 'The Justice System of the Federal Republic of Germany'.
8. Foisneau, 'Mass Arrests and Persecutions of "Nomads" in France, 1944–1946'.
9. Milton, 'Persecuting the Survivors'.
10. Margalit, 'The Justice System of the Federal Republic of Germany'.
11. Lauenberger and von Wedemeyer, *Ede und Unku*.
12. Jana Müller, *What Happened to Unku?* (Alternatives Jugendzentrum, 2008).

Notes

13. Petre Matei, 'Compensation Claims from Romania in the ITS Collections. Between the Victims and the State', *Jahrbuch des International Tracing Service* 5 (2016): 160–86); and 'Roma in 1980s Communist Romania and Roma Discourse on Holocaust: Between Compensation and Identity', in *The Legacies of the Roma Genocide in Europe since 1945*, ed. Celia Donert and Eve Rosenhaft (London, New York: Routledge, 2022).
14. Elena Marushiakova and Vesselin Popov, 'State Policies under Communism' (Council of Europe open-access working paper, 2013), https://rm.coe.int/state-policies-under-communism-factsheets-on-romani-history/16808b1c58 (accessed 11 November 2022).
15. Mateo Maximoff, 'Germany and the Gypsies: From the Gypsy's Point of View', *Journal of the Gypsy Lore Society* XXV (1946): 104–8.
16. Anja Reuss, '"Returning to Normality?": The Struggle of Sinti and Roma Survivors to Rebuild a Life in Postwar Germany', in *Jewish and Romani Families in the Holocaust and Its Aftermath*, ed. Eliyana R. Adler and Kateřina Čapková (New Brunswick: Rutgers University Press, 2021).
17. Eve Rosenhaft 'Strangers in Their Own Land: Romani Survivors in Europe 1945', *National WWII Museum*, September 2021, https://www.nationalww2museum.org/war/articles/romani-holocaust-survivors-1945 (accessed 18 September 2022).
18. Hilberg, *The Destruction;* Slawomir Kapralski, 'The Memory of Genocide and Contemporary Roma Identities', in *The Nazi Genocide of the Roma. Reassessment and Commemoration*, ed. Anton Weiss-Wendt (New York, Oxford: Berghahn Books, 2013).
19. Miriam Novitch, *Le génocide des Tziganes sous le régime nazi* (Paris: Comité pour l'érection du Monument en mémoire des Tziganes assassinés à Auschwitz, 1968); María Sierra, 'Creating Romanestan: A Place to Be a *Gypsy* in Post-Nazi Europe', *European History Quarterly* 49, no. 1.2 (2019): 272–92.
20. Grattan Puxon and Donald Kenrick, *The Destiny of Europe's Gypsies* (London: Sussex University Press, 1972).
21. Gilad Margalit and Yaron Matras, 'Gypsies in Germany – German Gypsies? Identity and Politics of Sinti and Roma in Germany', in *The Roma: A Minority in Europe. Historical, Social and Cultural Perspectives*, ed. Roni Stauber and Raphael Vago (New York, Oxford: Berghahn Books, 2007).
22. Nadine Blumer, 'Commemorating Sinti and Roma and Jews in Germany's National Narrative', in *The Nazi Genocide of the Roma. Reassessment and Commemoration*, ed. Anton Weiss-Wendt (New York, Oxford: Berghahn Books, 2013).
23. Franz, *Zwischen Liebe und Hass*.
24. Kapralski, 'The Memory of Genocide'.
25. Ilsen About and Anna Abakunova, 'The Genocide and Persecution of Roma and Sinti. Bibliography and Historiographical Review', 2016, https://www.holocaustremembrance.com/resources/publications/genocide-and-persecution-roma-and-sinti-bibliography-and-historiographical (accessed 8 September 2022).
26. Puxon and Kenrick, *The Destiny of Europe's Gypsies*.
27. Zimmermann, *Rassenutopie und Genozid*.
28. Milton, 'The Context of Holocaust'; Milton, 'Gypsies and the Holocaust'; and: Friedlander, 'Step by Step: The Expansion of Murder, 1939–1941'; and *The Origins of Nazi Genocide*.
29. Benz, 'Vom Vorurteil zum Massenmord'; *Memorial Book*.
30. Lewy, 'Himmler and the 'Racially Pure Gypsies''; and: Gilad Margalit, *Die Nachkriegsdeutschen und 'ihre Zigeuner'. Die Behandlung der Sint und Roma im Schatten von*

Auschwitz (Berlin: Metropol Verlag, 2001); and *Germany and Its Gypsies. A Post-Auschwitz Ordeal* (Madison: The University of Wisconsin Press 2002).

31. Karola Fings, Herbert Heuss and Frank Sparing, *From 'Race Science' to the Camps. The Gypsies during the Second World War* (Hatfield: University of Hertfordshire Press, 1999); Donald Kenrick, *The Gypsies during the Second World War. In the Shadow of the Swastika* (Paris: Hatfield, Centre de Recherches Tsiganes/University of Hertfordshire, 1999).

32. Anton Weiss-Wendt, *The Nazi Genocide of the Roma. Reassessment and Commemoration* (New York, Oxford: Berghahn Books, 2013).

33. Celia Donert and Eve Rosenhaft, *The Legacies of the Roma Genocide in Europe since 1945* (London, New York: Routledge, 2022).

34. Eve Rosenhaft, 'At Large in the "Grey Zone": Narrating the Romani Holocaust', in *Unsettling History. Archiving and Narrating in Historiography*, ed. Sebastian Jobs and Alf Lüdtke (Frankfurt: Campus, 2010).

35. Huub van Baar, 'From "Time-Banditry" to the Challenge of Established Historiographies: Romany Contributions to Old and New Images of the Holocaust', in *Multidisciplinary Approaches to Romany Studies*, ed. Michael Stewart and Máton Rövid (Budapest: Central European University, 2010), 153–71.

36. Ljiljana Radonic, '"Unadaptable People" – Roma and "Our" Victims in Post-Communist Memorial Museums', in *The Legacies of the Roma Genocide in Europe since 1945*, ed. Celia Donert and Eve Rosenhaft (London, New York: Routledge, 2022).

37. Berger, *Unter den Brettern hellgrünes Gras*; Ceija Stojka's memoirs are available on her namesake website, 2019, https://www.ceijastojka.org/; Karl Stojka, *The Story of Karl Stojka: A Childhood in Birkenau* (Washington DC: United States Holocaust Memorial Museum, 1992).

38. 'Don't Forget the Photos' [virtual exhibition slideshow], Alternatives Jugendzentrum Dessau and University of Liverpool (n.d.), https://dontforgetthephotos.wordpress.com (accessed 3 September 2022); Eve Rosenhaft, 'A Photographer and His "Victims": Reconstructing a Shared Experience of the Romani Holocaust, 1934–1964', in *The Role of the Romanies. Images and Counter Images of Gypsies/Romanies in European Cultures*, ed. Nicholas Saul and Susan Tebbutt (Liverpool: Liverpool University Press, 2005).

39. 'Forgotten Victims: The Nazi Genocide of the Roma and Sinti' [virtual exhibition slideshow], United Nations, August 2020, https://www.un.org/en/exhibits/forgotten-victims (accessed 3 September 2022).

40. Wanda Jakubowska, *The Last Stage* (in Polish *Ostatni etap*) (Film Polski, 1948); Alexander Ramati, *And the Violins Stopped Playing* (in Polish *I skrzypce przestaly grac*) (Studio Filmowe TOR and Roberts/David Films, 1988); Toni Gatlif, *Korkoro*, ed. Monique Dartonne (Production Princes, France 3 Cinéma and Rhône-Alpes Cinéma, 2010); Étienne Comar, *Django*, ed. Monica Coleman (Olivier Delbosc, Marc Missonnier, 2017); Joanna Kos-Krauze and Krzysztof Krauze, *Papusza*, online feature film (New Europe Film Sales, 2013) https://www.youtube.com/watch?v=Lemo7DK7e3c (accessed 9 November 2022).

41. Müller, *What Happened to Unku?*; Navarro, *Mi Holocausto – My Holocaust*.

42. It benefitted from research conducted in collaboration with the project Beyond Stereotypes: Cultural Exchanges and the Romani Contribution to European Public Spaces (BESTROM) and the Universities of Seville, Liverpool, Helsinki and Krakow.

43. Gerhard Baumgartner, Irmgard Bibermann et al. *The Fate of European Roma and Sinti during the Holocaust. Teacher's Manual*, trans. Chris March, Austrian Bundesministerium für Bildung und Frauen, the Fondation pour la Mémoire de le Shoah, Paris, and the

Notes

International Holocaust Remembrance Alliance (n.d.), https://www.romasintigenocide.eu/en/home (accessed 3 September 2022).

44. Rosenhaft, 'Strangers in Their Own Land'; Maria Sierra, 'Philomena Franz, Narrator of the Romani Holocaust', BESTROM (n.d.) (https://bestrom.org/blog-2/105-philomena-franz,-narrator-of-the-romani-holocaust) (accessed 4 September 2022); 'Giving Memory a Future. The Sinti and Roma in Italy and around the World', USC Shoah Foundation, 2015, https://sfi.usc.edu/education/roma-sinti/en/conosciamo-i-roma-e-i-sinti/chi-sono/nel-'mondo-e-in-italia'.php (accessed 3 September 2022).
45. Michel van der Burg, *Westerbork Films by Rudolf Breslauer* (Westerbork Films Collection, UNESCO Album, uploaded 20 January 2020) [filmed at Westerbork, The Netherlands in 1945; Settela appears at minute 6:21] www.openbeelden.nl/media/1223905/WESTERBORK_FILMS_COLLECTION__UNESCO_ALBUM__20200120 (accessed 4 September 2022).
46. Aad Wagenaar, *Settela* (Nottingham: Five Leaves, 2005; repr. 2016).
47. Cherry Duyns, *Settela, Gezicht van het Verleden* (Vera de Vries for VPRO, 1994).

Chapter 4

1. Levi, *The Drowned and the Saved*.
2. Annette Wieviorka, *L'ère du témoin* (Paris: Plon, 1998).
3. Viktor Frankl, *Man's Search for Meaning, an Introduction to Logotherapy* (Boston: Beacon Press, 1959), 20.
4. LaCapra, *Representing the Holocaust*.
5. Rosenhaft, 'The Gypsy's Revenge'; Julia von dem Knesebeck, *The Roma Struggle for Compensation in Post-War Germany* (Hatfield: Hertfordshire University Press, 2011).
6. Levi, *The Drowned and the Saved*.
7. Paul Steinberg, *Speak You Also: A Survivor's Reckoning*, trans. Linda Coverdale and Bill Ford (New York: Metropolitan Books/Henry Holt and Co., 2000; Kindle edn), Chapter 'Digression III'.
8. Levi, *The Drowned and the Saved*, 173.
9. Simon Laks, *Music of Another World* (Evanston: Northwestern University Press, 1989).
10. Nico Rost, *Goethe en Dachau* (Barcelona: Contraescritura, 2016).
11. Sonneman, *Shared Sorrows*, 39,77.
12. Steinberg, *Speak You Also*, Chapter 'Hindsight'.
13. Frankl, *Man's Search for Meaning*.
14. Margalit, 'The Justice System of the Federal Republic of Germany', 196.
15. C. stojka, *Wir Leben im Verborgenen*.
16. Rosenberg, *A Gypsy in Auschwitz*, 126–7.
17. Franz, *Zwischen Liebe und Hass*, 101.
18. C. Stojka, *Wir leben in Verborgenen*, 97.
19. Quoted by Reinhold Lehmann in his interviews with Franz in: Franz, *Zwischen Liebe und Hass*, 98.
20. C. Stojka, *Wir leben im Verborgenen*.

21. Berger, *Unter den Brettern hellgrünes Gras*.
22. C. Stojka, *Nous vivons cachés. Récits d'une Romani à travers le siècle* [we lived in hiding, a Roma woman's twentieth-century memoirs] (Plounéour-Ménez: Éditions Isabelle Sauvage, 2018).
23. Zwicker, 'Journeys into Memory', 77.
24. Lily van Angeren, '*Polizeilich zwangsentführt'. Das Leben der Sintizza Lily van Angeren-Franz* [kidnapped by the police: the life of Sintizza Lily van Angeren-Franz] (Hildesheim: Gebrüder Gerstenberg, 2004).
25. Karl Stojka, *Auf der ganzen Welt zuhause: Das Leben und Wandern des Zigeuners Karl Stojka* [the whole world as home: the life and wanderings of Gypsy Karl Stojka] (Vienna: Picus Verlag, 1994); and *The Story of Karl Stojka*.
26. van Angeren, '*Polizeilich zwangsentführt'*.
27. Walter Winter, *WinterZeit. Erinnerungen eines deutschen Sinto, der Auschwitz überlebt hat* (Hamburg: Ergebnisse, 1999) The English language version cited earlier is the one used here: Winter, *Winter Time*.
28. Winter, *Winter Time*, 35.
29. Ibid., 123.
30. Otto Rosenberg, *Das Brennglas* (Berlin: Eichborn, 1998); and *A Gypsy in Auschwitz*.
31. Ewald Hanstein, *Meine hundert Leben. Erinnerungen eines deutschen Sinto* [my one hundred lives: a German Sinto's memoirs] (Bremen: Donat, 2005).
32. Hanstein, *Meine hundert Leben*, 9.
33. Winter, *Winter Time*, 57.
34. LaCapra, *Representing the Holocaust*.
35. Zwicker, 'Journeys into Memory'.
36. Eve Rosenhaft, 'A Photographer and His "Victims": Reconstructing a Shared Experience of the Romani Holocaust, 1934–1964', in *The Role of the Romanies. Images and Counter Images of 'Gypsies/Romanies' in European Cultures*, ed. Nicholas Saul and Susan Tebbutt (Liverpool: Liverpool University Press, 2005).

Chapter 5

1. Levi, *The Drowned and the Saved*, 16.
2. Barbara H. Rosenwein, 'Worrying about Emotions in History', *American Historical Review* 107, no. 3 (2002): 834–6.
3. Joanna Bourke, *Premature Burial and the Mysteries of Death* (Oxfordshire: Routledge, 2020).
4. William M. Reddy, *The Navigation of Feeling. A Framework for the History of Emotions* (Cambridge: Cambridge University Press, 2001).
5. Viktor Frankl, *Man's Search for Meaning*.
6. *Memorial Book*, 1523, 1498.
7. Steinberg, *Speak You Also*, Chapter 'Digression III'; Frankl, *Man's Search for Meaning*, 33.
8. Rosenberg, *A Gypsy in Auschwitz*, 78–9.
9. Levi, *If This Is a Man*, Ch. 17, 'The Story of Ten Days'.

Notes

10. Franz, *Zwischen Liebe und Hass*, 9.
11. Kapralski, Martyniak and Talewicz-Kwiatkowska, *Roma in Auschwitz*, 75.
12. Hanstein, *Meine hundert Leben*, 47.
13. C. Stojka, *Wir Leben im Verborgenen*, 22.
14. Winter, *Winter Time*, 45, 46.
15. C. Stojka, *Wir Leben im Verborgenen*, 20.
16. Frankl, *Man's Search for Meaning*; Simon Laks, *Music of Another World*, 97.
17. Lily van Angeren, 'Polizeilich zwangsentführt', 74.
18. C. Stojka, *Wir Leben im Verborgenen*, 37.
19. Laks, *Music of Another World*, 6.
20. Winter, *Winter Time*, 110.
21. Frankl, *Man's Search for Meaning*, 95.
22. Hanstein, *Meine hundert Leben*, 78.
23. Franz, *Zwischen Liebe und Hass*, 69.
24. Steinberg, *Speak You Also*, Chapter 'The Verdict'.
25. Rosenberg, *A Gypsy in Auschwitz*, 38, 40–1.
26. Winter, *Winter Time*, 39.
27. Sonneman, *Shared Sorrows*, 148.
28. Rosenberg, *A Gypsy in Auschwitz*, 57.
29. Winter, *Winter Time*, 76.
30. C. Stojka, *Wir Leben im Verborgenen*, 39, 40.
31. C. Stojka, *Wir Leben im Verborgenen*.
32. Steinberg, *Speak You Also*, Chapter 'One Sunday in Spring'.
33. *Memorial Book*, 1504.
34. Rosenberg, *A Gypsy in Auschwitz*, 110–12.
35. Ceija Stojka, *Nous vivons cachés. Récits d'une Romani à travers le siècle* (Plounéour-Ménez: Éditions Isabelle Sauvage, 2018), 97.
36. *Memorial Book*, 1518.
37. Hanstein, *Meine hundert Leben*, 52.
38. Ibid., 53, 69.
39. Rosenberg, *A Gypsy in Auschwitz*, 109, 53, 69.
40. Franz, *Zwischen Liebe und Hass*, 88.
41. Frankl, *Man's Search for Meaning*, 42.
42. Franz, *Zwischen Liebe und Hass*, 67.
43. Rosenberg, *A Gypsy in Auschwitz*, 71–2.
44. C. Stojka, *Wir Leben im Verborgenen*.
45. Sonneman, *Shared Sorrows*, 167.
46. C. Stojka, *Nous vivons cachés*, 88.
47. van Angeren, 'Polizeilich zwangsentführt', 68.
48. Rosenberg, *A Gypsy in Auschwitz*, 64.

49. Hanstein, *Meine hundert Leben*, 45.
50. Rosenberg, *A Gypsy in Auschwitz*, 65.
51. Winter, *Winter Time*, 50.
52. Rosenberg, *A Gypsy in Auschwitz*, 27.
53. van Angeren, 'Polizeilich zwangsentführt', 83.
54. Ibid., 70 *et sequentes*.
55. *Memorial Book*, 1510.
56. Rosenhaft, 'The Gypsy's Revenge'.
57. C. Stojka, *Wir Leben im Verborgenen*, 27.
58. Hanstein, *Meine hundert Leben*, 43.
59. Winter, *Winter Time*, 122.
60. Franz, *Zwischen Liebe und Hass*, 81.
61. Rosenberg, *A Gypsy in Auschwitz*, 116.
62. Rosenhaft, 'The Gypsy's Revenge'.
63. Rosenberg, *A Gypsy in Auschwitz*, 128.
64. Winter, *Winter Time*, 120–1.
65. Franz, *Zwischen Liebe und Hass*, 82.
66. Franz, *Zwischen Liebe und Hass*, 71.
67. Rosenberg, *A Gypsy in Auschwitz*, 100.
68. Winter, *Winter Time*, 62.
69. *Memorial Book*, 1510.
70. Levi, *If This Is a Man*, Ch. 4 'Ka-Be'.
71. Franz, *Zwischen Liebe und* Hass, 15.
72. *Memorial Book*, 1497.
73. Rosenberg, *A Gypsy in Auschwitz*, 18.
74. Winter, *Winter Time*, 8–9.
75. Hanstein, *Meine hundert Leben*, 10.
76. van Angeren, 'Polizeilich zwangsentführt', 18,31.
77. Winter, *Winter Time*, 11.
78. *Memorial Book*, 1497.
79. Jean Améry, *At the Mind's Limits. Contemplations by a Survivor of Auschwitz and Its Realities*, trans. Sidney Rosenfeld and Stella P. Rosenfeld (Bloomington and Indianapolis: University of Indiana Press, 2009), 41.
80. van Angeren, 'Polizeilich zwangsentführt', 46,50.
81. Ibid., 64.
82. Kertész, *Fateless*.
83. Rosenberg, *A Gypsy in Auschwitz*, 24.
84. Sonneman, *Shared Sorrows*, 136.
85. Laks, *Music of Another World*, 18.
86. Frankl, *Man's Search for Meaning*, 19.

Notes

87. Nico Rost, *Goethe en Dachau*, 284.
88. Rosenberg, *A Gypsy in Auschwitz*, 103.
89. van Angeren, '*Polizeilich zwangsentführt*', 75.
90. Rosenberg, *A Gypsy in Auschwitz*, 69.
91. *Memorial Book*, 1511.
92. van Angeren, '*Polizeilich zwangsentführt*', 90, 102.
93. Hanstein, *Meine hundert Leben*, 9.
94. Winter, *Winter Time*, 93.
95. Rosenberg, *A Gypsy in Auschwitz*, 86.
96. *Memorial Book*, 1527.
97. Winter, *Winter Time*, 87.
98. Hanstein, *Meine hundert Leben*, 164.
99. Charlotte Delbo, *Auschwitz and After* (New Haven-London: Yale University Press, 1997).
100. Sonneman, *Shared Sorrows*, 113.
101. van Angeren, '*Polizeilich zwangsentführt*', 100.
102. Rosenberg, *A Gypsy in Auschwitz*, 68.
103. Sonneman, *Shared Sorrows*, 169.
104. Winter, *Winter Time*, 15.
105. Rosenhaft, 'The Gypsy's Revenge'.
106. Eve Rosenhaft, 'A Photographer and His "victims"'.
107. Winter, *Winter Time*, 30–1.
108. Franz, *Zwischen Liebe und Hass*, 13.
109. Ibid., 31.
110. Hanstein, *Meine hundert Leben*, 25.
111. van Angeren, '*Polizeilich zwangsentführt*', 26.
112. Rosenberg, *A Gypsy in Auschwitz*, 12.
113. Marianne C. Zwicker, 'Journeys into Memory'.
114. Anne-Marie Gentily, 'Un *Sionisme* gitan: conversation avec Vaida Voevod III', *La Terre Retrouvée* 15, no. IX (1961).
115. Lorely French, *Roma Voices in the German-Speaking World* (New York, London: Bloomsbury, 2015).
116. van Angeren, '*Polizeilich zwangsentführt*', 114,156–7.
117. C. Stojka, *Wir Leben im Verborgenen*, 97.
118. Zwicker, 'Journeys into Memory'.
119. Ibid.
120. Franz, *Zwischen Liebe und Hass*, 10.
121. van Angeren, '*Polizeilich zwangsentführt*', 7.
122. Hanstein, *Meine hundert Leben*, 165.
123. Winter, *Winter Time*, 122.

Annotated Bibliography

1. This is a revised version adapted from a book originally published in Spanish by the author under the title *Holocausto gitano. El genocidio romaní bajo el nazismo* [Madrid: Arzalia, 2020]. Just as some parts of the book itself, geared to Spanish readers, have been deleted or altered, this bibliography of recommended readings omits publications exclusively relevant to the original.

INDEX

Abakunova, Anna 111
About, Ilsen 111
Absolon-Růžička, Antonin 79, 85
abuse 13, 17, 60, 62, 82–4, 99, 107, 127, 153
Achim, Viorel 57, 67
Ahnenerbe 72–4
Améry, Jean 161, 164
And the Violins Stopped Playing 116
anthropological observation 27–30
anthropometric ID cards 38, 62–4
anti-fascist Resistance 95–6, 161
anti-Gypsyism 2, 13, 16–17, 41, 100, 103, 128–9, 134–5
   de-Nazification 102
   genocidal trajectory 65
   German occupation 63
   nationalist projects 47
   Nazi regime policy 47–52, 57
   post-war 129
   and Zigeuner 128
anti-Semitism 47–8, 58, 100
Antonescu, Ion 67
Arendt, Hannah 6, 66
'Aryaneity' 72–3
asocial/asociability 36–7, 40, 48–9, 60, 62, 101, 103
Auschwitz-Birkenau extermination camp 3, 45, 51, 57, 59, 64, 74–9, 82, 86–9, 101, 118, 127, 131, 141, 143, 149
Auschwitz Decree 46, 57, 72, 74–8, 89, 101
Auschwitz *Zigeunerlager* 78–87, 93–4, 136, 153, 166

Babbitt, Dinah 92
Baker, Else 76, 88–9
Benz, Wolfgang 58, 78, 100, 111
Bergen-Belsen Camp 89, 97–8, 107, 137, 148–51, 164
Berger, Karin 176
BESTROM ('Beyond Stereotypes: Cultural Exchanges and the Romani Contribution to European Public Spaces') research project 116–17
blogs and websites, historical research 116–17
Blumenbach, Johann Friedrich 27
Blumer, Nadine 108
The Bohemian Girl 33
Bormann, Martin 73–4
Borrow, George 24, 28–9
Boursier, Giovanna 66

British Gypsy Lore Society 30
Broad, Pery 76
Buchenwald 67, 79, 87–8, 90, 131, 135–6, 154

capital punishment. *See* death penalty
Carmen (Mérimée) 24–5, 32–3
Centre for Research on Racial Hygiene and Demographic Biology 53, 74
child abduction 27, 31
childhood memoirs 160–1
children at concentration camps 87–93
Communauté Mondiale Gitane 106
concentration/extermination camps 3, 7, 45, 47, 49–50, 57–9, 62, 67–9, 72–4, 85, 89, 98, 101, 106, 108–9, 139, 145, 150–1, 158, 162, 173
confiscation of properties 60–4
Convoy Z 64
corporal punishment memoirs 151–5
criminality/criminology 18–19, 37–8, 78, 101
Czerniaków, Adam 65

Dachau Camp 48, 89, 107–9, 127, 131, 135, 165
D'Almeida, Fabrice 84
death camp survivors 149
'death marches' 88, 98, 133, 136, 148
death penalty 16–17
Delbo, Charlotte 168
deportation 7, 45–50, 58–9, 74–5, 87–9, 102–4, 162, 164
Dillmann, Alfred 38, 52
discrimination, Nazism 47–52, 58, 68, 99, 108, 135
Django (Comar) 116
documentaries, historical research 116–17
Donert, Celia 40, 112

Egyptians/Bohemians 13–14, 17
Ehrhardt, Sophie 57, 102
Eiber, Ludwig 47, 60
Eichberger, Joseph 102
Eichmann trial in Jerusalem 6, 66, 105
Einsatzgruppe 7, 43, 65, 70–1
emotions, survivors' memories 139–40
   anger and sympathy 155–7
   disappointment and distress 167–72
   enduring wounds 151–5
   expressive resource 140–1
   fear/terror 145
   guilty feeling memoirs 164–7

Index

history of 139–41
home longing memories 158–64
language of 140
vindication 141
Enzensberger, Ulrich 135, 137
eugenic/eugenic culture/eugenecists 40, 49, 67
Europe's Roma/Romanies 13–15
   to Auschwitz-Birkenau camp 101
   constraints 18
   motion pictures 116
   regulatory instrument 19
   and Second World War 44
   slavery and forced labour 17–18, 60
executions 64–72
exhibitions, historical research 113–15

Ferdinand VI of Spain 18
First World War 5, 16, 33, 36
Foisneau, Lise 103
forced labour 16–18, 58–62
   minors 87–9
Forel, August 40
Frankl, Viktor 124, 128, 140–1, 143–4, 150, 165, 167
Franz, Philomena 4, 34, 54, 78–9, 84, 95, 100, 108–9, 111, 116–17, 129–31, 137, 142–3, 149–52, 155–60, 169, 173, 174–7
Fredrick II of Prussia 17
Friedlander, Henry 46, 111
Friendländer, Saul 66

genetic criminality 77–8, 101
ghettos 64–72
Gilsenbach, Reimar 104
Gitanos 4, 17–18, 28
Glück, Leopold 30
Goebbels, Joseph 60
Gran Redada (the mass raid) 18, 109
Groome, Francis H. 29–30
Guttenberger, Elisabeth 79–80, 82, 84, 141, 159, 161
'Gypsies'/Gypsyism 2–4, 13, 59, 100–1. *See also* *Zigeunerlager*
   fictional portrayal/images of 20–1, 23–4, 30–3
   'Gypsy plague' 7, 39, 41, 46–7, 49, 52–3, 67, 71–2, 74, 102–3
   'Gypsy vengeance' 156
   'Gypsy' women 24–6
   novels and stage plays 19
   Orientalism and 22

Hancock, Ian 5, 118
Hanstein, Ewald 136, 138, 142, 144, 149, 152, 154, 156, 159, 166–7, 169, 173, 176–7
head shaving humiliation 153
Heddebaut, Mónica 64
Heimweh 158–64
Heydrich, Reinhard 46, 52–3, 58

Hilberg, Raul 47–8, 106, 111
Himmler, Heinrich 30, 46, 52–4, 58, 66, 72–4, 77–8, 80, 93, 101, 131
Historikerstreit 107
Hitler, Adolf 1–2, 41, 51, 73–4, 125, 136, 145, 175
Hobsbawm, Eric 20
Höllenreiner family 147, 150, 164, 168–9
Holler, Martin 46, 70–1, 97
Horvath, Hermine 80, 153, 157, 165
Höss, Rudolf 31, 72, 80, 82, 95
humiliation 140, 151–3
hunger/malnourishment, camp system 81–2, 107, 135, 149–51

identification cards 38–9, 54–5, 73
imprisonment 47–8, 60, 63, 67–9, 81, 109, 136, 145, 164–5, 167
intentionalism/functionalism, genocidal 44, 61, 69
International Holocaust Remembrance Alliance (IHRA) 114, 117
International Romani Union 5, 106

Janouch, František 90
Jardin d'Acclimatation Anthropologique (anthropological acclimatization garden) 33
Jews/Jewish 4, 41, 44, 48–9, 53, 60, 70–1
   confiscating properties of 60–1
   ghettos 65
   survivors 128
Joachimowski, Tadeusz 94
Joseph II of Austria 17
Justin, Eva 54–5, 57, 89, 101–2, 128–9, 135, 153, 170–1

Kalderash tales 33
Kapralski, Slawomir 109
Karsten, Leo 102
Kay, Alex J. 44, 69
Kertész, Imre 79
Klemperer, Victor 124
Klímová- Alexander, Ilona 36
Knesebeck, Julia von dem 125
Knox, Robert 27
Kommers, Jean 31
Korkoro (Gatlif) 116

LaCapra, Dominick 4, 125, 137
Lackenbach Camp 1, 58, 65, 73
La Gitanilla [The Little 'Gypsy' Girl] (Cervantes) 33
Laks, Simon 85–6, 127, 143, 164
Laubinger, Erna (Unku) 55–7, 104, 116
Lebzelter, Victor 36
Leni, Riefenstahl 20, 25–36, 50
Levene, Mark 41, 71, 77
Levi, Primo 81, 83, 85–6, 94, 123, 125–8, 139–42, 158, 165

211

Index

Lewy, Guenter 6, 45, 72, 111
Lípa, Jirí 62
Liszt, Franz 24
Little Egypt/African Egypt 14
Lombroso, Cesare 37–8
looting 61–2

mala vita (the underworld) 31, 37
Margalit, Gilad 53, 102, 111
Marzahn internment camps 48, 50, 89, 135–6, 145, 153, 163, 174
Mauthausen 57, 67, 74, 86, 150
Maxglan Camp 50–1
Maximoff, Mateo, *Journal of the Gypsy Lore Society* 105
May, Kurt 103
memoirs 123–9
    bewilderment/testimonies 142–5
    of corporal punishment 151–5
    death camp survivors 149
    Hitler's rise to power 145
    in-camp discipline 143
    political power 173–7
    rituals owed to dead 154
    by Roma survivors 130–8
    testimonial literature 124–9
Mengele, Josef 57, 81, 90–4, 126, 157
Mérimée, Prosper 24, 32–3
Mettbach, Reili 95, 127
migrations, Romanies 13–20
Milton, Sybil 100, 111
Montreuil-Bellay Camp 64
Morgan, John E. 17
Mosse, George 27
Motadel, David 46–7
Müller, Jana 116–17
municipal internment camps 48, 50, 57–8
museums and memorials 112–14
musical culture 18, 24, 33–4, 85–7, 135, 178
Muslim/Islam 46–7

Nazi camp system 52, 60, 74, 80–9, 98, 126–33, 141, 143–5, 150, 154, 157, 164, 167, 173, 177
Nazi racial policy 4–7, 14, 30, 41, 72, 103, 128, 133, 134
Nebe, Arthur 52–3, 73
Neumann, Thomas W. 99, 134, 137
1936 Berlin Olympic Games 48, 135
Nirenberg, Jud 61
nomad/nomadism 16, 30–1, 34, 36, 40–1, 60, 98
Novitch, Miriam 106
Nuremberg laws 47, 49, 129, 162
Nyiszli, Miklós 92, 125

Paczkowski, Edward 22, 84
St Pantaleon-Weyer Camp 58–9

Papusza (Kos and Krauze) 116
'pariahs' 94, 127
Perski, Marian 86
personal identification 38–9
Peter, Maria 76, 82, 84, 149, 166
Petropoulos, Jonathan 61
photography/motion pictures 115–16
Pike, David 86
Pittard, Eugène 30
Porrajmos 5
prisoners' forced labour 16–18, 58–62, 87–9

racial medicine 87–93
Rastplatz Marzahn 48
Ravensbrück 79, 82, 88, 95, 97–8, 131, 133–4, 144–5, 147, 150, 153, 155, 157, 165–6, 169
Reddy, William M. 139–40
Reich Criminal Police Department (RKPA) 52–3, 57
Reindhardt, Django 34, 63, 116
resistance activities 94–8
Ringelblum, Emmanuel 65
Ritter, Robert 30, 40, 48, 50, 53–5, 57, 72–5, 77, 82, 89, 101–3, 153, 170
Romani activism 3–4, 106–8, 135
Roma/Romani
    children's behaviour 57
    deported to Auschwitz Decree 74–8
    fear of persecution 145
    at ghetto 65–7
    killings of 70–1
    legislation 16–17, 21, 36
    music/musician 85–7, 135, 178
    Muslim communities 46–7
    national rules 45
    Nazi policies against 13, 17, 46–7
    persecution of 100–5, 123
    personal identification 38–9, 54–5, 73
    racial stereotype 24–5, 52–3, 77
    research and dissemination 110–19
    reservation 72–4
    scientific expertise 27
    survivor memoirs 130, 140 (*see also* memoirs)
    victims of Nazi violence 105–10
    women's role in Romani culture 175–7
Rosenberg, Otto 50, 85, 89, 97, 129, 135–8, 141, 145, 147–59, 163–6, 169, 173–6
Rosenhaft, Eve 112, 115, 125
Rose, Romani 108
Rost, Nico 127
Rotaru, Ionel 106–7, 174

Sachsenhausen Camp 113
Samudaripen 5
'sauna,' humiliation 152
Schmidt, Helmut 108

Index

school memoirs 160–1
scientific expertise/ 26–33, 52–8
Second World War 4–6, 13, 16, 44, 46, 58, 140
sexual assault/abuse 83–4, 153
Sinti 36, 41
slavery 17, 21, 27, 58, 60
Solonari, Vladimir 67
Sonneman, Toby 60, 127, 130, 164, 168
Steinbach, Settela 117–19
Steinberg, Paul 126, 128, 141, 145, 147–8
stereotypes 20–6, 34, 113, 177
sterilization 40, 47–52, 55, 57, 93, 101, 105, 153
Stojka, Ceija 89, 97, 114, 129–33, 136, 138, 143–4, 147–8, 150–4, 157, 159, 173–6
Stojka, Karl 89, 114, 132–3, 169, 176
Strafkompanie 83

Talewicz-Kwiatkowska, Joanna 83
Teatr Romen 35
terror-based discipline, prisoners 145, 147–8
Theresa, Maria (Empress) 17
Third Reich rule 5, 17, 44, 64, 66, 74, 162–3
Traverso, Enzo 5
Trevisan, Paola 67
Trollmann, Johann (Rukeli) 51–2
'*tsiganes nomades*' 64
Tyaglyy, Mikhail 65, 71

Uschold, Rudolf 102
U.S. Holocaust Memorial Museum 61, 98, 114, 133
Ustasha violence 68

van Angeren, Lily 132–4, 143, 152–3, 159–60, 162, 165, 168, 173, 175
Verzetsmuseum 118

Wagenaar, Aad 118
Weisbach, Augustin 30
Weiss-Wendt, Anton 6–7, 47, 112
Weltzel, Hans 115
'White Gypsies' 47
Wierzbicka, Ludwika 92
Wiesenthal, Simon 106
Wieviorka 124
Winter, Erich 99, 134
Winter, Walter 49, 59, 99, 130, 134–5, 137, 149–62, 166–9, 171–4, 177
World Jewish Congress 100
Wurth, Adolf 55, 57
Wüst, Whilst Walter 73

Yoors, Jan 95–6

Zanko, Alexandre 33
Zentralrat Deutscher Sinti und Roma 108
'Zigeuner' 3–4, 27, 30, 46, 48, 53, 128
Zigeuner-Buch 38
Zigeunerlager 57, 78–87, 89–94, 97, 133–6, 148–51, 166
Zigeuner Mischlinge (ZM) 54–5
Zimmermann, Michael 36, 40–1, 99, 111–14, 134, 137
Zwicker, Marianne C. 174, 176